Road Trips

BY THE SAME AUTHOR

West of Kabul, East of New York
Destiny Disrupted
The Widow's Husband
Games Without Rules

Tamim Ansary

Road Trips

*Becoming an American
in the vapor trail of The Sixties*

San Francisco

Library of Congress Control Number: 2016913254
ISBN: 978-0-578-18526-2

Published by Kajakai Press
www.mirtamimansary.com
Illustrations and cover copyright © 2016 by Elina Ansary
Printed in U.S.A.

This is a work of nonfiction, but most names have
been changed to protect the privacy of people whose
lives happen to have crossed the author's.

For Deborah, Jessamyn, and Elina

And I think over again
my small adventures
when with a shore wind I drifted out
and thought I was in danger.
My fears—
these I thought so great
for all the things I had to get and to reach
and yet
there is only one great thing,
the only thing—
to live to see,
in huts and on journeys,
the great day that dawns
and the light that fills the world.

Inuit Song

Prologue

The Black Stone

Once upon a time, so long ago that the memories seem like fairy tales now, I lived in a tiny town called Lashkargah, on the banks of the Helmand River, in southwestern Afghanistan. Today, as I write, Lashkargah is the capital of an insurgency against whatever-you-got, with bombs going off every day, some dropping out of the sky, some exploding out of the dust. But when I was a child in the late 1950s, Lashkargah was the nerve center of a U.S. funded development project that was building dams and roads and canals and experimental farms, and my father was the administrative vice-president of this gigantic project. He was the first Afghan to marry an American woman and bring her back to the country to live with him, and the government blackballed him for the crime, but eventually he gained forgiveness, and by 1958, he had secured his high position in the Helmand Valley Project, and so we made our home in this little fairy tale of a town.

The year I was ten, a rumor reached Lashkargah that somewhere near the Iranian border, in an area without roads, cities, or known villages of any kind, there stood a mountain made of alabaster. As you may know, alabaster is a fine-grained stone that takes a high polish, like marble except that alabaster is filled with swirling bands of color. If a mountain of this stuff existed in Afghanistan, the government wanted to find it and mine it. My father was assigned to look for it, and so he mustered a crew, a caravan of engineers, geologists, cooks, drivers, and other officials.

At the last moment he decided to take me along. For ten-year-old Tamim, this was an indescribable thrill, because ten is still in that age before sexuality sets in, when boys are particularly tuned into the resonance of adventure. It's just about the last pure moment of that age. In that brief bubble of time, my favorite author was H. Rider Haggard, who wrote 19th century fantasies set in a mythical Africa. I was oblivious of course to any racist overtones in his narratives. I read a version adapted for ESL students, which stripped away Haggard's overblown Victorian language and reduced the novels to pure plot and fabulist scenery. Every Haggard book revolved around a quest for some legendary treasure in "deepest Africa," for in his day Europeans romanticized Africa as a place of mystery comparable to Star Trek's "space—the final frontier." Haggard portrayed the continent as an endless jungle filled with jewel-encrusted temples, strange monsters, frightening magicians, and lost cities.

I had just finished *King Solomon's Mines*, and its prequel *Allan Quatermain*, and I took both books along on our quest for the alabaster mountain. As we jounced across roadless terrain, I huddled next to the window, reading about stolid Allan Q, and dashing Sir Henry Curtis, sank into the story so thoroughly that I was *on* that boat running down the oily river...I *saw* the mighty serpent come slithering out of the green water. We men hacked it to death—but too late to avoid the rapids sucking us into a great hole in the cliffs. Desperately did we paddle, but the current shot us into utter darkness through which we flew for hours until we emerged into a vast underground world lit by needles of sunlight from the cracks above—whereupon, to our dismay, we saw crabs as big as horses swarming toward us...

Sporadically, I looked up from my reading and by God, our own quest was scarcely less hair-raising. There we were, inching through a narrow canyon. Or screeching to a stop because the road ahead was crumbling. Or bursting forward to escape an enormous boulder dislodged from the slopes above...

On the afternoon of the second day we halted at the edge of a vast basin filled with sand dunes. The bluff extended out of sight to either side, and the basin's far shore was lost in the distance. All we could see were dunes stretching to the horizon. This was *Reg-i-Rawan,* "Flowing Sands," part of the famous "Desert of Death."

The sand looked as yellow as straw and was mounded up like countless haystacks, fifty to a hundred feet high. Each dune had a scallop-shaped bite taken out of it by the wind. Every scallop was the same size and set at the exact same angle—just the sort of place Allan Quatermain might have stumbled upon.

The men were discussing what to do. Going around might take days! So should we descend to the floor of this basin and strike south? Getting down was no problem but could we navigate across such a wasteland?

I stood with the men, legs akimbo, hands on my hips, lips pursed, nodding sagely at points raised, just as if I were part of the decision-making process. I was really living in a Haggard novel then! It's not that I was confused about what was real, but I was not pretending either. Haggard's fictional Africa and my real Afghanistan shared some *essence.* When I was huddled in the car, reading his story, I was right there on the underground lake, and even though I had read the story before, when those enormous crabs appeared, my pulse hammered, some part of me believing that this time it could end badly.

Now, standing outside the car, I imagined being right where I actually was. It felt so real! The fact that it *was* real subtracted nothing from the romance of how real it *felt.*

Our *direwar* laughed at us. D*irewar* just means "driver," but in Afghanistan these professional drivers were versatile road warriors. They knew how to navigate through trackless gullies and how to tell when flash floods were coming. Our *direwar* was the legendary Khalifa Musa, he of the bristling moustache, who assured the brass that he could get us across the flowing sands, no problem.

Had he been here before, my father asked?

Not here, he said, but places like it, and he trusted God. This was good enough for my father. Our whole caravan descended to the Flowing Sands and headed south. But halfway across, our biggest truck made a horrid grinding sound and stopped dead.

Khalifa Musa stepped in to quell the panic. The men should stretch their legs and have a snack; he would fix the truck. We all piled out. The men sat in the shade, but I amused myself by climbing the scalloped face of a giant dune. None of the men paid the least attention to me, which was good, for the attention of grownups generally involved telling small boys what not to do. Climbing the dune was like climbing a hill of water. Every time I stepped up, my feet sank down. It made me laugh, it was so much fun. Eventually, gasping and clutching, I made it to the top. And from there I just flung my body into space. Why not? The dune did not contain one single pebble or impurity. I could not land on anything but sand that flowed like water. I was flying.

Meanwhile, Khalifa Musa gathered a number of turbans and spread them on the sand, overlapped slightly. Wrapped around a head, an Afghan turban looks like a strip of cloth, but spread out, it's about three feet wide and twenty feet long. Five turbans gave him a substantial working surface. With help from other *direwars*, Khalifa Musa took the engine out of the truck, disassembled it, polished each individual piece, manipulated a few of them somehow, put the engine back together, and bolted it into the truck again. When he turned the key, it sprang to life. Four or five small parts remained on the turbans, but he tossed them in the back of the truck, explaining to my father, "Those were extra," as a doctor might speak of an appendix he had just removed.

We took off and the truck ran like a puppy. The Rovers stayed healthy, and another day's journey brought us to the fabled alabaster mountain. Like all mountains, however, it looked to be made mostly of dirt. It was covered with alabaster boulders but unpolished alabaster, it turns out, looks just like any other rock. Nonetheless the workers set up our huge airy tents, and laid out blood-red Turcoman carpets as ground cover. They fired up big brass samovars with hot charcoals so the men could have tea. That evening, we dined on skewered meats roasted over an open fire and rice baked in heavy iron pots with hot coals piled on their lids. Afterward, we sat in a circle , drinking tea and telling stories in the unsteady yellow light from kerosene lanterns. I could sense the utter blackness of the night outside. There was no human habitation for miles. I shivered with delicious dread.

Delicious because it was adventure-dread which differs from real fear. It's enjoyable because it includes the certainty that everything will come out all right in the end. Adventure-fear is what you get from a tense book. I felt it on that expedition because I was nestled under the protection of my father and his buddies, grownup men who would certainly prevent the order of the universe from being violated. Bandits and wild animals might attack us, but the central characters of our story—me, my father, and those of the men whom we knew personally—would survive. That's how it always is in stories.

The next day, as the men examined the alabaster boulders, I ambled away to gather the smooth, black pebbles I spotted here and there. Further and further I roamed from camp until—turning a corner—I found myself amid a jumble of broken boulders separated by the cracks and runnels that flash floods had carved— for in mountains such as these, where the sun bakes the soil hard, when rain falls at high altitudes, not one drop soaks into the ground. It all comes down the slopes, gathering force and weight, until it breaks upon the deserts in sudden torrents that toss car-sized boulders around like marbles and gathers into rivers that cut their own notches pouring over cliffs. Then the floods end, the water disappears, and the desert suddenly looks bone-dry again, no trace left of the flood except the chaos of boulders and the notches over which waterfalls had briefly poured.

At the dead end of one such gully, I came across bedrock. It was black as the pebbles I had been gathering, black as the stone at the heart of Mecca. Unlike the rest of the alabaster, this stone was polished to a high sheen because it was situated right where a waterfall splashed whenever there was a waterfall.

But waterfalls existed here only three or four times a year, and only for a few hours each time. So it must have taken tens of thousands of years, maybe even hundreds of thousands, to buff this black stone to such a gleam. That's how long it must have been sitting here, unseen until I came along. It made a guy feel like Allan Quatermain, by God.

Later, when my father asked me how I had spent the day, I told him about the black stone. He and a couple of other men followed me there to have a look. The stone impressed them and months later, when the alabaster mines were in fact being developed, my father had that stone dug up and transported to the stone-cutting factory in Lashkargah where it was sliced up. My father had one slab of that black stone made into a mantelpiece for us. When we moved back to Kabul that year, we took it along, and when we remodeled our house in Dehbouri, we had a fireplace built into our new living room: we paved the wall around it with bits of polished alabaster and embedded the black stone shelf above it.

I was ten when I found that stone. Five years later, my mother, my two siblings, and I went to America, my mother's world. My father stayed behind. My mother and siblings never returned, and I didn't go back for 38 years. During that time, the country went through a revolution, an invasion, a civil war, and finally a descent into the darkest of fanatical tyrannies. Finally, in 2001, a handful of terrorists linked to the infamous Taliban hijacked four planes, crashed two of them into the World Trade Center, one into the

Pentagon, and one into the ground near Pittsburg. This event brought Afghanistan slamming back into my life, as I've chronicled in another memoir, *West of Kabul, East of New York*. The following June, I headed back to Kabul to write a piece for a magazine about how the place had changed. By then, the U.S. military and their Afghan allies had driven the Taliban from power. No one could tell me what Kabul would be like, however—whether there was such a thing as a hotel in the city, or public transportation. When I landed in Kabul, I had no idea where I would stay.

Fortunately, I did have one cousin still living in the city, in her late father's house, somewhere near the old Soviet bread factory. Kabul, it turned out, was teeming with cabs: it was easier to catch one there than in New York City. I had no address for my late uncle's house, but my cabbie found the place easily with the iota of information I could give him.

On my second day back, my relatives took me to my old neighborhood, just to let me get a glimpse of the house in which I was born. This entire quarter of the city had been pulverized during the civil wars, and I wandered among heaps of bricks and chunks of wall, trying to guess which pile of rubble had been ours.

Then I saw it. I was standing in a rectangle formed by the remains of four walls, a shallow enclosure filled ankle deep with rusted artillery shells that looked like huge grains of rice. One section of the northern wall was more intact than the rest; it stood seven or eight feet high. Swirls of color in the wall told me it had once been paved with chunks of polished alabaster, a few of which were still in place. At the foot of that ruined wall, mixed in with the spent artillery shells, were fragments of black rock—the same rock I had found embedded in a gully where a waterfall appeared unwitnessed once or twice a year for hundreds upon thousands of years. The story that began back then had ended now.

I got to thinking about that journey with my father, and about other journeys I had made over the years. It struck me that every time one heads for a place that is far away and difficult to reach, the journey acquires a story-like arc. And the story isn't just about the destination or what happens on the road. It includes what led to leaving and what came of having gone. The journeys I recount in this book took place after I moved to America, when I was living in Portland, Oregon, in the vapor trail of the sixties, a decade that began with Woodstock and ended with Jonestown. These trips took place after the age in which boys are so attuned to the resonance of adventure that life itself feels like a story. They took place in that next age, when the dominant themes are love and sex and the fruitless longing for transcendence. And yet—even so—it all felt as real as that black rock while it was happening. How is it that, looking back, all one sees is story?

Running Free

The summer that men set foot on the moon, I decided to see if I could hitchhike across North America on five dollars and the kindness of strangers. It was 1969, two years after the Summer of Love, and the best minds of my generation were telling me that the cosmos would shower me with bounty if only I would "trust the Universe." This was so much the same advice trumpeted by my long line of Sufi ancestors back in Afghanistan that I could not help but take it seriously. It's true that the Sufis said "Allah" instead of "the Universe" but it came to the same thing, or so it seemed to me in the summer of 1969.

Trusting the universe does not come naturally, however. A man has to learn that skill and I had not yet mastered it. For that matter, I wasn't a really man yet, but a boy. No one could have been more timidly desirous of security and protection than I. But I figured, if I left home by myself with only five dollars in my pocket, and struck off across the continent, and ended up in places where no one knew or cared about me, I could force myself to trust the Universe. I lived in Portland, Oregon, so my goal was anywhere along the Eastern seaboard.

I was nineteen years old that year, and to most of my American friends I was still the Afghan Kid. I had been in the United States less than five years and had spent virtually all of those years as a dirt-poor scholarship student in expensive private schools surrounded by the sons and daughters of the rich, the very rich, and the super-rich. In high school, a private boarding school in Colorado, while all the other kids went skiing, I trudged to the nearest town with a bag of dirty laundry over my shoulder to wash and dry my clothes in the coin-op laundromat. Throughout my almost-five years in America, I was far and away the poorest person I knew, but the scholarship funds bequeathed to me by various schools kept me in a sort of degraded luxury.

Before that, in Afghanistan, I had been a pampered member of a privileged urban family living in a compound, sheltered from the rude men of the bazaar and from the tribal peasants who surrounded the city. In short, my life so far had taught me nothing about the nit and grit of the real world, nothing that might help me step up and take my place as a man among men. I badly wanted some romantic adventures to toughen me up and put me in touch with what was real. I pictured striding through mean cities with my eyes narrowed to slits against a cruel wind, my jacket collar pulled up around my ears, giving me that James Dean look of a man who has survived many a drunken knife fight and countless devastating encounters with beautiful girls. What I didn't want to be was me.

"Me" was a skinny, multi-lingual, culturally confused intellectual "Poindexter" with thick glasses: I had just finished my junior year at Reed College, to which I had transferred from a place called Carleton in the Midwest, a place so frigidly bound with staid social rules I figured I would never get laid there. At Reed, I had, in fact, cracked the virginity barrier and endured one love affair, a ruinous one to be sure, but not in the romantic ways I had envisioned. Marcy had come to an impromptu party at my house and singled me out from the herds of nerds with whom I grazed. Marcy and I lived together for six months, but we were a quarrelsome pair. I recognized that we were a bad match but assumed that if I let go of Marcy I would never again have a girlfriend—it was fortuitous enough that pretty Marcy had mistaken me for an attractive guy: I could scarcely hope for the same lucky accident to befall me twice in a lifetime.

When the school year ended, Marcy moved to Eugene to work for her mother. I stayed in town and got myself a job at B. P. John's furniture factory. Would Marcy and I get back together in the fall? I didn't ask, and she didn't tell.

B.P. Johns' was an assembly-line factory reeking of glue, petroleum distillates, and finishing oils, and I left work each day lightheaded and nervous about the brain cells I may have lost. But they paid three bucks an hour, handsome wages at the time. I was bringing in money by the bucket load and spending virtually nothing because I had moved into a house that rented for zilch.

The house was on Ivan Street. It rented for zilch because it was situated in the path of a projected freeway. The whole neighborhood was slated to be torn down, and the landlords were merely waiting for the protests and lawsuits to subside so they could sell their properties to the state at jacked up prices. In the meanwhile, they simply needed to keep their buildings occupied in order to qualify for certain tax breaks; or such was the tale I heard told about the Ivan Street house, a two story-building with a full apartment in the basement.

A recluse lived in the basement, and on him I never set eyes. I had the main floor to myself, a bathroom, two large rooms, and one small bedroom, plus a kitchen, which I shared with the people upstairs, a varying number of street rats from New York, all of whom had fled to Portland for various reasons having to do with petty crimes or emotional breakdowns. They made their living by shoplifting, and a good living it was, by the looks of the consumer goods they enjoyed. These street rats eventually became my best friends. Well, of course they did: we all had long hair.

My floor officially rented for 20 dollars a month. You may suppose that's what I meant when I said the place rented for nothing. Twenty dollars for a three-room suite in a house with a yard and plumbing that often worked must certainly seem as close as one can realistically hope to come to paying nothing for rent.

But it was better than that. The landlord had actually forgotten about this property. He never showed up to collect any money. Maybe the recluse sent him something, I don't know. I myself had no idea where to send a check, had I been so inclined, and for the others the question was moot: they were not so-inclined.

In one month at B. P. Johns, I saved the whole amount I was expected to contribute to my next year's scholarship at Reed, plus fifteen dollars. As soon as I had that much in the bank, I began to think about other ways to occupy my time.

It was then that I decided to see if I could hitch-hike across the continent on five dollars. Someone told me that hitchhiking was legal in Canada, so I thought I'd go up there for the journey. Of course, since North America is shaped like a triangle, going north adds many miles to the trip east, but I figured it was worth it. I had hitched in the United States but always with my heart in my throat, because hitchhiking was illegal here and because I was often carrying a couple of tabs of LSD in my pocket, this being, as I mentioned, the sixties.

A couple of days before I set off, I walked past a thrift store in lower downtown Portland, the once-slummy part near the river (urban renewal has since turned that strip of the city into a posh waterfront geared toward prosperous families.) In the store window, I saw a pair of black boots. My own shoes were pretty worn out, and, of course, I didn't have the money for a new pair. These boots in the window were going for a buck and a half. I tried them on and they almost fit! With two pairs of socks, they'd be perfect.

Not till I left the store in those boots did I realize I had launched upon a daring deception. This was the first pair of non-Poindexter footwear I had donned in my entire life. Something about the way the leather encased my feet, something about the pointed toes and the way those hard heels clacked on the concrete made me walk differently—made me stride.

After a short time, I realized that the boots didn't just cover my feet. They covered my whole self with a dangerous disguise. Bystanders looking at this boot-wearing fellow saw a case-hardened, street-smart tough guy, not the nerdy intellectual I actually was, son of Professor Ansary, sheltered scion of a high-status religious family in Afghanistan, pretty well-versed not only in the mysticism of ancestors like Khwaja Abdullah and Sheikh Sa'duddin but also in Hume's doubt about the existence of an objective reality and Kant's critique of pure reason. Yet, as soon as I put on those boots, the boots were in control: they told the little people to get the hell out of my way, else they'd get run over.

On the day of my departure, I was packing up my meager belongings to put them into storage in a friend's basement. I had the windows open to let a warm breeze into my big front room. As the room grew steadily emptier, the garish walls came into view, painted yellow and black by hippies before my time. In the end, nothing remained except a mattress in the middle of the room, and a cheap radio that could play only three stations, all of them AM. Today AM means "talk radio" but back then it meant lowest common denominator "top-forty" pop/rock hits.   On this day in 1969, all three stations were incessantly playing the ubiquitous pop hit of the moment, a song long forgotten now. The lyrics went:

> *In the year twenty five, twenty five...*
> *If man is still alive...*
> *If woman can survive....*

I was more into the likes of Frank Zappa and Doctor John, but you couldn't get that stuff on the radio, so I was listening to the available schlock. I had to admit, there was something strangely haunting about this particular top-40 hit—something about the sweep of time it proposed, for each stanza jumped a thousand years.

> *In the year thirty five, thirty five...*
> *If man is still alive...*

Sometimes the announcer would interrupt the song to bring bulletins and updates from the big news of the moment. A United States spaceship was approaching the moon. A couple of astronauts were going to land up there. On that very day, some fellow named Neil Armstrong and another man whose name I and most of the world have forgotten, were going down a ladder, rung by rung, to romp in actual moon dust. I was only vaguely aware of the whole event, and quite impervious to its drama.

To me, it seemed like nothing more than money talking—landing on the moon represented no invention, no new scientific discovery, no breakthrough to a larger truth. It was just an engineering feat. Anyone could go to the moon if they had enough time and money, was my attitude. Anyway, what was so exciting about the moon? It was just a rock.

Now, Canada—*that* was a different matter! I imagined a land covered with snow, walruses dotting the landscape, baying polar bears rearing up on distant hills. A man—well, a boy, really—hitch-hiking across this forbidding landscape with only five dollars in his pocket—now *that* would be a feat, if he made it. And the boy certainly would make it. All he had to do was trust the universe.

> *In the year forty five, forty five...*

Okay, I have a confession. I had more than five dollars on my person. I had another ten dollars hidden in my underpants. It constituted all the rest of the money I had in the world just then, not counting what I had put away for Reed next year. I was thinking I would hitchhike all the way east within Canada and hitch again once I got back into the United States, but I would buy a bus ticket to get back across the border from Canada to the United States. I figured the Universe would give me a pass on that bit of cheating. I vowed to forget I even had ten dollars hidden in my underpants, which wasn't easy because that ten-dollar bill kept sliding into—well, never mind the details.

The Road

Striding and strutting and looking dangerous in my new shit-kicker boots, I pipsqueaked my way to the freeway ramp where I got a ride the moment I stuck out my thumb. In fact, I got a series of good rides. Near Seattle, a couple of guys from Vancouver picked me up. They were headed home and promised to get me across the border but advised me to lie to the Canadian authorities and tell them I was going to Vancouver just for the day. Otherwise, the authorities would assume I was a draft dodger. This was the late sixties, remember: Vietnam. The draft. The antiwar movement. The fib would be easy to put across because I had no suitcase, no bag, no backpack, nothing but a wallet in my pocket, the clothes I was wearing, and those boots on my feet. The young guys said they would cover for me, and they did, which was a good thing because only after I crossed the border did I remember that I still had two tabs of blotter acid in my wallet.

Crossing the border was a great surprise. There was no snow on the other side, no polar bears, and no walruses. Canada looked just like the United States. They even spoke English up there.

And then the details get hazy. All I remember of Vancouver is trying to walk across it, to the transcontinental highway running east, and the light slanting low across the rooftops, stretching all the shadows out long, creating sharp contrasts, buttering the shabby wooden frame buildings with an orange glow. I was getting hungry by then, for I had eaten nothing since breakfast, and the kindness-of-strangers thing was not kicking in any victuals at this point. I worried that the Universe had spotted the ten dollar bill in my underpants and pegged me for a cheater.

Or perhaps I had not suborned my will sufficiently to the will of the universe. I was still trying to make things happen, which my best-friend Ralph called "pushing the river." He had recently joined an Indian religious cult headed by a guru named Kirpal Singh, so he presumably knew a thing or two about trusting the Universe. From his instructions I knew what I was supposed to do—go with the flow, accept whatever happened. I was pretty certain I would get the knack of it as soon as I got out on the open highway, beyond the range of all possible safety nets. In the meantime, however, random doubts kept poisoning my innocent faith.

For example, it was getting rather cool. I could not afford to check into a motel room, not even the cheapest one. I was waiting for the universe to do its vaunted thing, find me a place to flop for free, but since the universe was showing no such inclinations yet, there was nothing I could do but keep walking. But I wasn't sure I could just keep walking very much longer. 'Cuz the boots sorta' hurt.

Then I passed a shabby diner and smelled hot grease. It struck me that I had done the hard part now: I had made it across the border into Canada. Only 3,000 miles to go now. Maybe I could break into that five. I deserved a reward.

The grilled cheese sandwich at that diner was pretty good. The French fries dripped deliciously with grease. A cup of coffee and a slice of cherry pie rounded out the meal, all for less than two bucks. Meanwhile, even in Canada, the radio kept wailing:

> *In the year fifty five fifty five*
> *If man is still alive...*

Because this was 1969, when hair-length was a raucous issue, some drivers slowed down as if to pick me up, but as soon as I started trotting toward them speeded up, just enough to stay ahead of me, just to see how far they could make me trot before shooting away in a cloud of smoke. A couple of times, a car veered and aimed straight at me, and I had to jump back into the ditch beside the highway to avoid being hit. Other hitchhikers along the road later told me that one of us had been killed this way by a driver who forgot to take his side mirror into account. But mostly, the hostile drivers felt disheartening. It was difficult to sustain a belief in the essential goodness of the Universe when strangers were trying to run you down because they didn't like your hair.

Hitchhiking teaches a special lesson, no matter where you are, and the lesson goes like this. You're a lonely nobody on a featureless highway. No one will stop for you. Humanity is a torrent of callous creeps and life is a bucket of shit. You might as well be dead.

Then you get a ride. Whoever stops for you is never whom you'd expect. And because one human being out of the roaring river of human indifference has shown you an iota of goodness, you are instantly transported to the heights of faith and love for humanity. In the next two to ten minutes, your perspective gets weirdly shifted, because the people you meet start out looking like some category but turn out to be individuals, only loosely assignable as types.

The ride that took me out of Vancouver was a clattering old pickup truck that stopped about a hundred yards up the highway from me. I had been teased by two or three pickups just like this one already, so I wasn't about to start trotting. An old geezer poked his head out of the truck window to stare back at me. Then he started to back up. I suspected a trick, so I slowed down and got ready to jump, in case he was going to try running his truck over my squishy body. But then he stopped. So I started forward with a cat's caution. When I opened the door and slid in, he said at once, "I got a big old pistol right under the seat here, boy, I could blow a hole in you bigger'n a horse, got that? Just in case you got any ideas, sonny."

"I got no ideas, sir."

"Good." And no more was said about his big ol' gun. After that he was just a garrulous old farmer gabbing a nonstop stream of country gossip, which saved me the trouble of having to say anything except uh huh and gee and ain't that amazing, and even that must have lapsed after a while, because I don't remember much more about that ride, nor about the many that followed. I only remember that night kept giving way to day and day to dusk and dusk to night as I inched across North America.

Along the way, I caught up with another hitchhiker and we ambled and rambled together and fell in with a third fellow by and by, a short guy named Robert, with a big nose and a mop of curly black hair. Robert was headed for Montreal. Like me, he was short on money. He told us he could always go back to Vancouver, because he was tight with the Gypsy Jokers, a motorcycle club there, the northwestern version of the Hells Angels. The two clubs disliked each other and often fought pitched battles that left many bikers broken or dead. I knew this from other sources, but Robert told me all about it again. The Jokers didn't take shit from anyone. Robert did not seem especially tough and he looked like he might take shit from a few someones, but the bikers had befriended him, and so he was enamored of them and of himself for having made that connection. He could hardly talk or think about anything but the Jokers back in Vancouver.

The other guy of our group was more or less local, and he knew a rope. Not "the ropes," just one rope. He knew of a hillside overlooking a certain fruit stand where, if you hovered till about nine o'clock, you could get something to eat, because after the place closed, the proprietors threw out any fruit that would not keep till the next day. As soon as they drove away, you could swoop down and get the fruit out of the trash. Some mighty good eatin' there, the local guy told us. But we had to get there quick and find a good place to hide because others would be after that fruit too. The moment it was safe to swoop, the hills would come alive with hungry hobos. We would have to stay alert and stay ready.

We crouched companionably in the darkness among the trees, we three, watching the bustle around the well-lit fruit stand. Then—being inexperienced and naïve—I leaned into the light to see what exactly was going on down there, and the fruit stand owner saw me. He came right to the edge of the woods and shouted up into the trees. "Hey, you there," he shouted. "What are you doing? What do you want?"

The others shushed me but too late: I had already blurted, "Just passing through, sir. We heard you throw away some fruit at the end of the day. We're hungry."

"Who's we?"

"Me and a coupla' friends."

"Come on down, then. I'll give you a bag of peaches."

Sheepishly, the three of us clambered down to the fruit stand and received our paper bag full of oozing peaches. We took it to the highway, and shared it out. In the course of my life I have twice experienced the absolute heights of gourmet satisfaction. Once was eating at Paul Prudhomme's restaurant in New Orleans just before he became the world's most famous chef. The other was this bag of over-ripe peaches.

But some part of me wriggled with uneasy shame as the juices ran down my gullet. Some part of me wondered what my relatives back in Afghanistan would think if they knew I was in a squalid town in the middle of nowhere, begging for rotting fruit. My father had been the country's deputy minister of interior for a brief period and later the press attaché at the Afghan Embassy in Washington D.C. What would he say if this got back to him? How would he feel?

Still, this was the experience I had wanted. I was one of the common folk now! On the road! Toughening up!

The three of us got a ride together that night. It's hard to believe that anyone would have picked up three scruffy-looking young men at night, but someone did. The local guy veered off at some point, but Robert and I continued hitching east together. Fellows joined up with us and fellows dropped away. The configuration of the pack traveling together kept changing, but I always had friends. And the friendships I formed and forfeited along that road struck me later as a metaphor for so many of the relationships I have formed and forfeited in my life: people I came to know because we happened to be on the same road at the same time, going the same way for a while.

I remember one fellow hitchhiker asking if he could borrow a quarter from me to get a soda out of a machine. "Borrow?" I said, laughing at his phrasing. "When do you suppose you'll be giving it back to me?"

"Oh, you'll get your quarter back," he said. "Just not from me."

The Detour

By the time we reached Regina, it was just Robert and me. Others had come and gone, but he and I seemed strangely joined. Regina posed a challenge because it was big. The Trans-Canada highway went right through town, but we couldn't get a ride on the side that went in. Those rides would only take us toward or to downtown Regina. If we wanted a ride headed further east, toward Toronto for example, we would have to walk across the city and hitch a ride with someone coming *out* of town on the other side.

Walking across a major city is no joke. Imagine crossing the entire length of any substantial city on foot—Omaha, say. Now imagine you've been walking, riding, walking, riding for a week, eating only sporadically and sleeping in fits and starts. What's more, as we reached the eastern outskirt of Regina, we saw a disheartening sight: clumps of other hitchhikers dotted the highway all the way to the horizon.

When we came abreast of the first two hitchhikers, they gave us a horrible glare. One of them growled: "Keep moving, assholes."

Of course, I saw what etiquette demanded of us in this situation. We couldn't set up ahead of these guys. If we tried, we would come to blows. I looked back and saw more hitchhikers coming, an endless stream of them.

"Gee, Tamim, we'd better hurry," said Robert. We picked up our pace, walking briskly past one set of hitchhikers after another. We must have walked at least a mile before we came to the end of that line. Any car that picked us up would have to have driven past at least fifty other choices. It was hard to see why any driver who had rejected fifty other hitchhikers would decide to stop for us, but what could we do? We set up, and stuck out our thumbs, and when another tired, shabby looking long-hair dragged his ass close, we glared daggers at him and muttered dangerously, "Keep moving, asshole."

Hours passed. Cars passed. The sun sank. In the fading light I noticed something scribbled on a nearby telephone pole by hitchhikers before our time. I walked over for a closer look and saw one short sentence penciled above three dates, two of which were crossed out—like this:

> Albert Smith was here
> ~~July 15, 1969~~
> ~~July 16, 1969~~
> July 17, 1969

Good God! Could this be? Could some hitchhiker have waited by this pole for three days without getting a ride? July 17 was just a week ago. I pointed out this grim graffiti to Robert. "I'm hungry," was his only retort. "Let's put our money together, you and me: see what we can get."

I turned out my pockets: a single dollar and some change remained of that five. I didn't mention the ten hidden in my underwear. Robert had no bills, just coins. Our joint savings added up to a little over two bucks. What to buy with this pitiful sum? Bread? Milk? Soda?

In the end we decided to spend our pittance on a bag of tobacco and some rolling papers: it seemed liked the best possible use. After all, nothing we could buy in the way of food would amount to a gnat's worth of nutrition divided between the two of us. We'd eat it, get a glimpse of satisfaction, and then suffer fresh and fiercer cravings.

A bag of tobacco, on the other hand, would give us hundreds of smokes, and smoking kills hunger.

So we got some tobacco, Bugler brand, with Zigzag papers of course; but getting it meant giving up our post by the telephone pole and walking past scores of hitchhikers to a tiny store. When we headed back we realized we would have to go on past our previous spot, to the very end of the ever-lengthening line. Along the way, Robert spotted a small two-lane blacktop that branched off into the woods.

"Where does that go?" he wondered.

"North," I said, stating the only fact that seemed to matter. "We're headed east."

"Well, I don't know," he said. "Let's check it out."

He pulled a tattered map out of his backpack and spread it open on the dirt. We crouched over it to study the region around Regina. The map had few details, but it seemed to show that we were standing at the mouth of a small road that looped up through a town called Yorkton and down again to the main highway. If we caught a ride north along this rural loop, we might conceivably skirt the patch where lonesome hitchhikers went to die, and get back to the highway at a better spot way further along.

What could we lose? Without discussion Robert and I started up the country road. Ten minutes took us around a bend and put us beyond sight of the main highway. Here, we had fewer opportunities to get rides but no competition. Other hitchhikers? Hey, to all appearances, except for a few crows barking in the treetops, we were the only animal life in the landscape, although there must have been lizards and mice in the weeds and worms burrowing beneath our feet.

"Anything to get out of Regina," Robert said.

When I say "fewer opportunities" I mean "none." Not one car passed by. We had our tobacco, though, so we rolled cigarettes and smoked peacefully in the dark, and I marveled at our camaraderie. We two had traveled from opposite ends of the Earth to share this same moment of hardship and adventure. Truly, humanity was all one.

Finally, around the curve came one of those long vans built to carry large families. Unbelievably, this car—the very first car to come along—stopped for us. Our luck was turning! It belonged to a family of genteel, provincial gentry with cultivated accents and civilized manners, headed back to their farm in the far north. They could take us as far as Yorkton, they said.

We were excited. All the way to Yorkton! Why that would get us to the middle of the 200-mile loop through the north. One more ride like this would get us back to the main highway. These were pleasant people too. The group included a healthy young man with a blond beard, his pretty, sun-browned mother, a woman in her late forties, clad in an embroidered blouse and a square-dancing skirt, and his father, who was a perfect postcard of a country squire, simultaneously refined and rough-hewn—a George Sanders look-alike. Several well-behaved children sat in the back, I didn't count how many. These cultured folks elicited our stories and recounted anecdotes about life in Canada. They talked about farming, but also about books and ideas. I discussed Schubert and Debussy with them, while Robert snoozed.

Once again, the wondrous yo yo of hitchhiking had popped us from the pits to the heights. Meanwhile, the darkness thickened, and the woods disappeared into a black pudding of night. Gradually, then, the conversation dwindled until nothing cut into the sleepy silence except our tires humming on the blacktop.

Almost four hours later, a few ticks past midnight, we arrived in Yorkton.

"This is where we'll have to let you off," said George Sanders.

"Thanks, man! Thanks for everything!" We stumbled out and our saviors drove away.

Then we looked around. What sort of place was Yorkton? Well, barely a place at all, it seemed.   Behind us loomed the forest, ahead of us a darkness crowded with the dim shapes of unlit houses. I counted two pedestrians in the scene, but that included Robert and me.

It was too cold to contemplate sleeping outdoors. We *were* quite far north and it *was* past midnight. Besides, when you're tired and hungry, you feel colder. I was shivering. I remembered reading somewhere that people could die of "exposure" even if it wasn't very cold. They could die if their body temperature dropped precipitously outdoors. The article I read was titled "Hypothermia, Killer of the Unprepared."

Unprepared was me. Robert at least had a backpack and a jacket. I had nothing but my faith in the essential goodness of the Universe. Books and movies show vagabonds like us sleeping in barns, but we were not in barn country. Here in Yorkton, we would have to break into someone's garage, which would push us across a line from romantic vagabonds to petty criminals.

"We have to get indoors," I said. Frankly, I was starting to feel a little nervous. "We have to find someplace warm to get some shuteye, man."

"Maybe we can find some heads," said Robert.

Before and after this time, "head" was slang for bathroom. But at this moment in history, at least for drug-ingesting young people in the know, "heads" was slang for "drug ingesting young people in the know." I guess young people always have a sense of solidarity vis-à-vis their elders, but I wonder if there was ever a time--before right now, the age of the millennial techies—when the young felt quite such cultish solidarity as the young people of the sixties, at least those of us who knew something was happenin' here and Mr. Jones didn't know what it was. Not that all young people belonged to the cult. There was never an adequate term for our subset of the baby boomer generation. "Movement" was too small, movement just referenced the politicos. Hippies didn't do it, they were just one branch of this thing. Peaceniks didn't do it; longhairs no; freaks no; seekers no—these were all part of a single greater thing that had no name. Back then, we knew who we were. Later, we discovered that some of us weren't one of us. Later we discovered that there was no Us.

But in 1969, the dream was not just alive but peaking—the notion that secret knowledge existed and that some folks had broken through to it. Certain signs marked the cognoscenti: long hair... experience with psychedelic drugs...Clothes could exhibit membership in the cult. I for example had those boots and fairly long hair. The boots alone might have signified countrified shit-kicker but long hair changed the meaning of the boots. Knowledge of rock and roll was part of it too, and opposing the war in Vietnam, and understanding that Mao was cool, that blacks were oppressed, and that American history was a sham—these were exhilarating insights shared in a conspiratorial fashion among an elite minority of millions. And within this minority, the burgeoning subset who had experienced LSD were the heads, short for "acidheads."

I was a head. I had broken through at Carleton, my first college, even though Carleton was not the cutting edge of hip. When I arrived, Carleton still had "frosh week" during which time freshmen had to wear little green hats called beanies, and sophomores were officially encouraged to haze them. Campus life featured "slave sales" of attractive freshman girls as school-sanctioned fundraising events. There at Carleton, I bought some LSD from another student, got myself an experienced guide, name withheld because he later won a seat in some state's legislature (probably as the get-tough-on-drugs candidate). The point is, when Jimi Hendrix sang "Are you *experienced?*" we heads knew exactly what he was asking.

Robert had taken LSD at a Ken Kesey "acid test" and later had dropped acid with members of the Grateful Dead, or so he claimed. I had taken it three times at Carleton, each a personal interview with God Almighty, and a dozen or so times at Reed, where it had become a much more casual affair—indeed, it was at Reed that I took to carrying a couple of tabs around in my wallet just in case I found myself in a time and place suitable for satori. I had, as I've mentioned, two tabs in my wallet at that very moment.

Heads were like brothers and sisters in some super Masonic organization. Here in Yorkton, for example, if we found some heads, we would certainly have a place to crash. But what were our chances of finding any heads here? I had to scoff at Robert's hope. "Do you remember where we are, man? Yorkton, Canada, 100 miles north of Regina! Where are we going to find any *heads* here?"

"In a laundromat," he said.

"A laundromat?"

"Trust me," he said. "If there are any heads around here, we'll find them in a laundromat."

"Why a laundromat?"

"Because they're open all night and you can hang in 'em for free.'

Heads did not hang out in bars, you see. Acid was at one end of an axis, alcohol at the other. We acid heads despised those drunks. We called what we did getting high and what they did getting low.

I could offer no alternative to Robert's plan, so we started working our way through town, looking for a laundromat. The curbs, I noticed, were about two feet high, making the streets look like dry canals. Robert noticed this too, and we puzzled over it as we climbed laboriously up from the street to the sidewalks. What did people in wheelchairs do around here? How did old ladies cross the street? These high curbs showed the ignorance of city planners up here in backward Canada. And yet some formless doubt niggled in the back of my brain. Maybe, just maybe, the high sidewalks signified something we had not fathomed.

Then it began to rain. Just a few fat drops at first, but enough to make me say, "Omigod, we'd better find something quick."

"We'll be okay once we find a laundromat."

And then the rain started coming down in sheets, an instantaneous transition from plinkety-plink to roar. We took off like frightened cats, looking for an awning, anything, running blind until we came to a curb--whoa! There we had to stop dead.

Where a street had been, a river now flowed. Did I say flowed? Wrong word. Raged was more like it!

"This way!" cried Robert, and he sprinted for the next corner as if the water would be lower there. I followed him, but of course came only to the banks of another torrent. So we headed for the third corner, utterly drenched now, shielding our faces from the storm, while sudden rivers roared all around us.

Then, as if someone had turned off a spigot, the rain stopped. Within minutes, the night turned warm and pleasant. We remained as wet as creatures dredged from a lake, however, and we could not get to any shelter now, because the downpour had turned our entire block into an island.

Wretchedly we schlumped around the fourth and final corner— only to see—yes!—a laundromat! No mistaking those open doors, that neon glare. We staggered inside and good heavens: five or six guys about our age were lounging about on the washing machines. Guys with long hair. *We had found the heads of Yorkton!*

My admiration for Robert skyrocketed: locating heads in this backwater took a level of street craft I could only dream of acquiring. We didn't have to present any credentials to these heads, didn't have to prove our bonafides, it was enough to appear in the dead of night looking as we did and to have long hair. They knew what we were, we knew what they were, and suddenly life was grand: we had found our people.

"Oh, man, are we glad to see you. We just blew in from the coast," I said, "We're hitching through. You know anyplace we can crash?"

"The coast?" they exclaimed in wonder. "The West Coast? You been in Frisco?"

"Just came from there," said Robert, "after a stop in Vancouver--I was tight with the Jokers, you know."

"He's dropped acid with the Grateful Dead," I added.

"Hey, we took some Owsley once," said one of these Canadian boys.

Owsley was a famous maker of LSD, part of the crowd that hung around with Ken Kesey and the Dead. Here in Yorkton, Canada, the mere fact that we were "blowing in from the coast" made us superstars. These fellows didn't merely want to help us. They wanted to impress us.

"I took some Purple Haze one time," another of them bragged..

Robert sat down to discuss the various brand names of acid with these boys: Sunshine, Purple Haze, Jack o'Lantern, Owsley, Blue Streak--and then the talk turned to all the different forms in which LSD was dispensed. The locals wanted our wisdom on which was best. Robert analyzed the virtues of blotter acid versus tab acid, discoursed on the dangers of dividing a pill in which the acid was poorly distributed, techniques for heightening the effects once they started to come on. And of course, each of us had to tell about a time when we took acid that was way too strong and what we'd seen and done when we were flying on rocket fuel like that.

I, however, did not participate in the discussion much. I was dead on my feet. All I wanted was a warm bed and a pillow. If these guys knew where we could crash, I wanted them to take us there now. They said "Jack" would be able to accommodate us. He'd come by later. Then they went back to discussing acid.

I tried to hint that while Jack's place sounded fabulous, we weren't choosy. We'd crash at anyone's "pad," could we pleeeaase, just go there now? But I couldn't hasten them

No, no, they insisted. Only Jack's pad was cool enough for cool guys like us, heads from the Coast, radical dudes who knew the Dead by name and hung out with Gypsy Jokers! They were not worthy. And we didn't have to stoop to the level of them, Jack would come by soon—oh, we'd dig Jack, they assured us. Jack was on our level. *He'd* taken enough acid to explode a horse. Two tabs of Owsley back-to-back one time. He'd even hitched to Regina once and seen the Cream live.

But the only thing that interested me about Jack right now was his pad. And his only trait seemed to be his absence.

"Can't you call him?" I ventured.

But apparently Jack didn't like to be called. Not by these guys. Jack would show when Jack showed. He was that kind of guy. "He'll be here."

Gradually it dawned on me that these fellows were younger than we assumed. They weren't really heads. They were high school students. They all lived with their parents. No way would they be taking two raggedy real-life acid-gobbling heads from The Coast home with them. We'd have to wait for Jack, their slightly older friend, probably the only one of the bunch who actually had a place of his own.

Finally, I lost patience and stalked outside to get a breath of air. And there, in the middle of Nowhere, Canada, sometime past midnight, out of the deserted night, came a big, bluff, red-faced, hearty, jolly, glad-handing, middle-aged man in a quality trench coat over an expensive suit. He came striding right up to me, thrust out his hand, and boomed. "Mackenzie! Harold Mackenzie! How you doing? How you doing?"

My guard went up. My radar locked into the ON position. I was instantly thinking pederast, or cop, or the wrong kind of drug dealer. But Mr. Trenchcoat wasted no time explaining why he wanted my friendship. He had just busted out of a maximum security wedding party that his wife had insisted he attend. He'd never wanted to go to in the first place, see, and now he and she had gotten into a big fight—not his fault—and he wanted to buy me a drink so he could tell me all about it.

"I'm with friends." I pointed toward the laundromat.

"Bring 'em along, I'll buy all of you a drink. Come on."

By "drink" he meant coffee. The waters had receded enough now that we could wade across the street, so Trenchcoat led us all—Robert, me, the five local heads—to an all-night diner. He bought each of us a cup of coffee so weak a baby could have drunk it safely and commenced to tell us the particulars of his quarrel with his wife.

He was, it turned out, an open handed, open-hearted, bombastically cheerful good guy with no ulterior motives. He just wanted someone to hear him out and agree that he was right and his wife was wrong. He sat with his back to the door and held forth, his big face shining down upon us with the florid warmth of an aging sun, a red giant. For the price of a cup of coffee, we seven young men gave him all the sympathy he could absorb, and he left us fully satisfied. We never saw him again.

But thanks to the cup of coffee he had bought us, Robert and I were now entitled to sit in this booth all night because that was the rule at an all-night diner: if you buy something, you can stay as long as you want. And if the thing you bought was coffee, you could help yourself to unlimited refills.

The staff didn't try to roust us. Why should they? They were just minimum wage dead-enders trying to get through the night. The local fellows hanging with us stopped mentioning their mythical older friend and we stopped asking. Clearly, we would never get a place to crash out of these pseudo-heads. At least, we had a place to sit all night and stay dry even if it started raining again. We drank coffee to stay awake and rolled endless smokes out of our bag of Bugler-brand loose tobacco to stave off hunger and the radio kept wailing "In the year sixty-five sixty-five ...if man is still alive..."

We weren't in danger anymore, we were okay now, and yet, after a while, I began to think that hell might be very much like this all-night diner in Yorkton. An ever-lasting version of this boggled the imagination. The lighting in this place was like the lighting in every all-night diner: garishly bright fluorescence coming at you from all angles, flattening every surface, erasing every last crack of shadow. Every object had the etched clarity of a Hustler Magazine gynecological porno shot. My head felt distended like a hot air balloon and my vision like a bubble-thin translucent sheet stretched over the scene. One thought kept gnawing at me. I had made it only a third of the way across the continent so far, and my five bucks were already spent.

The diner was never packed but never deserted. Traffic kept trickling through, a constant buzz of late-night low life that ground my wits to dullness. And yet every few minutes something triggered my flight-or-fight reflexes. So I was half dozing, half dreaming, and at the same time jolts of adrenaline were zapping my senses sporadically.

Once, for example, two big blond guys with hair combed up into duck's ass swirls came staggering in. They had cut lips, bruised eyes, and bloody faces and yet they radiated rollicking aggression: young, drunk, and angry, they had obviously been in one fight and were spoiling for another. It happened that a couple of Royal Canadian Mounted Policemen were sitting in a booth near theirs, enjoying a quiet cup of coffee and some slices of pie. The Mounties looked exactly like Mounties are supposed to look-- correct in their bearing, neatly uniformed, loyal, and trustworthy.

The punks began to badmouth the officers. One sniffed at the air ostentatiously. "You smell something? I smell bacon. Woo hoo! Sure does smell like pig in here."

And his friend said, "Let's cut some slabs offa' that, make us a pig samwich."

"*Taste* like shit," the other opined, "Cuz they *is* shit now, ain't they, eh?"

They went on like this, doing everything in their drunken power to spark a fight with the Mounties, but the Mounties studiously ignored them, drank their coffee, ate their pie, and walked out: neat, precise, correct, and polite.

Our new friends whispered warnings to us about these dangerous "greasers," but we were already on alert. We knew about greasers. Greasers were the opposite of heads. They were into violence instead of love. They listened to country music instead of rock. Greasers didn't smoke grass or do LSD; they drank beer or even, in extreme cases, whiskey. They got into bar fights and were usually racists. They hated heads.

Heads were therefore scared of greasers. We lay low when greasers came around, knowing they would beat the pulp out of us if they noticed us. The local fellows said these particular greasers would have been pounding on us right now, if the Mounties had not distracted them. But with the Mounties gone, there was no one to draw their attention away from us. At this point, the local boys sheepishly slipped away, to their warm beds and snug homes. But we didn't have to worry: the greasers followed them out.

Along about 4 a.m. Robert began to nod out. That, however, violated the only other rule at an all night roadside diner: you cannot nod out.   I kept poking him and he kept stirring, then sinking back into torpor, Eventually I figured I should let him sleep because we were going to need at least one functional brain between the two of us to handle the rigors of tomorrow. So I used my body to shield Robert from the gaze of the cooks and I drank his coffee as well as mine to make it look like two of us were drinking, and I smoked our smokes and chattered to my sleeping buddy as if we were having a conversation, even though only one of us was talking (which has sometimes been true even when the other guy was awake.)

The Greaser

Finally, sunlight began to mix with and then replace the neon glare. Dawn had come. By 6:00 a.m. truckers were stopping in for breakfast.   The graveyard shift went home and a new set of workers took over the grill. I told Robert we had to hit the road. He could barely open his eyes and grumbled that he wanted to stay in the coffee shop but this struck me as a really bad idea. During the graveyard shift, when business was slow, we could occupy a booth on the strength of the single cup of coffee someone had bought us many hours ago, but now, with the morning crowd filling up the joint and spending real money, the management would want us to start buying or get going. Besides, in the bright, clean light of day, they would see us as vagrants and maybe call the cops.

"Let'em," said Robert. "What's the worst the cops 'r gonna do? Arrest us? Let them. I'm done, man. At least, we'll get a place to sleep." He said this several times as if he were joking but then started to take himself seriously.

I could not listen to this option. The son of the eminent Mir Amanuddin Ansary, the grandson of the famous Einuddin, the king's own physician back in Afghanistan in the old days, locked away as a vagrant in some jail cell in remotest Canada? Unthinkable! Impossible to endure even the thought of the shame my father would suffer if he ever heard, if God forbid the story were told to him in front of strangers.

"No, no, no," I insisted. "Let's not give up. We can do this." I rousted Robert out of there and dragged him to the highway with me, I force marched the two of us down the road to where the town gave way to countryside and the only cars coming would be headed someplace far away. Robert grumbled incoherently, staggering and stumbling and resisting. He had zero left in the energy tank. How could this be, given that he had actually caught some shut-eye, while I hadn't slept a wink? Actually, that's probably the reason: once you fall asleep, some kind of morphic chemical gets into your bloodstream and makes it harder to shake off the grogginess. I read that somewhere.

Anyway, I figured if I could just get us into a car, we'd be okay. I stuck out my thumb and the traffic blasted past us, dramatizing the indifference of the universe to our petty existence. But I braced against it as one must to get a ride, scraping up the last drops of optimism from the bottom of my soul to give my face an appealing brightness. Robert, however, couldn't do it, couldn't fake good cheer.

"Let's get back to town and turn ourselves in," he said. "Come on! It's a good deal. They keep you in jail for a couple of days, and it's okay, they treat you good, they give you three squares a day, man, and then they put you on a bus to the next town, I heard."

"You heard this where?"

He shrugged and gestured vaguely at the road that vanished in each direction. "You know."

I had heard very different things about jail. I had heard the guards beat you and so did the other prisoners. I didn't want to get beaten for three squares a day, no sir.

And I didn't have to. Suddenly, a wall of fact glistened between us, a wall only I could see—because Robert didn't know my secret: that I wasn't actually broke. that I had ten dollars hidden in my underwear. In my case, giving up didn't have to mean going to jail. It could simply mean walking back into Yorkton and buying a bus ticket to the next big town on the main highway.

But I couldn't tell Robert about the money, not now, not after we'd knocked about for so many days as brothers in poverty. It wasn't just the prospect of the withering look he'd give me. The crucial deciding factor was more concrete. Ten dollars would not be enough to save us both. It might get one of us out of this place, but not both. As I stood there, looking at Robert with this crucial fact percolating in my subconscious, my conscious thoughts and feelings went through a rearrangement.

Mere hours ago, I had been marveling at what different roads we had traveled to end up as comrades on the road and how little those differences really mattered. Who cared if I grew up in Kabul and he in Modesto, if I was a Reed College student while he was a high school dropout, if I was well versed in Heidegger and Kant while he was in good with the Gypsy Jokers? We listened to the same music, we shared the same political attitudes, we'd both seen where a guy could fly on LSD—we were brothers!

But now, in the cold light of day, with just enough money in my possession to save one of us, our similarities seemed trivial to me, our differences profound. Who was this guy, really? An ill-educated hood who bragged of his closeness with a motorcycle gang. What did we have in common? We liked the same music? Not even that, actually! Sure we both liked the Grateful Dead and Bob Dylan, but who didn't. The crucial test came after that. What else did he like? Three Dog Night. He had mentioned liking

Three Dog Night. *Three Dog Night,* for God's sake! This man wasn't my brother, he was a stranger!

My analysis was not wrong. He was in fact a stranger. Even if we had gotten a ride together at that moment, we would have parted ways forever a few miles further down the road. That's true. But I've thought about that moment many times since that day. At the time, I thought I was weighing the various factors and making a decision, but in retrospect I see that I wasn't thinking at all. My thoughts and attitudes were simply adjusting themselves as necessary to fit the choice I had already made. I've seen whole populations go through this process since then: all the op-eds and punditry, for example, that seem to precede but which actually only rationalize a nation's decision to go to war.

Robert and I stood there for a moment not saying anything, looking into each other's eyes. His were red, bleary, and brimming with despair. "Well," he said, "Do what you want, man. I'm going into town, turn myself in. I'm a vagrant."

Even then he didn't move and we stood silently.

"So what are you going to do?" he said finally.

"I'm going to keep hitching."

"All right, then. Goodbye," he said.

He crossed the highway, and we stood on opposite sides, both of us with our thumbs out, one of us hitching east, the other one west. A car soon stopped for Robert and took him back toward Yorkton. I never saw him again, of course.

I kept my thumb out, Dylan singing in my head, *with the cold eyes of Judas on him, his head began to spin.* My hitching stance was pro forma. I knew no one was going to stop for me. The universe rewards good faith, openness, and trust, not guile, greed, and dishonesty. I had earned no favors from the Sacred Oneness. I was only giving the road another fifteen minutes to avoid any risk of running into Robert back in town. As soon as it was safe, I intended to head in and catch a bus to wherever ten dollars would get me.

But wouldn't you know it, no sooner had Robert vanished than a car stopped for me. Had Robert waited five more minutes, he would have gotten out of Yorkton too. Instead, he would languish in jail tonight and I, the lying scoundrel with ten dishonest dollars hidden in his underpants, would escape. What kind of message was the universe trying to give me? I ran to the car and jumped in (only at that moment realizing that I had ended up with the tobacco and rolling papers Robert and I had bought together). The car didn't move. I glanced at the driver and saw a young man, five or six years older than me, mid-twenties, but all I could focus on was his light brown wavy hair glistening with hair cream oil and combed into a gleaming pile atop his head.

I had gotten into a car with a greaser, and the car wasn't moving. The intentions of the Universe began to take color and shape. The greaser stared at me with a big grin spread all over his face. I figured he was smiling at the thought of what my bones would sound like, breaking.

"Um...which way you headed?" I stammered, thinking that no matter what he said, I'd say I was headed elsewhere.

"East," he said dreamily.

We were on a highway that only went east and west, and I was hitching on the side that went east. "Oh," I said. "Well ..." But I could think of no excuse for getting out of the car. Besides, I didn't want to tell one more lie, not just after the Universe had given me this pass on my one big basic lie. "Me too," I admitted. I waited for him to take off, but he just kept sitting there, grinning, dreaming.

Then he started talking. "Three days ago," he said, "I was in Toronto. My wife sent me to the store to buy some milk. It's only two miles from the house to the store but on the way, I saw a beautiful blond girl standing next to the road with a Russian wolfhound as big as a horse. She was hitchhiking, so I stopped for her and she got into the car with me. Her dog filled the whole back seat. I said, 'Where are you going?' She said 'Edmonton.' Then she said ' How about you?' and I don't know what got into me. I said, 'Me too," and I hit the gas.   I never went home, I never called my wife, nothin'. I've just spent three days with this girl. I drove her a thousand miles and I let her off and she walked away, her and her dog, and man, I am in love. I am in love, man, and I never even fucked her. Never touched her. I'll probably never see her again. Where did you say you were headed?"

Some deep part of me exhaled.   "Back to Highway One and then east as far as you can take me. What's your final destination?"

He grinned that same dreamy, foolish, heartbreaking grin. "The grave, man. But Toronto before that. My wife's going to kill me."

"Toronto will do," I said diffidently, but my heart was romping. Toronto was pretty much on the U.S. border. I couldn't believe my luck. Now, when I least deserved it, the Universe was finally showering me with bounties. Hard to make heads or tails of this Universe and its whimsical ways.

That was the longest single ride I got, not just on that trip but ever in my hitch-hiking career. I drove 1,000 miles with that greaser called Kookie, and man, I got to like that guy, strange though it was for us to be together. Ten or twenty miles after he picked me up, we saw a couple of my fellow longhairs hitching. My new pal slowed down and stared at them balefully, then speeded up and hurled on by. I remember so clearly what he said next. "How'd you like if I picked up one of them butchers?" He chuckled at the very notion of taking such a foolish risk.

"Butchers?" I said. "What do you mean?"

"Didn't you see 'em? Them long-haired fellows, they're always hopped up on dope, you let one of 'em into your car, he'll slit your throat ear to ear 'fore you know it."

"Is that right?" I could not help but let my hands creep up to my head. Was Kookie blind? Did he not know he had one of those "butchers" in his car right then?

But when I touched my head, I realized something. Having been on the road for ten days now with no shower and no sleep, my hair had grown extremely slick with natural oil, and by constantly running my fingers through it, combing it back to keep it out of my eyes, I had draped it over my head till it was lying down flat and slick.

To Kookie, I looked like a greaser. And the rest of my outfit could fit that interpretation as easily as any other: my black, steel-tipped cowboy boots, my jeans, my denim work shirt, especially since I had lost the headband I was sporting when I left Portland.

At one point, early in our time together, Kookie flipped his glove box open and said, "Need some grease?" Yes, he actually called it grease. He handed me a tube of Wildroot Cream Oil. I had seen advertisements for that brand of hair cream in Afghanistan, cartoon strips that appeared on the back pages of the comic books we sometimes got from visiting Americans. They featured a character who looked like Dick Tracy but captured crooks by dint of having used Wildroot Hair Cream Oil. I had even used Wildroot hair cream oil a few times myself, as a teenager in Kabul, because greased-up Elvis-style hair was popular among young men there. We never called it grease though. We called it cream.

As we drove along, mile after endless mile of Canadian prairie, Kookie told me about his life. He married young, dropped out of high school as a result, and lived in the shadow of his wife's family. They were an Indian family, I don't know what tribe. She was a forceful woman herself, and she had five huge, domineering brothers. Kookie worked in a family-owned auto shop with these five. They outnumbered him, they outranked him, and the powerful family into which he'd married completely owned and squelched him. At the shop, he worried constantly about doing the wrong thing. "You get a car in to fix, man, there's lots of times there's going to be a frozen bolt you can't reach in there and when you get a wrench on it, finally, after you've skinned your knuckles to the bone and got grease bleeding into the cut, it breaks off on you, and then you're fucked, because the customer never believes a thing like that is just God's way of flippin' the finger on you, it's always your own fault, and there's always trouble about it, even when there's nothing you coulda' done, no way you were getting that bolt out without breaking it." Kookie's days were filled with fault, and all of it his.

Then one day he went to the store for milk, picked up a hitchhiker, and disappeared for a week. "I never even fucked her," he kept repeating in solemn wonder. "Man, I am going to remember that girl till the day I die."

I bet he did too. I mean, if that cross-country trip looms so dramatically in my mind, I can't imagine what place it holds in Kookie's life: his one wild breakout. And I wonder who that girl was, too, and what she remembers about Kookie, if anything. I think about the three of us, scattered across the globe now, who knows where, each of us on the prow of our own history, three lines that intersected through that one moment near Winnipeg over 40 years ago.

We listened to the radio the whole time: country mostly with a few AM pop radio stations thrown in there. The 2525 song was started to fade out. AM radio had found a replacement for it, a Seals and Croft song that I still sometimes hear in greatest-hits countdowns: "Summer breeze ... makes me feel fine....blowing through the jasmine of my ... miiiiiii-hi-hiiiiiind ." There was still residual news about men landing on the moon but I don't remember what remained to be said about it. As I said before, the whole event seemed dull to me, and Kookie had a similar view. "Well," he said, "they put some men up there. It's just a rock now." I liked that observation: all that splendid technology, and what was the achievement? They took what had been the moon, and turned it into "just a rock."

The weather was wonderful, the grandest middle of the best summer in North American history—1969! And we were good buddies, Kookie and me. When he found out I had only ten dollars, he told me not to even think about paying for meals, he'd take care of me. I couldn't help him drive, because I didn't know how to drive yet, but he didn't care about that either. He just wanted an audience for his stories about The Girl with the Dog as Big as a Horse, and I was a good audience, because I didn't just listen, I marveled with him, I adored his girl vicariously through his reminiscences.

What strikes me now is that he never felt a need to fake a romantic triumph with her, never used her to celebrate his own prowess, sexual or otherwise. He only wanted me to confirm that something wonderful had happened in his life, so wonderful he'd take it to his grave and even on his last days be elevated by the memory of it, and I was glad to oblige, because this was the reason I had set out across the continent with (fifteen) dollars: to witness at first hand miracles that would reify and magnify my belief in the essential goodness of the Universe.

It's true that when I set out I was thinking more in terms of *myself* meeting up with a blond girl and her Russian wolfhound. In my visions of that miraculous encounter, falling in love definitely played some part, but this was good too, the mere story of it, the fact that it happened in this other fellow's life, this was good too. In a sense it didn't matter who it happened to. The fact that it happened to *anyone* proved that the Universe was a compassionate and beneficent papa with a bag of miracles to dispense to lighthearted souls gifted with enough trust and daring to take spontaneous risks. It didn't matter who received the blessings as long as I knew about them and believed in them, and I did.

The Ashram

Toward the end of my time with Kookie, I started to feel hyperaware of the LSD in my pocket. Hitching across a border with that acid felt risky. The time had come to buy a bus ticket. My ten bucks got me all the way to Syracuse with enough left over for potato chips but I was then down to three pennies. It felt great to be back in a land I knew, but any way you cut it three pennies isn't much. I had to go to ground somewhere safe. I could have headed straight to D.C. where my mother lived, option A, but that felt *too* safe. I had hit the road to experience the sacred, but all I'd done so far was almost starve, almost drown, almost go to jail, almost get beat up—and witness someone else's transcendence.

So I decided to exercise Option B. I would take the road that led to Ralph Garner, my best friend. .

Ralph had just graduated from Dartmouth. It was there that he had converted to the religious teachings of Kirpal Singh and become a Satsangis or a "worshipful meditator", as his followers called themselves. At the time, Ralph outlined the guru's promises to me in very physical terms. He said Kirpal Singh taught a meditation technique that connected one to a mystical stream of sound, a sound most people could not hear. After a while, this stream carried one away, as a breeze carries a feather, carried one up out of this world and into a realm known as the Astral Plane, which was higher and better than the Earthly plane but was only the first of many levels above ours, each progressively less physical and more spiritual. Those who stayed with "the program" would eventually rise to the highest level, the purely spiritual one, where they would merge with God.

Kirpal Singh proclaimed the Astral Plane real and tangible. Ralph reported some of the descriptions he had heard: in the Astral Plane, the breezes were visible: they looked like mother-of-pearl. When they played across a person's skin, the sensation was pure pleasure. Thoughts and wishes materialized instantly there. If you wanted to fly you imagined yourself flying and suddenly you were doing it.   Once you were in the Astral Plane, you actually experienced these things and saw the truth of Kirpal Singh's philosophy for yourself. If you didn't like what you saw, fine: you could drop out. As Ralph put it, Kirpal Singh didn't ask you to take anything on faith.   He promised to *show* you. Ralph said he would get with the program, and if he didn't make it to the Astral Plane, or if he got there and it wasn't as advertised, he'd know the whole thing was bogus.

So you see, this wasn't one of those "cults" you hear about.

I remember something else he told me after he found Kirpal Singh. We were coming out of a movie theater where we had just seen Zeferelli's *Romeo and Juliet*. Ralph said, "That movie expresses better than anything I could possibly say, why I am on this path with Kirpal Singh."

"Oh? How so?"

"Because what the movie says is true: the world is pain. Love leads to pain. Not having love leads to pain. Everything that can possibly happen to you in the so-called Real World is painful. It's pain now or it's pain later because all good things come to an end. Kirpal Singh offers a ticket out of all this pain. Now that I'm with him, I don't have to deal with pain because I'm on the express train to bliss."

I was young and therefore impressed. But I was also me, and therefore skeptical. The express train outa' here—I had a hunch no such thing existed, but I made my own second derivative of Ralph's resolve. I too would scrutinize this Kirpal Singh thing, but not by joining his cult. I didn't have to, because I had a pal on the inside. I'd wait to see what Ralph found out. If he reported that the Astral Plane was real and he'd been there, I'd get a ticket and board the train to bliss too.

Now that Ralph had graduated from college, he expected to be drafted soon. He would probably hear from his draft board by fall. While he waited, he was spending the summer in New Hampshire at a spiritual retreat called the Sant Bani Ashram. I could go there and have a place to sleep and food to eat, even with zero money. And at this point, I do mean zero. Even my last three cents were gone. I don't know where I spent them. Those three cents I musta' squandered.

Hitching to the ashram took most of a day and Ralph exulted to see me. The ashram featured incredible beauty and absolute peace. A slow-moving, saintly old woman presided over the place. Ralph was thrilled to introduce her to me as the lovely soul who had introduced him to "Master"— the term everyone used for the guru-guy. Once or twice I might have heard him referred to as "Kirpal Singh," but mostly it was Master this and Master that.

The ashram had once been a working farm. It had a few old farm houses, lots of trees, and a few atmospheric cows browsing and grazing in the distance. It had the greenery of a New England summer. It had flies and bees buzzing in tall grass. A man named Kent, another Satsangi living at the Ashram, was a stained glass craftsman and had set up a workshop in a former chicken coop. He taught me how to use his equipment, how to stretch lead and cut glass to make objets d'art, and how to solder thin copper foil for finer items, tighter seams. I loved that work.

I was attracted to it especially because life on the ashram was...how should I put it? Did I say peaceful? Yeah, but peaceful doesn't quite capture it. Did I say spare? Yeah, there was a certain spare quality to the physical environment. The rooms had no furniture except mats on the floor. The built-in bookshelves had no books or magazines except for fat volumes of Master's thoughts. No pictures hung on the cleanly whitewashed walls except for framed portraits of Master, a benign looking elderly Indian gentleman with a thick, white beard.

In fact, Kirpal Singh was a dead ringer for an elderly relative of mine back in Afghanistan, a fellow known as MawMaw, who lived with us in Kabul and moved with us to Lashkargah, and who took care of us kids and told us fabulous stories and killed our beloved dog because he was jealous of the attention we gave it. MawMaw, too, looked benign and had a white beard like "Master." My mother loved that old man dearly until she discovered that he exploited our trust in him to steal our family blind. I don't mean to say that Kirpal Singh was a thief, a fake, and a criminal. I only wish to make the point that you can't tell anything definitive from looks. But if looks do prove anything, then Kirpal Singh was a very, very kindly old man. It's just that his kindly mug was the only image to be seen at Sant Bani Ashram. So yes, "spare" was another apt adjective for this place, and yet "spare" does not quite nail it either.

Did I mention slow? Slow applies too. Very little happened at the Sant Bani Ashram. We were awoken each morning at the crack of dawn, we all enjoyed a slow, spare breakfast of banana bread and tea, and then the Satsangis began their meditations which, from the outsider's point of view, consisted of sitting for hours on end without moving or speaking. Uh...may I be excused now?

In short, yes, slow too describes life at the Sant Bani Ashram but even "slow" doesn't get to the essence of it. A better word would be...

Boring! Ah! There's the word I'm looking for. Life at the Sant Bani Ashram was *borrrrrring*.

Boring boring boring boring!

Okay, granted, boring to me because I was not on the bus to bliss, not in the process of leaving this world so that I could never again be hurt by love, hate, or indifference. But during those days at the ashram, I came to realize I would never board that bus, because my program was exactly the opposite of Sant Bani's. I wanted to feel the raw embrace of life itself. I wanted to experience love, hate, and every other passion. I wanted to plunge into the thick of the world, and care, and do, and be hurt, not for any masochistic pleasure but for the realness of it all. I wanted the memory of pain for later, because I wanted to know some truth that I deemed accessible only through suffering. It seemed to me then (and seems to me still) that no insight worth having can come easily. The monumental and essential truth couldn't possibly be sitting by the side of the road where all you've got to do is sign right here, or be available in some booth where all you've got to do is drop a coin in the slot. To me then—and to me now—nothing you can have by signing on the line and doing as told could be worth having except in a small way. A vacuum cleaner is clearly useful, you can put something like that on your credit card, that's the sort of thing you can get the more-or-less easy way. But it seemed to me that any spiritual harvest you could get in that same way would be on a par with a vacuum cleaner.

The Satsangi enterprise didn't interest me because they were busy earning spiritual vacuum cleaners, from my perspective. I joined their meditations the first couple of mornings, but then I could take no more. On the third day, I decided to skip the meditation session and work quietly in the stained glass workshop while the others were doing their thing.

But when I knocked off at noon and went to join the Satsangis for lunch, Kent had an issue to raise. He felt so passionately about this issue that the veins bulged in his temples as he spoke. While all the others watched in scandalized embarrassment he addressed me directly. "Tamim," he said, "I did NOT set up the glass workshop for people to work in during Satsang."

Discomfort filled the room like expanding foam, plugging every social crack and crevice. Kent bulged at me and glowered at my silence. Even Ralph bristled disapproval of me. I felt humiliated and betrayed, and searched for an adequate response, and could not find one. Rarely had I felt so angry as I did at that moment. I wanted to make Kent taste the same humiliating displeasure he was causing me. But in the end I just bowed my head and said, "I'm sorry, Kent. It won't happen again." I felt like a coward and hypocrite for buckling. I should have confronted him, I later thought. I should have told that whole group what I thought of their bus to bliss. But there were fifty of them and one of me, and so, contemptibly enough, in that setting, I found myself unable to speak out.

Ralph and Kent were driving south that weekend and had already agreed to take me with them, so I had to tolerate a few more days of excruciating boredom in the Place Where Time Had No Meaning. Dressing me down made Kent feel pretty good about himself, which led him to forgive me and thereafter to treat me with the gentle, compassionate understanding appropriate to a man bound for bliss.

In those last few days, the one bright moment came when our whole ashram visited another spiritual resort nearby. I realized I had met the "guru" of this other ashram at Carleton College. Back then he called himself Richard Alpert. Originally a professor of psychology at Harvard, he and his fellow professor Timothy Leary were among the first to take LSD and it bonged them right out of their mindset. They lost or quit their jobs and began to preach the gospel of turning on, tuning in, and dropping out—in fact, I think it was Alpert who coined that famous phrase although Leary got the credit.   Alpert came to Carleton in that period and delivered a memorable lecture. He told us that according to some study or other, the average college dropout now had a higher IQ than the average college graduate. We all laughed and clapped, and he said, "You laugh but...here you are." Which made us laugh and clap again. Mainly, though, on that night he told us about acid. He didn't praise it or promote it. He just told us what had happened to him when he took it. It didn't give him pleasure, he said; it gave him insight. It opened his eyes to what was real.

My friend Ralph, who was at Dartmouth then, had already taken LSD and had good things to report, but I had hesitated to try it until I heard Richard Alpert. He tipped me over the edge. A few weeks later I met a film student who was selling acid to finance his art projects. I bought two tabs from him and took one. Two hours later, all I felt was nervous—and pissed off. I was ready to take the second tab, but a guy I knew came along and said, "Wait a minute, Chester. Smoke a joint with me first." We smoked a joint and got stoned. "Big deal, this is just grass," I said. "I've been stoned before. I wanna' trip. Where's the acid?"

I guess I was hoping for hallucinations.   I went back to my room for the second tab. The room was full of guys smoking dope and listening to the Rolling Stones. The Satanic Majesties album. I was all set to join them when suddenly the interconnectedness of everything snapped clear. I saw—no, not saw: I *felt* how, when any one thing shifted, the relationship of everything to everything shifted. It was happening right then. It was happening always. It was happening everywhere. In every second of my life, I changed the universe, the universe changed me, everyone changed everyone, and it was all happening simultaneously, because All Is One. I jumped out of my chair, blown-away-amazed, grabbed the nearest saggy, droopy, stoned guy, pointed to him, and hollered, "That's grass,"   then pointed to myself and yelled, "This is acid."

He nodded and sank back into the music, while I wafted up from the room and became part of the transcendent realm that Richard Alpert had talked about.

Now that I was meeting him again at this ashram, he called himself Baba Ram Dass. He sported a beard and wore Indian-style all-white holy-man clothes. After an (excruciatingly boring) joint meditation session, a bunch of us gathered around Ram Dass to chat, and I found him just as witty, interesting, and authentic as he had been when he called himself Richard Alpert. This man really was seeking something: not a formula but an authentic breakthrough—just the thing I was looking for.

He told me that his problem with LSD was that you always came down. In an effort to stay in that transcendent realm he kept taking more and more acid, until at last, one day, he took so much, he lost track of who he was amidst the eruptions of revelation, and when he groped for it, all he heard was a voice asking "Who is this? Who is this?" That was his moment of crisis, but he dealt with it by asking himself the following question: "Who is asking 'Who is this?'" That question brought home to him that what he had always hitherto called "himself" were like garments. He could put them on, he could take them off. Deep inside all the garments was his real self: a pinpoint of consciousness. That pinpoint was the only Real Thing. He went off to seek a way to be in this consciousness all the time. He humbly admitted he wasn't there yet, but he thought he might have found a way to *get* there through meditation.

Unlike Kirpal Singh and his devotees, Richard Alpert/Ram Dass had lively, original ideas worth talking about and discussing, because his ideas might change yours and yours might change his. Kirpal Singh had his immutable truth. You sat down and heard what it was and either said I-accept or not-for-me. Conversation was not part of it because his program would not change because of you. The only possibility was that you would change because of it. I didn't care, therefore, if Kirpal Singh had a point. To me, it was inherently the wrong sort of point.

On the appointed day, Ralph, Kent, and I climbed into a car and headed south. Somehow, as we approached New York, we got on a road with no exits and so we ended up going through the tunnel to New Jersey. On the other side we explained our mistake to the toll keeper, and he let us go back through the tunnel without charging us a toll. But on the other side we got on the same wrong highway and ended up in the suburbs north of the city. Twice, we'd aimed our car at the biggest city on Earth and both times missed it.

Ralph and Kent decided this was a sign. The Universe was trying to tell us New York was too big, ugly, mean, and non-spiritual. We should stay out of it. They decided to go back to the ashram. They said I was welcome to come along.

But I did not want to go back to Sant Bani Ashram. Even that single distant glimpse of New York had sparked a hunger in me. Technically, I was on my way to the safety of my mother's house in Washington D.C. and having squandered all my money, I should no doubt have stuck to that plan, but instead I asked Ralph and Kent to let me off and lend me a dime. They couldn't get into Manhattan, but I was betting I could do it, with my thumb and a prayer. It wasn't just the thrill of metropolis calling to me. I knew a girl in New York. I had her phone number in my wallet.

Soulmates

When I say "knew," I don't mean "knew her well." I don't mean I knew her so intimately well that I had ever actually seen her face or heard her voice. But I knew her all the same: we were soulmates.

Or so I had been told by our mutual friend Phoebe Sutton. Ah, Phoebe Sutton! Let me pause to reminisce a little about Phoebe Sutton. She and I overlapped for a year at Carleton as freshmen and quickly formed a best-buddy bond. Phoebe had short, bobbed hair and wore glasses behind which she had a tendency to blink. She stood five foot eight which she considered way too tall for a girl. I knew this was her opinion of herself because she told me so within five minutes of our meeting. Her own feeling about her height gave her the gangly gawkiness of a camel. She spoke in rapid bursts and looked at the world with a fetching combination of curiosity, naiveté, and excitement. She was the first in a long line of women who shaped me by seeing in me qualities I didn't have, thereby inciting me to acquire those qualities so as to deserve the approval I was already getting. Phoebe thought I was a poet, so I wrote poetry. Phoebe thought I deserved a beautiful girlfriend, so I formed the same opinion about myself. Phoebe toiled hard to hook me up with someone suitable, and I was happy for the help. Phoebe didn't think she herself was nearly good enough for me, and therefore I didn't think so either. Phoebe discovered that I was interested in a girl named Ruth who lived in her dorm. She went on a spying mission for me, found out everything I needed to know to ask Ruth out, and got us dating. After each date, she collared me for a long chat about how it had gone, hanging breathlessly on my report, and offering helpful advice at key points. Ruth and I didn't last long, I barely remember her, but those after-date chats with Phoebe still linger.

Long after I knew Phoebe, I realized I adored her, but only once during our year of palling around did the least suspicion of my attraction to this girl even enter my own conscious mind. It happened in the late spring of our freshman year, when some group produced a "Bohemian night," meaning that they turned our Midwestern college "tea-room" into a simulacrum of a fifties-style beatnik coffeehouse--a sad simulacrum, to be sure: a sorry, shallow, Minnesota–style gosh-you-betcha' imitation of a Greenwich Village dive. My best friend KC made an appearance at that event. He stood at the mike and growled a long string of senseless words, while another friend of ours pounded on a garbage can lid. Later, when someone asked him what the hell he thought he had done, he said he had delivered "some of my best beat poetry, by God."

Phoebe Sutton was doing duty as a waitress that night and she had dressed to fit the theme. Her costume involved leaving her glasses back in her dorm room. Yes, that old cliché came to life before my eyes: Phoebe took off her glasses. The rest of her costume consisted of a pair of black tights under a man's long white dress shirt over breasts unfettered by any bra: in 1967, this was a daring departure from social norms. She left one more button unbuttoned than the Midwestern fashion of the day considered quite appropriate, and she finished the look with a long string of fake pearls.

When she came up to take our coffee order, I reeled. Phoebe! Buddy! Izzat you?

She sat down to chat with me, and of course her voice and words instantly turned her back into my cozily familiar Phoebe: she punctuated her conversation with self-deprecating little hoots and embroidered it with an idiosyncratic set of pseudo-nervous gestures—years later, Diane Keaton caught the essence of Phoebe Sutton perfectly with her portrayal of Annie Hall, thereby turning the Phoebe I knew into an icon that captivated all of America; but when I knew Phoebe, neither of us had an idea she was Annie Hall; she was just my Carleton buddy.

That night at the faux fifties-coffeehouse, I was caught in a pincer-grip of cognitive dissonance: being with Phoebe was just as comfortable as it had ever been: she was good ol' Phoebe, same jokes, same voice...But those legs, my God, where had those come from? Sheathed in those black tights! Five foot eight wasn't tall enough for legs like that: she needed to be seven feet tall and most of it below the waist to accommodate such gams. And that loose shirt with the suggestion of breasts bobbling underneath! I knew Phoebe wasn't a boy, but I had never thought of her as a girl either, she had been in some third, female best-buddy category. Now I realized my best-bud was totally hot. I made some elliptical mention of this discovery to Phoebe, carefully couching it in language that would not sound like I was hitting on her, but she laughed and oh-pshawed it out of consideration, dismissing the impression she was making on me: so it was working, she inquired? So she was actually managing to trick the eye momentarily into imagining that she had what Ruth and all those other desirable women had? Well, that was a bubble soon popped, alas. Then she leaned across the table and confided a bit of news: she was leaving Carleton next year, transferring to the University of Colorado at Boulder.

"Why?" I said.

"Because it's a party school."

"A party school?"

"Yes. Open dorms, guys and girls can get together. It's the virginity thing, Tamim."

"Ah! The virginity thing," I murmured. "Hmm."

I knew it well, this virginity thing. Would that I had known anything else in the world as intimately well as I knew this virginity thing.

"I just feel hung up by it," Phoebe went on. "I can't go on with my life till I get this virginity thing out of the way. I figure I'll go to this party school and just make it happen. Simply make it happen. You know? And then I can relax and figure out what I want to do with the rest of my life."

We discussed her conundrum in solemn, friendly terms until the evening ended, and then she went back to her dorm, and I went back to mine, where I stayed up late into the wee hours, lamenting with my friends, all virginal nerds like myself, the lack of "babes" in our lives.

Well, I make that long tangent by way of introducing Liz Croce, the girl in Manhattan whose phone number I was carrying in my wallet. Liz and Phoebe had grown up together in Brookings, South Dakota. They'd been best friends since childhood. Phoebe thought of herself as restrained, conservative, inhibited, staid, shy, and conventional, and she passionately admired people who were wild, uninhibited, creative, poetic, and unfettered. In this category she placed two people above all others: Liz and (for some reason) me. Naturally, therefore, Phoebe felt that Liz and I should get to know each other and I, well: I was interested.

Liz had blazed a rep as a rebel in her small town. She was an only child, born late in life to rigidly religious Presbyterian parents. From Phoebe's accounts, I pictured her dread parents as the couple in Grant Wood's American Gothic. When Liz got to high school, she waded into trouble. Nowadays, "trouble" would mean shooting crack, gangbanging, or at least breaking windows. But in 1967, in South Dakota, the trouble had to do with writing and speaking poetry. It's true, of course, that Liz wasn't reciting Edgar A. Guest. *Blonde on Blond* still lay in the future, but Dylan was already spouting words like *don't wanna be a bum, you better chew gum, the pump don't work 'cuz the vandals took the handles* and before him there was Kerouac, spraying stuff like *why the wild ground and bodies bare and breaks--I quaked when the giver creamed, when my father screamed, my mother dreamed.* Who can fathom what is happening to a girl who starts speaking in tongues like that? In fairness I should add that some of her parents' alarm also had to do with Liz's urge to seek out consciousness expanding drugs, but poetry was the main marker, the most palpable sign of her departure from the ways of normal folks. It would be wrong to say her parents disapproved of this departure. Their feelings went way beyond disapproval. They thought their child had gone insane. They locked her up in the house to keep her from her friends, all of whom they considered agents of Satan. Liz tried to run away, but the cops caught her and dragged her home. Her parents then did the only thing they *could* do: committed her to a mental institution. I mean what *you* do if your kid started spouting poetry?   Liz spent some months in that institution. When she got out, she knew enough to act chastened and keep her mouth shut, but she was merely biding her time, waiting for her 18th birthday.

When Phoebe first told me about this girl, Liz was living at home, caged in her room and cut off from the world. She was allowed to write to oldest-friend Phoebe but not to communicate with anyone else on Earth except her parents and through them with school authorities and church leaders. Phoebe felt her friend needed the sunshine of similar minds and classified me as one such mind. She arranged that I would write to Liz, she would enclose my letters with hers, and Liz would send responses to me in envelopes addressed to Phoebe. That was the plan.

I wrote to Liz pronto, and what I wrote was crazy surreal stuff because that's what Phoebe admired. "The moondog howls in the swamp at the edge of midnight where only God's chosen orchids bloom and only when the sun is in Scorpio..." I wrote.

That's not an actual quote, mind you, just my present day approximation of what I think I might have written back then: the first words that rolled off my tongue, anything that sounded cryptic.

My letters inspired Liz to write back equally nonsensical pseudo-Dylanesque verbal streams, on scented stationary, in a spidery little hand, with a thin-tipped pen, decorating the borders of her letters with floral and geometric designs and with icons that looked as if they might have significance in some unknown culture. Thus did we become pen pals. Every week or so I sent her a letter and every week or so I got one back. If we had opened up to each other authentically even the tiniest bit in those letters, we might have cultivated a really deep relationship.

But in all of that voluminous correspondence, I did not learn one single personal fact about Liz nor did I impart any. It was all moondogs and orchids, Satan's sweat and heaven's beads. She never asked what I was studying, whether I had a girlfriend, what I wanted to do or be in life, nothing. She never asked why I had such an unusual name, and if she knew that I was from Afghanistan I don't remember that she ever asked about it. That stuff all belonged to the trivial Earthly plane. We were meeting on a higher level.

That summer she managed to escape from home, and our correspondence slacked off. The next year Phoebe was gone from my life too, but just before I started at Reed, on a road trip through the Rocky Mountain region, I stopped in Boulder and hunted up Phoebe Sutton. She had taken care of the virginity thing by then, and in so doing had acquired a sleepy, cat-like sensuality, which I was permitted to witness but not touch.

Phoebe told me Liz had landed in New York and gave me Liz's mailing address. I kept meaning to renew our correspondence, but life kept happening. Later, I did drop Liz a mundane note to let her know I was in Oregon, going to Reed College. Liz sent me her phone number and told me to look her up if I was ever in New York. It was the shortest letter I had ever received from her and the only one ever to convey any concrete information, but it was still on scented notepaper and decorated with hearts, stars, and mystical symbols. I had that letter in my pocket now, right in there with the two panes of just-in-case blotter acid.

The Liz'n'Me Club

I alighted from Kent's car, bummed a dime from Ralph because that's what a phone call cost in those days, and hitched into the heart of Manhattan. It was five or six o'clock in the afternoon by the time I called Liz. She answered on the second ring and sounded thrilled to hear my actual voice at last! Was I staying in New York, she wanted to know? Would I stay with her, she pleaded: pleaaaaaase? She had a tiny place, a one-room apartment, only one bed—but what did space matter among friends, especially two so close as we?

Oh boy, I was thinking. Yes, of course, I pictured sex--but in the most romantic terms. The two soul mates meet at last. And she would be lovely. And there would be hunger between us—a hunger hard to sate with mere sex, but we'd try, oh we'd try.

Yes, I said, I *could* stay with her. I had no money for a taxi or even for the subway, so I walked the 40 blocks or so to Liz's apartment in the heart of Greenwich Village. The city amazed me: everywhere else, urban density thins out after you hit the core. Here, I seemed to land in the core and no matter how long I walked, I saw no sign that I was getting out of it. I just walked and walked through block after endless block of downtown and more downtown, the density stacked up high in buildings that reflected the twilight back and forth between towering banks of windows.

Down below 14th street, the city just got better. Life felt like a movie. Smoky little bars lined both sides of the street, and my stride turned rhythmic to match the electric guitar music wailing out of those dark little doorways. Here I was in a place as thickly crowded with artists and poets as the fields outside our compound in Kabul were with fat-tailed sheep, camels, and dogs on days when the nomads pulled into town.

I made it to Liz's building and she buzzed me in. Three flights of steep stairs brought me to an open door restrained by a chain, and there she was: two shining eyes in a small, round, freckled face—that's what I saw first. What she saw was a guy with long hair, horn-rimmed glasses, sunburned skin, frayed levis, black boots.

"Tamim?" she ventured.

"Liz?"

She shut the door to release the chain and flung it wide. "I am soooo glad to see you! To *meet* you," she added.

"We've already met," I declaimed.

"Ah..." she sighed. "In the deepest way!" She stepped away from the door, giving me room to enter. Her apartment was about the same size as the largest closet in my current house. I noticed this only vaguely. I was still busy taking in the sight of Liz, trying to reconcile what I was seeing with what I had imagined on the way up here and what I had pictured during our two-year correspondence.

Her skin had a sun-starved urban pallor against which her freckles stood out. Her russet hair was gathered into a couple of sweet little pigtails. Her face was small, round and made up entirely of smaller constituent round parts—round cheeks, round eyes, a round pert little nose. She was short and just plump enough that Zap Comics cartoonist R. Crumb would have seen her as ripe. Her thighs stretched her levis in the way that R. Crumb liked to depict, her ass was round in the seat of the levis, and she had disproportionately large, R. Crumb-pleasing breasts. She was R. Crumb's dream girl. I took in the incongruities of her: the plain cotton T-shirt, the unglamorous blue jeans, and the corn-fed cowgirl look, overlaid now with a layer of later experience, a hint of excess suggested by the creases below her eyes, the eyes of an urban night creature. It all added up to "cute." Somehow it did not immediately add up to sexy, but she was certainly cute, and I could hope that as I relaxed into her presence she would begin to look sexy too.

She held out her arms, but it was more like that Jesus Christ pose you see on postcards, not an invitation for me to come closer and be physical. She began to speed-talk: "I'm so glad you called, I'm so glad you're here. You know, some guys, I wouldn't even let them come up to my apartment much less ask them if they would stay with me because they'd make it into something sexual, you know? But you're different. I can trust you. I know you live on a higher plane, it's so great to be with someone like you where you know it's a spiritual relationship and it's not going to turn into something crude and crass, like physical or something, you know? I mean you're incredible, Tamim, because you're different, you're not like other guys."

I puffed with pride about my difference from other guys, although at the same time, deep down, secretly, I had to admit, even at the time, I felt a little disappointment about my elevated consciousness. As usual her words pulled me into the shape they described. I felt inescapably locked into becoming the guy she was praising. Already I was rearranging my fantasies to make this be exactly what I had been looking forward to with Liz, an elevated, spiritual interaction. We would smoke a few joints and talk about cosmic things, this would be oh-so-good, none of that ugly physical stuff.

"How long can you stay?" she chirped. "At least a week, I hope! I'm going to this big rock concert upstate, everyone's going to be there, the Airplane, the Dead, even Dylan maybe, it's near where he lives, but not if I have to go alone, will you come with me? Please, please, will you come?"

"Uh... sure...but...I—"

"But what?"

"I've just hitched across the continent. I'm busted. I mean, flat broke, Liz. I don't have a dime. Not one penny. "

"Oh!" she scoffed. "A dime! A penny! That's just money. If you're worrying about money, stop worrying. I have money. I'll get you a ticket, I've got this...like..." She paused, having come to the verge of a humiliating confession, then bit her lower lip and blurted it out: "I have this straight job, like in an office you know? It's awful and I'm, like, a slave, they really suck the soul out of you, but I mean, what's it for if you can't take your spiritual twin to the greatest concert ever? I mean everyone's going to be there, did I mention Dylan? And everyone will be getting high..."

"Well," I said. "Okay. We'll go."

So far, I had been with Liz for five minutes, and already I'd agreed to spend the night with her but not touch her and to go to a rock concert with her, not in the city but someplace upstate. This was, to my mind, more than enough business. Now I was hungry. I was about to ask Liz what she had in mind for dinner, when she blurted out, "Hey! So you've just hitchhiked across the country? Ohmigod, that's so cool!"

"Mostly across Canada," I noted.

"Oo, double cool. Canada! If I were a man, that's where I'd go, even if they didn't try to draft me. Canada is all about peace, man. Far out! So you've been hitching?" And then she did a double take. Something hit her. "So you're used to it, huh. You must be good at it," she exclaimed. "I want to hitch to Boston, but it's hard for a girl. You want to hitch to Boston with me? I'd love that. Let's hitch to Boston together, wouldn't that be so cool? You and me, on the road together. Wanna'?"

"Okay," I said. "Let's do that someday. Sure. When might you want to go?"

"Right now!" She had just settled onto a huge pillow but she jumped up again.

"Now? But I just got here."

"So you're still in the traveling mode. And I'm ready. What do we need?"

"To hitch? Nothing, really."

"Nothing? So we can just hit the road?"

"Well, we have to figure out which road ... and we have to get to the right freeway ramp..."

"That's easy! I've got a map, I know the city. So you into it?"

I didn't want to say no. I didn't want to say I was tired and hungry, and I just wanted to have some dinner, drink some beer, smoke a joint, have some sex, and crash out. Cool people in the know always want to go and go. They always long to find out what lies beyond the horizon, a thirst they can never quench because no matter how far they go, the horizon is still out there, unreached and unreachable.

I didn't want to be the guy who stopped reaching for the unreachable. Also, I didn't want to take a stand on what Liz and I should do together. I didn't want to commit to *my* version of the Liz'n'Me club, lest it cost me my membership in the Liz'n'Me club. I was only an affable member of the club, by no means a troublemaker, certainly not someone who was going to buck the rules, just someone who needed a little clarification. What were they again, the duties required of members? That upon arriving in New York City, one get the hell out of New York City? Fine, fine, no problem. That's pretty much exactly what I myself had been wanting.

"Hitch to Boston," I said. "Cool. Let's go. We're already late."

And we *were* late. The sun had set. We'd have to hitch to Boston in the dark and I didn't even know what we were hitching to in Boston. Before I knew it, though, we were on a ramp, and then we were in the back seat of some car hurling north in the dark, and the couple giving us the ride were telling us they were fascinating people themselves, did a lot of traveling, and they were not tourists, wherever they went they got down among the people and did what the people did, in Spain, in Zambia, in New Zealand and Brazil other exotic places.

When they finally lost interest in us and started conversing with each other, Liz told me why we needed to go to Boston. It had to do with the big concert she had mentioned. She had given some fellow money to buy a whole bunch of tickets for her, and we were going up there to take delivery. She wanted to be able to give tickets to all her friends. I understood the feeling. Extravagant, ruinous generosity is an Afghan thing to do, a way of racking up prestige among friends. I understood Liz's motives. She was just trying to be a good Afghan.

It took Liz and me six rides to get to Boston. Everyone who picked us up knew about the big concert next weekend, and all of them—even that rich couple who traveled to places like Zambia and Brazil and got down among the natives—were planning to be there. Every single person had his or her own idea of what bands would be playing at the concert. Some said Big Brother, some said the Airplane, others said Ritchie Havens, Buffalo Springfield, even Jimi Hendrix—the list went on and on. It was an impossible list, of course, but if even half of those bands showed up, this would be a monster concert. Even a quarter of them—but what were the chances? Really.

I murmured some mention of this to Liz , but my doubts bounced off her like pebbles off the windshield of a Mack truck. "I've got a vibe about this one," she kept insisting.

We made it to Boston before midnight and found Liz's friends. They lived in an apartment on Beacon Hill, a very sparsely furnished apartment. No rugs in that place, just bare hardwood floors covered with grime. One room had a thrift store couch in front of a TV and empty beer cans littering the floor all around it. In the kitchen, I saw an overflowing trashcan and splashes of spaghetti sauce crusted on the counters. Excellent acid rock was thundering out of enormous speakers, slithering guitar lines wrapped around sturdy columns of bass boom-boom: early San

Francisco sound, Quicksilver Messenger Service, I judged, or Moby Grape.

A large number of men and women seemed to live in that apartment. The men were older guys, in their mid- to late-twenties or maybe even hitting their early thirties, rough characters with black leather jackets and beards.

The women had hard faces too, and they looked worn. Some of them were cooking foul-smelling soup in big tureens in the kitchen, but they were moving slowly as if "tired of themselves and all of their creations." Some of them had tattoos, which were visible because they weren't wearing much: baggy shorts, flouncy skirts, halter tops that displayed wide expanses of bony chest between baggy breasts, or blouses left carelessly unbuttoned to reveal grimy cleavage and any amount of mammary flesh. Skirts were allowed to flounce carelessly and if a skirt crept up a thigh it was never decorously tugged back down.

None of this aroused me, because it had no flirtation in it. The women didn't seem to feel beautiful in their own bodies Their attitude seemed to be: why bother to keep myself covered, what have I got worth looking at? Such was the feeling I got anyway. One of them plopped wearily on a couch with broken springs and her butt on impact raised a cloud of dust from the aged seat cushions; when she pulled her legs up to sit cross-legged, her skirt tented and I saw that she was naked underneath: her pussy staring out at me like some squat black-bearded troll.

Our arrival had set off a brief flurry of interest, energy, and activity, but that soon died away. Everyone went back to slouching around listlessly. No one was sleeping, but no one seemed especially awake either.

Liz didn't appreciate the scene. She announced that we had come to get the tickets. The woman with the troll between her legs said she was going to the concert. The hard ones with the halter tops and tattoos said they were going, wouldn't miss it. Yes, they all agreed, this would be a great one. But no one went to fetch the tickets. Liz pressed for information, but the women were too drained and were feeling too worthless to respond. "Why ask me," was their attitude. "What would I know?"

And the men? One of them, after all, had taken Liz's money. Which one exactly I didn't know and Liz no longer seemed sure either. For one thing, they were hard to tell apart, these men, and we couldn't talk to them because they would not stay still. They kept scurrying in and out of the room.

When they breezed in, all bristling and wire-bearded, their attention was a sex organ, poking, probing. They looked at Liz and saw nothing but a fresh one with nice boobs, not spent like the other cows around the place. Their sexual interest in Liz was all I saw and for selfish reasons. It wasn't that I felt jealous. Liz had lost all flavor of fantasy for me within our first hour together. But we were together and I felt obligated to protect her. If trouble started I would have to be her knight, and I didn't want to be a knight.

The men kept giggling weirdly, jostling one another, and disappearing into some room in the back of the house, only to pop out again. Liz couldn't pin them down about the tickets. They kept answering her questions with jokes or changed the subject or gave back no answer at all. Finally Liz said all right, forget the tickets, just give me back my money; but they only cracked more jokes. Meanwhile, they were trying to get some complicated project off the ground in the next room. It wasn't working and this fact was just so funny. In ones or twos or small clumps they came out to report to their comrades or demand advice or tug someone back to help.

Finally, they got on my nerves. Liz stood to lose a lot of money here, and these guys needed to pay attention. What the hell were they doing back there anyway? The next time one of the bearded dudes went back, I followed him. Pushing through a door, I saw a little ring of them clustered around a Bunsen burner or some such device. Were they conducting a chemistry experiment? No, it looked more like a medical procedure. One of them had a thin rubber tube tied around his arm. His sleeve was rolled up above the tubing. One of the others had a hypodermic.

The instant I walked in, a guy lying on a mattress at the back of the room fumbled in the blankets and then snatched up a toy gun and pointed it at me. For just a flash of a moment, I marveled at how real it looked. Then I realized it looked real because it was real. I was looking into the barrel of a hand gun.

The moment lasted no longer than the time it took to think, "Hey that toy gun sure looks real, hey, that's no toy gun, it is real." One of the women bustled in, swept up to the guy with the gun, and knocked it aside as diffidently as if he were holding a carrot. "What are you doing, asshole, that's Liz's friend," she snapped. He giggled.

The men conducting the medical experiment were still trying to find a vein in the one fellow's forearm. The man on the mattress put his gun back under the blankets, and he and the woman fell to jawing at each other like that jaded couple in *Who's Afraid of Virginia Woolf*. Liz showed up at my side and saw the guy with the needle. She looked down, and following her gaze I noticed more hypodermics scattered across the floor. I could feel Liz's body stiffening up next to mine.

"Liz," I said, "I want to leave. What do you want to do?."

"I want to leave too," she said.

She shouted some kind of good-bye to her friends, or whatever they were, and we hurried out the door. No one paid any attention to our leaving, just as no one had paid much attention to our arrival. But when we got to the bottom of the stairs, one of the women came to the doorway and shouted something. Liz dragged herself reluctantly back up the stairs. I couldn't hear what passed between them, but Liz came back with an envelope. The men had squandered Liz's (and many other people's) money on "smack," it turned out, but three or four tickets had somehow ended up floating around the house, and the woman had slipped a couple of them to Liz. She would catch hell for it later, but at least Liz now had two incredibly overpriced tickets to a concert someone was supposedly promoting at an improbable place called Woodstock.

She Felt a Vibe

We had no place else to stay in Boston, so we got back on the highway and headed right back to New York, even though the hour of the wolf (4 a.m.) was nigh. The trip to Boston had unnerved me and a jagged weariness was now tearing up my innards. Back at Liz's flat we lay down, and went to sleep in our clothes. When we woke up it was afternoon. Liz got right on the phone and renewed her quest for tickets to the big rock concert. She still had money to squander, and she still wanted me to go with her.

But I had seen and heard enough. "You know something, Liz? This concert is a scam."

"What?"

"It's a scam. Think about it. Dylan and Jimi Hendrix on the same stage? When did that ever happen? One of those guys is going to open for the other? I don't think so. Not to mention— who else did you say? Jefferson Airplane? Dream on, Columbus. Not in this world, not in our lifetime. Don't you see? There's some totally unscrupulous, underground hype machine churning out these rumors. Let's not get fooled!"

"I have a vibe," she kept insisting.

"Me too," I said, "but my vibe is saying, don't fall for this. There is no way anyone is going to get all those bands signed up to play at one concert, but even if they did, it wouldn't be in some cow pasture in upstate New York."

"I think you're wrong," she said, shaking her head. "Have you been there? They have heads up there now."

"I don't deny it—"

"It's groovy up there. It's a scene."

"Might be, might well be. There are heads everywhere now— even in Yorkton, Canada—I saw 'em myself—but *these* bands, man? The Airplane? The Dead? How much did you say these tickets were?"

"Not that much. The bands are going to play for free, I heard."

"Oh sure. Bands like Ten Years After are going to show up in some podunk place called Woodstock and play for 'the people' out of the goodness of their hearts. Come on! Bands like that are not really heads anymore. Some of them used to be, maybe, but they're stars now. Music isn't a spiritual thing for them, it's a business."

"Even if Dylan is the only one, it's worth it," she said,

Liz was going to feel betrayed if I left. I knew that. But rebellion had risen inside me. We could talk all day, but my heart had made up its mind. I didn't want to be mashed between the sweating flesh of strangers and feel like I was about to pass out while music turned into torture—I'd been there, done that. The Cream concert in Minneapolis. The Who, that time at the Coliseum. And I sure didn't want to be in the same crowd as those Boston hooligans. "Whoever shows, it's going suck, Liz. I mean, everyone we've met says they're going. At least 50,000 people are going to show up. Even if it's Dylan he'll just be this tiny speck. What's fun about that?"

"Everybody's going to be high," she said.

"You'll have to fight to get near the music."

"If only we could score some acid!"

Suddenly I realized how I was going to get out of this. "Liz," I said. "I've been on the road for such a long time, I've got go to ground somewhere. I'm heading down to Maryland to rest. But I have these two tabs of acid I've been carrying with me since I left Portland. I've just been waiting for the right place and moment to take 'em, but I don't think it's going to happen. You go on to this Woodstock place, and take my two tabs of acid with you. Take them both and do what you want with them. Give them away, take one and give the other away, whatever you want. I'm going to skip Woodstock, but at least my acid will be there."

This was a plan Liz could accept. My acid would be there. This was cosmic enough to strike her as destiny coming to fulfillment and to convince her that she could satisfy the universe by letting me go. So we parted company and I went south alone, to Silver Springs, the suburb of Washington D.C. where my father had so recently been the press attaché at the Afghan embassy, and where my mother still lived.

A week later, I went to a light show at the Smithsonian with a friend. We were sitting on the floor, waiting for the show to begin when a couple of "heads," a girl and a boy, lanky twenty-something-year-olds, plopped next to us. Both looked like they had taken some powerful hallucinogens and were just now in the lift-off stage. Both were almost physically giving off light, as if they'd been rubbed so hard they were emanating static electricity. When they settled next to me, they did not simply occupy their own space in a decorous and expected manner but leaned lovingly and unashamedly against me and all other available neighbors, like young cats in first heat, seeking the blessed relief of flesh-against-flesh contact, except that there was nothing sexual about this rubbing and lolling. In fact, there was something sweet about it, something mysteriously sweet.

"*Were you there?*" they whispered.

"Where?" I said.

"Woodstock!"

"Nah. I was going to go, but I met all these people—"

I launched into my explanation of why I didn't go to Woodstock, but these two interrupted me to say, "Oh, man. You shoulda' been there!"

"Why? Was it good? Who was there?"

"Who was there?" they exclaimed. "*Everyone was there!*"

"Everyone? Really? You mean Dylan showed up?"

"I don't know. I don't know if he showed up, man, I don't know who showed up, there were lots of bands, they were playing, it was raining, people were dancing, getting high, making love, it was like—oh man. If you weren't there, you'll never know. You just hadda' be there."

So, that's how I hitched 4000 miles on $15 in quest of the ultimate hippie experience and managed to miss Woodstock by mere inches. That's the story. But *did* I miss it? The standardized narrative of that time pinpoints Woodstock as *the* emblematic hippie moment, in which case it wasn't just my two tabs of acid that made it to the festival. I was there myself because at that moment Woodstock, in the larger sense, was everywhere. In retrospect, however, I also see what I could not see then: I wasn't really on a road trip, I was in a story called *Road Trip*. The protagonist was a reckless, romantic, lovably foolish figure, passionate to a fault, nimbly living by his wits, not unlike the main character in Knut Hamsun's *Hunger*. I wasn't him, but a guy can pretend and perhaps, by pretending skillfully enough, make it real.

Running Scared

In 1972, it was still the sixties, only more so. The U.S. was still up to its neck in Vietnam. Nixon was still president and campaigning for re-election by touting a "secret plan" for ending the war. Massive music festivals had become the norm. Bands like Blue Oyster Cult were wearing Gothic makeup and breaking decibel records. In Portland, no one ever thought twice about smoking dope in a public place because who ever got arrested for a little thing like that? And at the end of that year, one gray November day, I realized I might commit suicide if I didn't get to the East Coast lickety split to see a certain someone. Six weeks later I came back cured of suicidal depression--and thereby hangs a tale.

The tale begins three years earlier as a fairy tale. I had just come back from my hitchhike across the continent. It was September of 1969, and my last year of college was about to begin. The cross-continental adventure had left this little semi-Afghan boy all puffed up with a sense of power. He thought he was a new man. He thought he had learned a precious spiritual secret on the road: how to let go and *trust the universe*! I mean to say, when you're standing by some God-forsaken highway in the middle of nowhere with cars hurling past you, and you're waiting for one car out of all those cars to stop for you, there is nothing you can do to make it happen. All you can do is wait. And waiting patiently—isn't that the essence of letting go?

The glow that came from crossing the continent on nothing but pluck and luck lasted until the first time I had to wait in a slow line at a grocery store. It then became plain I hadn't learned a goddamn thing about patience. And the first time I found myself within 50 feet of an attractive girl, I realized I was still the same out-of-place, insecure, tongue-tied "Half-Afghan" boy I had been before I hit the road.

That September I had good reason to feel insecure: no real friends, no social network, no place to live, no money. I went to the Ivan Street House, where I had rented a pair of rooms before my adventure, hoping to get my old suite back, but all the people I live with had moved out, and the whole ramshackle mansion had come under the control of one gangly guy, who let me know at once that he didn't need no more stinkin' roommates.

"You've got the whole place filled?" I stared incredulously past his shoulder. This house had five rooms upstairs, two downstairs, two bathrooms, and a complete in-law apartment in the basement, and all the rooms I could see from the front door (including my old suite) looked empty.

"No," he said. "It's just, I'd rather live alone. See..." He scuffed at the floor with a threadbare sneaker. "I play piano?"

"Oh! Music? I love music, the louder the better, are you kidding? What kind of music do you guys play?"

"It's just me. Acoustic piano. I play..." He hung his head in shame. "Classical?" then added, "I don't want anyone to hear me."

I couldn't reason with him. He wouldn't budge. There was nothing for it but to find another place to live. Unfortunately, this close to the start of school, rooms-for-rent in other people's communal houses had all been gobbled up, so I went looking for Marcy. She'd been my girlfriend the previous year, and maybe she still was, hard to tell. In those last months of junior year, she and I and a couple of other women had rented a cheap place several miles from campus, an isolated little house jammed between a lumberyard, a junkyard, and some railroad tracks. We were cut off from campus life, and two of us in that household didn't get along.

Unfortunately, those two were Marcy and I. She considered herself a woman of the people and had nothing but contempt for effete intellectuals. I considered myself an artiste and had a lofty disdain for the beer-swilling masses. She said the Stones were the best band in the universe because they were earthy and real; I said the Beatles because they were subtle and complex. Her favorite book was Eldridge Cleaver's *Soul on Ice;* mine, Romain Rolland's novel about the fictional composer Jean-Christophe.

Marcy mocked my pretensions relentlessly. I defended myself with withering analyses of her skewed logic—she was given to statements like, "Redheads are good at music. I know because I met a redhead once." I think she might have said such things just to goad me.

Being with Marcy was better than being with no one but not much better, and she didn't think so either. Since we never said we were breaking up when we parted for the summer, I guessed that technically we were still together. I went looking for her to see if she might help me gather a few strays and start a new communal house. Meanwhile, I had to line up a place to crash each night, which wasn't hard actually: this being the sixties, you didn't have to be close friends with someone to sleep on their couch. You just needed to have shared a cosmic moment. "Check out that sunset, man." "Right on, man." "Heavy." "Very heavy." "Can I sleep on your couch?"

I stashed my stuff in someone's basement, crashed in a different place each night, and spent my days hunting for Marcy, but everywhere I went, Marcy had just left. Was this her way of telling me I had been dumped? How outrageous! Now I really wanted to find her just to let her know that if anyone was dumping anyone, it was me dumping her. But when I finally caught up to her in one of those grungy Reed houses, she looked so dark and so pretty, I just wanted to hug her. She however folded her arms to forestall any hugging and stated coldly, "You owe me fifty dollars."

Something about a phone bill. I never understood what. My pride was too wounded to demand an explanation. I could only punish her by asking in the coldest possible voice, "Where should I send the check?" She gave me an address and then left, and I let her go, and in so doing, let go of all our shared friends, most of whom were her friends anyway. No big loss: I had never felt close to any of them, one on one. It's just that I had no friends of my own. Or acquaintances even.

Ghost Town

All this was actually typical of Reed College, which was a ghostly social environment. Don't get me wrong, Reed was and probably still is an intense and wonderful place. It had and still has a stellar intellectual pedigree, which made it my kind of school because I was one of those four-eyed head cases who actually loved to study. Reed also had a long reputation for radical ways. Some said the college was founded by leftie journalist John Reed who witnessed the Bolshevik revolution and wrote a classic admiring account of it in *Ten Days that Shook the World*. That connection was apocryphal, it seems. The only thing the college shared with the journalist was a certain spirit. Reed's first president was arrested in downtown Portland for leading an anti-draft protest during the First World War—how cool is *that*?

But Reed also had a famous institutional affection for people who didn't fit into conventional society. In my day, this meant that each Reed student had been the single most alienated person at his or her high school or previous college. They were drawn to Reed in hopes of finding their own kind. And their own kind was just what they found. But when you concentrate a thousand such people in a small space, you create a microcosm in which no one is ever so uncool as to say hello to anyone else.

And it was more than a thousand, actually. A thousand was only the official enrollment. At least that many more had dropped out but had not gone away. They were still part of the Bohemian nimbus that surrounded the school for twenty or thirty blocks. They lived in the communal houses in those neighborhoods, they haunted the campus coffee shop, they came to Reed parties. Some of them eventually dropped back in. Some dropped back in, then out, and then repeated the whole maneuver.

The dropouts were not losers defeated by the rigors of this college. As a group, they were possibly more distinguished than the ones who attended straight through. One of my friends must have done a total of two years over the course of five and never did graduate, but he was a theater guy, so even when he wasn't enrolled he was acting in the student plays, and later he kept coming back to direct; later still, he went to New York and helped create iconic television shows such as *Homicide, Life on the Streets*, and *The Wire*. Another dropout in our circles later wrote *A Walk in the Woods,* a Pulitzer-prize winning play about two world leaders talking disarmament. And there was Ry Cooder who'd sat in with Captain Beefheart's Magic Band the summer before starting college and dropped out during his first year to go play backup on the Rolling Stones album *Let It Bleed*. And there was Steve Jobs, who was also at Reed but dropped out quickest of all. Jobs didn't even finish a semester; but after dropping out, he kept going to classes as if he were still a Reedie, imbibing just the stuff that interested him. Reed was that kind of place.

Some of the people thronging the campus never had been and never would be Reed students. They were merely oddballs attracted to that cluster of crazies as flies to meat. Take, for example, short, pockmarked Brother Hubert: he always wore a dusty, ill-fitting, blue-gray suit that looked like he slept in it. He carried a well-thumbed dog-eared Bible under one arm and preached the gospel just outside the coffee shop to the students and dropouts of Reed College. Brother Hubert was a character straight out of Faulkner's *As I Lay Dying,* or Carson McCullers's

Wise Blood, so we sort of liked him: he actually thumped his bible as he shouted out imprecations and told us we were all going to hell. We Reedies sat on the steps in the sun, sipping coffee and sometimes clapping. We saw him as entertainment.

Then there was Robinson Hobbes, an older fellow who frequented the coffee shop. By "older" I mean he was in his forties, but that's just a guess. I was no real judge of age. Back then, anyone over 25 looked 40 to me. Anyone over 40 looked 80. Robinson Hobbes always wore what looked like an undertaker's suit. He had a black Russian-anarchist type beard and coal-black eyes, and he claimed to be the overlooked genius of the age, a philosopher who had created an architectonic structure of thought that encompassed and explained all of reality, if only anyone would pay attention. He called it The Theory of Difference Arranging, and it formed the reference point for all his remarks. If a few of us were discussing Vietnam or the evolution of rock music or why Camus's "Stranger" was so indifferent to his mother, Robinson might chime in with an opinion that inevitably began "According to the Theory of Difference Arranging..." Sometimes, in the middle of a hot discussion on some obscure point, Robinson would be likely to rumble, "Go back to the book—Chapter 22. Right there you'll see it says..." as if The Book existed on its own merits, quite apart from his having written it, and also as if any random person he might be talking to would certainly have read his (unpublished) masterpiece.

The coffee shop had a jukebox loaded with Creedence Clearwater, Jimi Hendrix, Jefferson Airplane, and the like. In the back booths, people sometimes lit up joints or toked up a little casual hashish. There were no cops on campus, law enforcement was never a concern. The whole environment of the college back then was so anti-authoritarian, no one would have thought to worry about breaking a silly ordinance like the one about weed. Cigarettes were 25 cents a pack, dispensed out of a squat machine by the counter, and the air was always thick with smoke. Any public place as smoky as that would feel sleazy to me now, but the smokiness of the Reed coffee shop struck me as glamorous. Sitting there, puffing on Gitaines, we all felt like Sartre except for the women, who all felt like Simon de Beauvoir.

At that moment, in the fall of 1969, ghostly social landscape though it might have been, Reed College was my entire home. Afghanistan, the land of my birth, was now part of another universe, which I figured never to see again. The Afghan government regarded immigration as treason, and when we—my mother, siblings, and I—left Afghanistan we had to hide the American passports we had secretly obtained and pretend that we were only going away to school and would soon be coming back. Apparently, since my mother was the first American woman to live in Afghanistan, her embrace of the country had some propaganda value, and her departure could be seen as criticism of the monarchy...

My father stayed. We were Americans now; he was an Afghan guy stuck in that universe—forever, I assumed. My sister was physically in Kentucky but our lives had diverged drastically. I had no idea where she was mentally or socially.

As for my mother, if there was a more solitary human being on Earth, I don't know who it could have been. She'd grown up in Chicago, the child of Finnish immigrants. Her father was an angry little working class agitator who would have been a Communist if only he could have gotten along with a single other Communist. He isolated his family from the rest of the Finns, and the Finns as a group were cut off from the larger society, first-generation immigrants who couldn't speak the language of the land. My mother didn't learn English until she started kindergarten. In college, she idolized Bohemians but they didn't know she existed. When she met my father she did the most Bohemian thing imaginable: she married him and moved from Finnish immigrant Chicago to (of all places) Afghanistan for God's sake, where she was sure to be the single most out-of-place person in every situation she encountered. I have to suppose she made this move because she wanted her circumstances to justify the alienation she already felt.

My mother passed her legacy of solitude down to us kids. I at least can attest that growing up in Afghanistan, I never felt Afghan, or American, or even "torn between two cultures." I only felt God-awfully singular. No matter who else was there, I felt out of place. The only time I felt I was among "my own kind" was at home with my mother and siblings and no one else. Even my father existed outside that charmed circle. That's probably why I gravitated to Reed.

Paying Marcy fifty dollars put a serious dent in my finances, for I then had only $200 to get me through the whole semester, and yet, the morning after mailing the check to Marcy, I bought a used bicycle, a 10-speed French racer, for eighty dollars. After this I could no longer afford to rent a room, but I hardly needed one: I could shower at the gym, study in the library, and sleep in the students' lounge, a three-room complex under the dining hall, featuring many plush couches, a TV set; and a glaringly bright game parlor stocked with pool tables and pinball machines.

One or two dozen night owls called these haunts their occasional home. On any given night, a subset of ten or twelve of us might be crashing there. We never exchanged more than curt nods on campus by day, but in that weird space, late at night, we were comrades who shot pool together, played cards, smoked cigarettes, and made fun of late night TV. I wouldn't say these guys were my friends. I didn't even know their real names, mostly; only their nicknames: "Easy"..."the Sultan"..."San Francisco Sly"... I, for some reason that I no longer remember, called myself Dog Mountain. "Sly" had his own pool cue, which he carried around unscrewed into two parts in a case that looked just big enough for a violin or a machine gun. He wore fedoras and wide, thrift-store suit coats and had a wispy little yellow beard. "Easy" was unkempt and unshaven and wore sweat shirts and baggy pants and sandals, and was often stoned on acid. He said his motto was, "If it feels good, do it." He was the only guy I knew who had a motto.

One night I was complaining to one of these acquaintances that I didn't have enough money to eat, and the guy scoffed. "What do you need money for? I'm down to nothing, and I dine like a king."

"How's that?"

"I scrounge," he said. "Don't you know about scrounging? Come with me, rookie."

Scrounging consisted of standing someplace in the college dining hall where people had to pass on their way to the dishwashing station. Quite often, students on a meal plan took more food than they could eat. Scroungers intercepted them on the way to the bussing window and took their untouched food. My new buddy assured me this was an ennobling experience. "It keeps you humble," he boasted.

I adopted an interested expression as if a method for staying humble was just what I'd been seeking. "I'll try it."

About twenty of us formed the hard core of scroungers. Hanging out in "scroungers' alley" gave us a bond of camaraderie, as if we belonged to an exclusive club of beggars. In fact, at the end of the year, the scroungers traditionally got together and cooked a huge fancy meal, which they dubbed the Beggars' Banquet, and they could do it, because most of those scroungers weren't actually poor. They had rich parents of whose wealth they were ashamed, so they sought penance in pretended poverty. The great thing was, a person like me, who was *actually* poor, could pretend to be a rich guy pretending to be a poor guy, and thus escape the humiliation of actual poverty. The students we scrounged from sort of admired us, and we regarded them with the benign superiority of hustlers toward marks.

At least, such was our group attitude. My own closely-held private sentiment included the anxiety that I might be an actual "beggar," not a noble "scrounger." I didn't tell my parents how I was getting by. My father would have been horrified, even though the Islamic world has a tradition of spiritually noble beggars known as "dervishes." I suspected he would not find me credible as a dervish. My mother might have tried to eke out a bigger allowance for me, which I could not permit. She had moved back to the United States when I did, longing for a home she had never found in Afghanistan and which, it turned out, she didn't have here either. Now, she had my little brother Riaz to support while struggling to make ends meet as an elementary school teacher. I could not lean on her.

Nor did I need to. Once I had a place to sleep and a way to eat, I stopped worrying about food and shelter. Like the protagonist of Celine's *Death on the Installment Plan,* I lived in a present moment that began yesterday and stretched as far into the future as early tomorrow. Since Celine's character was a child, his only preoccupation was play. Since I was 20, my every idle moment was consumed with craving a girlfriend.

In Afghanistan, where I grew up, boys might crave girlfriends, but they never got one. In Afghan culture, dating simply was not done. Boys did not approach girls outside their family and suggest that they meet privately for a little innocent fun. In fact, in my high school, when a boy asked a girl if he could lend her a pencil, it was seen as a shocking transgression, and the school administration had him beaten with a stick at a public assembly. That's how much Afghan culture frowned upon dating.

American culture was not like that; and thanks to my American mother, the values and attitudes I carried in my psyche were American ones, not Afghan. But values and attitudes don't get a boy a girlfriend. I understood that one must take some steps. I had no idea what those steps might be, however. From Marcy, I had learned nothing. She had taken all the steps. She chose me, hauled me into bed, and lived with me until she was done with me. I was on my own.

My first strategy—stroll about and hope some girl would fall in love with me—didn't work. What I needed, I decided, was an image. Girls were attracted to certain types of guys and I should try to look like one of those. I could never fake being a jock, but that category, thank God, did not exist at Reed. Rock'n'roll types were popular here—wild, extravagant, confident, and boldly sexual men who played electrified instruments—but I couldn't even tune my acoustic mandolin. Then there were student-leaders: they called meetings, led rallies, and had passionate convictions, which they voiced in stirring language that made other people feel guilty. I *certainly* couldn't be one of those.

Hailing from Afghanistan might have given me some exotic allure, but I couldn't play that card. For one thing it was false. As the second child of the first American woman ever to marry an Afghan, I was even more alienated in "the old country" than I was here. There I could never camouflage myself. People looked at me and they knew, talked to me and they knew. People who didn't even know me knew who I was: that guy from elsewhere. Here in America, I had a chance to blend in, and I was desperate to do it; but you can't blend in by advertising the features that make you a misfit. Which means those features are also off the table as a source of glamor.

Fortunately, no one who met me could guess that I was from anywhere else. I looked vaguely something-else but so do most Americans, and I spoke idiomatic American English without a trace of an accent, and I had all the same current pop cultural references as my peers. I loved the Beatles. Who didn't? I respected the Stones but considered them a notch below the Beatles. Who (except for Marcy) didn't?

The cultural memes that eluded me had to do with fifties TV, mostly. Once, someone "revealed" that Alice Cooper was really Eddie Haskell. I knew all about Alice Cooper, but who was this Eddie Haskell? When such references came up, I laughed at the same time as everyone else. It was like socializing in a mud bath with a bunch of people who see only one another's heads. From the neck up I looked like them. No one could tell that below the surface I was a freak—not as hippies used the term, but an actual freak.

Then one day, I hit upon an image I could viably cultivate. In those shabby streets paralleling the Willamette River, where thrift stores alternated with hippie boutiques, I spotted a pair of Frye boots, square toed and triple-belted, a daring fashion upgrade from the clunky black cowboy boots I had worn while crossing the continent (themselves a fashion upgrade from the humiliatingly handmade shoes I had brought along from Afghanistan.) I also saw a pair of wire-rimmed glasses that would make me look like a poor man's John Lennon. I bought both items, and later that same day I found myself in a downtown department store purchasing, with the last of my money, a pair of wide-legged bellbottoms. This was the most daring move of all, because only women had worn bellbottoms until "mod" fashion came boiling out of London's Carnaby Street, and in 1969, even though long hair and bellbottoms had become the cutting edge look for hip young men, it still took a *very* confidently masculine guy to wear women's clothing.

Was I that guy? Good heavens no, but when the madness receded, I certainly looked like a damaged soul, hardened by blows he didn't care to speak about. The checkered bellbottoms walked back to Reed, the boots clicking on the sidewalks. I figured if I said as little as possible, the outfit would get away with it, and no one would notice me inside. I was a little boy wearing Iron Man's suit.

Lily

Then came the afternoon of September 10th. I know it seems implausible that forty years later I would know the exact day I first saw Lily Edelstein, but the thing is, on that day, the Mets won a doubleheader and made it into first place for the first time in history. Believe me, I didn't care about this news at the time. Like most foreigners, I could not fathom baseball and had no idea who the Mets were except that they also sang opera. I certainly didn't know there was an "important" baseball game going on somewhere or that a baseball game could be important.

I only knew that it was a balmy afternoon and the sun was setting over the rhododendron gardens west of campus and the slanted light was the color of wheat. And soon, that an attractive girl was sitting on the steps outside the dining hall, reading aloud to a little group from a book called *The Adventures of a Rock.* One look at that slender, delicate face and I couldn't look away. Her curly hair was cut boyishly short and she was twisting one light brown curl around an idle finger as she read. Even now, I can recall her plangent contralto. Was her voice really so different from any other? That depends. What does "really" mean when you're talking about falling head-over-heels?

Standing on the edges of that little crowd that day, I fantasized what would happen when Lily noticed me. *Their eyes met, and at that moment—*

At that moment, The Sultan came galumphing up and grabbed my arm. "Dog Mountain," he yelled, "The Mets are ahead!" Apparently, somebody had just hit a homer, or a triple, or a foul or whatever they hit in baseball. I yanked my arm away but he wouldn't let go. "Don't you get it, Dog Mountain? This is history!" he bellowed. "Years from now, you'll be telling people you saw this game."

For a moment, I loathed baseball, but resisting the Sultan would only make him noisier, so I let him drag me away from the only place I wanted to be for the rest of my life, down to the student union to join a riotous crowd cheering the Mets.

And the irony is, The Sultan was right. Years have passed and here I am, telling you I saw that game. The moment *was* historic. Only later did I get the significance of it all. The Mets were baseball's iconic losers, but that year they went on to win the World Series and became a perfect metaphor for the Sixties, that era when all the underdogs got their day, when freaks became cool, and gallant little poor countries defeated gigantic, nuclear-powered, rich ones. That's how I know that September 10, 1969 was the day I first set eyes on Lily. I looked it up on Wikipedia.

A band was playing on campus that weekend and I wandered over, thinking I might bump into Marcy and we'd have The Conversation. The room had a raised perimeter around a sunken central pit. Couples were dancing in the pit. Singles were watching from the edges, each person positioned far enough away from any other to broadcast that he or she was not part of some herd of needy nerds but a proud individual, solitary by choice.

Blasting out of gigantic speakers in that huge, hot room was rhythmic thunder generated by the Portland Zoo, a local band fronted by Peter Langston who had recently graduated from Reed but like so many recent graduates and dropouts hadn't gone away. Langston played a kick-ass lead guitar and walked the earth with all the warping weight of a rock-and-roll god. That night Langston was on fire, and his band was kicking major ass. Every time Langston's guitar came soaring out of the cacophony, I lost my breath. In one of those breathless moments I saw Lily again, and the universe collapsed into a singularity. She was sitting on a table, wearing a red corduroy miniskirt, the full length of her amazing legs on display; and again, yes, she was twisting one boyishly short curl around an idle finger while gazing over the crowd, her eyes languidly half-lidded, her lips just barely parted.

I looked down and there was Marcy in the pit, dancing with some stranger. Marcy looked up. Her gaze skipped over some furniture, skipped over me, skipped over some more furniture, and I realized I had in fact been dumped, and here before me was this goddess. Can you spell destiny?

I decided to pluck up all my courage and ask her to dance. All my courage was, however, less than the amount needed to lift my feet. While I stood there, a lanky long-haired Frank Zappa look-alike came up and spoke into her ear, and she shook her head, whereupon I lost my nerve. A girl who turned down Frank Zappa would never look twice at an awkwardly out-of-place overly-intellectual pseudo-American/half-Afghan fraud like me. What was I thinking?

I left the dance depressed and yet elated. I wanted to tell someone about this girl but had no one to tell. And come to think of it, I had nothing to tell them. What was my news? *She existed*! That was a I knew. I didn't even know her name.

A few days later, strolling past me in scroungers' alley, she brushed against my elbow. Oh, thrilling contact! "Do you have a teabag?" I blurted.

She looked down at her stark tray on which there was quite obviously nothing but a single spoon, and said in a throaty contralto that made me swoon, "No... but I have some tea. Do you want to come back to my room with me?"

The John Lennon glasses and the checkered bellbottoms shrugged as if this were almost an imposition. "Okay," my lips choked out.

She led me to her room in Foster dormitory, a boudoir aromatic with femininity. A poster above her bed offered a quote attributed (wrongly, I've later discovered) to Anais Nin: "Not only to be loved, but to be told that I am loved, for the realm of silence extends far enough beyond the grave."   Lily presented me with three boxes of tea and lazily explained the virtues of each. I made a selection. She cracked a small joke but I didn't realize it was meant to be funny until too late. "A joke," she explained, so I emitted a forced ha-ha. The water boiled. We sipped tea. Brief bits of conversation burst out, separated by patches of agonizing silence.   I tried to justify my inarticulate discomfiture by mentioning that I was from Afghanistan. She assumed *this* was a joke and forced a chuckle. I didn't know how to correct her assumption. I drained my tea. I glanced at my wrist. I didn't have a watch. "Well," I said, standing up.

"You're going?" she exclaimed.

"Things to do." I shrugged the shrug of a mystery man nursing inexpressible sorrows no mere woman could solace.

"Okay," she said. "Goodbye then."

As soon as I was out of the dorm and away from her gaze, I fell to the grass, laughing with joy. Life had never been sweeter, funnier, or more delicious. But wait: she hadn't even asked my name. And come to think of it, I still didn't know hers. Now that I thought about it, the whole encounter had gone rather poorly.

Still, after that I saw her everywhere. Of course I did, because perception is not a screen upon which impressions fall willy-nilly but a hound that goes snuffling out into the world, looking for the single thing it wants. All irrelevant stuff blends into a featureless background upon which the only thing that matters can stand out. If Lily was anywhere in sight, Lily was all I saw. Even at a distance, I could pick her out by her gait, her dancer's grace: her spine straight up and down, her shoulders seemingly attached to invisible strings, the rest of her suspended below, floating along as if weightlessly. I did a little detective work and discovered that her name was Lily Edelstein.

The guy who told me this also said, "She's Tanzer's girl."

Ouch! But then, how could such a goddess not be *someone's* girl? And of course it would be someone like Rick Tanzer, a political activist who posted leaflets and was sometimes seen with a bullhorn exhorting people, and *on top of that* played drums for a rock band. It was like discovering that a hot movie star was already dating another hot movie star.

Oddly enough, however, Lily kept seeking me out. Apparently, even though she was Tanzer's girl, she was open to a Platonic friendship. We ate together when she found me scrounging, and she sometimes smoked a joint with me on the hillside overlooking the Rhododendron Gardens. It was early fall, before the rains started, and in that season there was not in heaven or on earth a more beautiful city than Portland, Oregon—all the more so because the rainless moment was so brief. If I hadn't known she was Tanzer's girl, I might have committed a fatal faux pas, like trying to kiss her.

Then one night, she ended up in my bedroom. This was not quite as exciting as it might sound because my bedroom, as I mentioned, was the student union. San Francisco Sly idled by, swinging the black leather grip that contained his pool cue, looking like a stylish 1920s mobster. He veered over to bum a cigarette, and I hoped Lily would be impressed by the kinds of dudes I hung out with. After Sly drifted off, we went on sitting side by side facing a big plate glass window. Then, reflected in the glass, I saw Rick Tanzer looming up. Then he was leaning down. Then he was stuffing his Mick Jagger lips right next to my goddess's neck—yes, burrowing his snout into her adorable curls, whispering in her ear.

What was a man to do? Yes, yes, she was Tanzer's girl, I knew that, I knew that, I was too well-behaved to dispute that fact, and yet—? And yet a proprietary spasm went through me. I felt wounded right in the honor, an organ I didn't even know I had. I felt like I ought to hit this guy. I had been in a few fights in my life, though never by choice, and I had won a fight once, when I was seven, by which I mean the other kid started to cry for his mommy (that counts as a win, right? When the other guy cries for his mommy?) But I had gotten the worst of every fight since then. Besides, nothing could have been less cool than a show of hostility at that moment. After all, what had Tanzer done? Leaned down and said something to Lily in her ear. Even if he had stuck his tongue in there, who was I to object? My tongue did not own her ear or any other part of her. My tongue had no claims to press here. She was *Tanzer's girl.* I lit another cigarette and stared sullenly at my image in the plate glass window, pretending not to notice what was happening *right next to me!*

Tanzer strolled away, and after a few minutes, inappropriately angry but trying to hide it, I offered to walk Lily back to her dorm. In the hall outside her door, I muttered. "What's the deal with you and this Tanzer?"

And she said, "Come in here," and pulled me into her room.

In the morning, we woke up bleary and haggard. Who knew bleary and haggard could feel so good? Curiously enough, the Earth's gravity had gone to half-strength during the night. Every step I took that day bounced me high, like those astronauts you see in movies of the moon landing. Inexplicably, I wasn't shy anymore. I caught a glimpse of a mirror, and holy shit—was that cool guy me? I stopped and checked and yup: that was me.

I knew then that I was living in a story, because only in fairy tales does the frog get the princess. Then again, was our connection so implausible? We came from nearly identical backgrounds. Well, her family was American, so different in that way. And her people were Jewish, mine Muslim, so different in that way. And yeah, she came from Chicago, I from Kabul, that was a difference too. Also, her parents were still together, her family still whole, not fractured like mine.

But still: her people were liberal intellectuals, steeped in books, art, and ideas, like mine. And the two of us could not have been more alike. Like me, she revered Bob Dylan. What's more, she loved the Beatles—what were the odds that we would both love *the same band*? She respected the Stones but considered them a cut below the Beatles. Wow! Was it possible for two minds to meld so uncannily? Our connection seemed...dare I say it? Telepathic!

If this were a movie, the next part would be a montage of shots. You know the kind: The couple are sharing a picnic in a meadow. The couple are riding bicycles through cobblestoned streets, zig-zagging and laughing about it. Holding hands in the sunset. Kissing. Making love—portrayed with artistic close-up shots: all you can see are intimations of flesh, tangled sheets, and moist locks of hair. And since this was the sixties, the montage would include a snippet of us at a Muddy Waters concert, higher than clouds, and in the rhododendron gardens, stoned on mescaline; and with a group of six or seven in a cabin at Cannon Beach, blitzed on LSD, smoking cigar-sized joints, and listening to Jimi Hendrix playing *Voodoo Child*.

My montage would include clips of Lily and me and four of her friends from Foster dorm, hurling down Interstate-5 in a VW van from which all but the driver's seat had been removed, on our way to California for Thanksgiving break. Lily and I had dropped Dexedrine, a type of speed. For me, it was a strange drug, because quicktime was my normal velocity, so the pills only made me feel normal, unusually so; except that when it was time to fall asleep, I didn't.   Which was fine with me: more hours to be awake with Lily? Bring it on!

We stopped at a restaurant at one point, and I saw a headline that made me scoop up somebody's discarded newspaper.   It was full of news about a man named William Calley, a platoon leader in Vietnam, who had ordered his guys to murder every man, woman, and child in a village called Mai Lai after raping the women and children. And they'd done it. They had followed his orders. We talked about this crime as we drove on. How could a whole platoon of draftees turn out to be unspeakable monsters? How did they all end up in the same squad? Or was there only one monster, who was able to exercise a demonic hold over his men? Who was this William Calley?

I offered a different speculation. Maybe Calley and his men were normal guys made monstrous by the war. Maybe the war was the evil thing and anyone caught in its clutches might do the unspeakable. My companions considered this and dismissed it. *They*'d never "follow orders" like that no matter what the circumstances.   But I wasn't sure I knew what I'd do in circumstances I could not even imagine.

All of us were against the war, but I alone had a personal stake in the issue, because I was the only senior in the car, and as soon as I graduated I would be drafted and sent to Vietnam, where I would be taking orders from men like William Calley.

My best friend Ralph had graduated from college the year before, and he was in boot camp now. When he got his draft notice, he submitted to it meekly because he turned to his guru for advice. Even though non-violence was supposedly central to Kirpal Singh's creed, he instructed Ralph to go into the army. "Don't worry," said the wise old man, "I will not let you commit any violence."

When Ralph reported this assurance to me, it made me queasy. If the whole war was a horrific massacre, would it be okay to contribute to the horror as a paper pusher? Would your guilt be diminished? How would you differ from those German clerks who filed paperwork for the Holocaust and later claimed they were just following orders?

No, the only role exempt from blame would be medic. It was the only role I could imagine myself playing in the war. I couldn't raise this issue with Ralph because he was in the army now, no backing out. His letters from boot camp remained cheery, but there was something weird about his cheer. He rhapsodized relentlessly about his meditation sessions but offered only scattered glimpses of boot camp. He did say his orders had come and he would be shipping out to Vietnam soon. He didn't say how he felt about it. And I felt reluctant to tell anyone I knew about my best friend's decision because deep-down I suspected the he was going to Vietnam not because he was following his guru's directive but because he didn't have the courage to resist the draft. I was ashamed of Ralph.

One girl in our group was from San Francisco, so we crashed at her parents' house for a few days and on those afternoons took the opportunity to stroll up and down Haight Street between Masonic and Stanyon. Shaggy people clad in embroidered clothing and wearing glasses with multi-colored lenses thronged the sidewalks, beads and amulets hanging off them like Christmas tree ornaments. These costumes had not become a cliché yet. Long hair was still a statement.

A few months ago, Greenwich Village had seemed hip to me, but the Village felt old compared to this. The village was Bohemian in a way that might almost be called conventional, part of a tradition that went back to the Left Bank. This—the Haight—felt unprecedented and raw: the Deadwood and Dodge City of hip, the true frontier.

From San Francisco, Lily and I parted ways. It was the first time we'd been apart since we got together. She went to San Diego to spend Thanksgiving with her grandmother and I hitched to Santa Cruz to see my old friend Shawn from Afghanistan days.

His father had been a doctor doing charity work in Lashkargah. Shawn and I had shared numerous boyish adventures, roaming the thousand-year-old Ghaznavid ruins downriver from our little town, playing at being smugglers, warriors and explorers on the thickly jungled island in the river that ran past our town, creeping through tunnels created by wild boars pushing their unstoppable weight through shrubbery so thick that boys like us could lean against it without feeling an inch of give.   But being on the cusp of adolescence, our biggest adventure had been the discovery of girls.

So I couldn't wait to tell Shawn that I not only had a girlfriend now, but she was the most dazzling girl in the world. As soon as Lily was out of my presence, however, something went wrong with me. There were no visible symptoms, but food lost its taste, jokes lost their funny, and all conversations seemed pointless. By the weekend, gravity had tripled. Moving was an effort, and thinking was impossible.

Everyone at Santa Cruz was buzzing about a big concert coming up at a place called Altamont. Bigger than Woodstock, people predicted. Santana would be there. The Grateful Dead. Even the Stones! Woodstock had taught me not to doubt such rumors. Every single person I met said they were going, and Woodstock had taught me that this was not a minus. Crowds were good, "important" concerts were sacred gatherings of the tribes. I had missed Woodstock; now the universe was offering me a second chance.

Then Lily called. "I can't bear it," she breathed. "I can't be without you. I'm going to fly to San Francisco tonight and take the van into town. Can you meet me at the Hilton?"

What to do? On one side stood the second cosmic gathering of my generation. On the other stood Lily. No contest. "Yes," I said, and we listened to each other's heavy breathing for a while. It was like a two-way obscene phone call except that we knew each other. Then we hung up, because what could words add? I told Shawn I had to leave at once. I had to hitch to San Francisco.

"What about Altamont?"

"Fuck Altamount."

I made it to the San Francisco Hilton just in time to see Lily step out of the airport shuttle. It was the edge of San Francisco's infamous Tenderloin. Our eyes met and time stopped. Corny. I know; but that's what happened. We stood there oblivious to the bums all around us burbling in their troubled sleep. We tried to speak but we couldn't. We tried to breathe but could only pant. She was as stricken as I. Two hearts beating as one! We lurched toward each other like zombies and as we moved closer came to life, and then the glad rush and the desperate hug as if by clinging to each other we could stop history.

Looking back, of course, I ask myself: "What was the big deal?" History marches on, 15 billion years and counting. What did those 10 or 12 seconds signify? How is it that decades later I can still remember the way neither of us could catch our breath?

I am writing in a context from which the historical Lily is not missing. I still know her. We correspond twice a year, once on each of our birthdays. She likes to read, she enjoys gardening, she shares her life with a charming partner. She's warm, intelligent, and well worthy of affection. Scientists have determined, however, that she is a normal member of the human species. Nothing magical happened between us. It was just biology. How strange to realize that almost everyone has felt this way, that this supernatural event is happening right now, to hundreds of thousands of people a day. And that most of us are imagining an event that does not exist.

World's Smallest Dog

Meanwhile, the war was heating up. President Nixon announced that he was adding another 50,000 troops to the 450,000 already there. His announcement had drawn a million people to Washington for the biggest peace demonstration in history; but Nixon had already told the media he wasn't going to be pressured into doing "the easy thing, the popular thing."

But there wasn't much reason to worry. Graduation was so far away, tra la! Seven months, for God's sake. Back then, everyone knew a nuclear exchange could break out at any moment, and if it did, the two superpowers would unleash enough weapons to destroy all life on Earth. From launch to detonation was expected to take 34 minutes. So anyone born between Hiroshima and the invention of the hydrogen bomb grew up knowing they might be living 34 minutes from the end. I put the draft out of my mind because the world might have ended by June and how could Vietnam matter to a guy who was spending every night with Lily? One must be high to fall far and I was soaring in those last months of college, at the tail end of the sixties, never suspecting that within two years I would be on the edge of suicide.

The first cloud appeared in March. The school year was coming to an end, and when it did, I would graduate and Lily wouldn't. Not that this spelled the end. Romeo and Juliet don't break up because Romeo graduates and Juliet is still in college. There was, however, one further trivial complication. Lily had decided to transfer to Antioch, a college in Ohio. Not to get away from me, mind you, just to get away from Reed. She wasn't leaving *me*, she was merely moving 2,400 miles away, just as my mother didn't leave my father (as I stoutly informed anyone who asked) she just moved to the other side of the world.

And there was that other slightly less trivial complication: the moment I graduated, I'd be draft bait. My friend Ralph had been in Vietnam since January, and his letters were ever more unhinged. Now he was pouring out streams of images hardly even interrupted by punctuation, relentlessly describing his sojourns to the astral plane. He didn't make one single comment about the bloody war he was part of, except for a curious remark he tossed into his florid torrents: "Wouldn't it be funny if I'm killed, and you get married and Lily gets pregnant? I might be back sooner than you think!"

Lily's birthday was coming up, and I felt desperate to get her something spectacular, something that could stand as a metaphor for our epic romance, a diamond, perhaps, or an original painting by Monet. Unfortunately, the most I could spend was a dollar.

Then one day, I walked into the Reed college coffee shop and saw a man in a long black overcoat standing at the counter, darkness ringing his eyes, like someone auditioning for *The Adams Family*. On his hand stood a perfectly proportioned hound. It had the familiar tapered snout, the soulful eyes, the floppy ears, but it was so tiny, it fit entirely on his palm. It wasn't a puppy but a full-grown dog, a freak of nature.

The guy saw me staring. "World's smallest dog," he said. "None smaller. One dollar. You want?"

One dollar! I shelled out my buck, and sure enough, Lily adored that tiny pooch, whom we named Annie. Every day from then until graduation, we spent hours fussing over that dog together as if over a child we had borne, always focused on Annie, never looking at each other. Then suddenly the end of the year had arrived.

The night before Lily's departure, we went to see fireworks at the college. Annie cowered in Lily's pocket, frightened by the noise. It struck me that night that I couldn't remember the last time Lily had said "I love you." On the way home, we set Annie down and strolled home arm in arm, enclosed in a bell of silence, the question I was not asking, the answer she was not volunteering.

Annie ran along behind us, keening. Every time we passed a house, she mistook it for ours and went bounding up the walkway to the front porch, yapping with glad excitement. Eventually, I realized what was going on. The universe was too big. Annie was too tiny. She wanted to be home, and we wouldn't stop moving, so she was trying to make each new place we passed *be* the home she craved by faking the joy of homecoming.

The next morning, a friend gave us a ride to the airport. I figured that as long as Lily said the three words to me before she left, all would be fine. It had to be just those three iconic words, not some interesting variation, not "I-love-your-sense-of-humor," nor even "I-really-love-you." Even "really" would diminish it. She could not say the three words in the car of course, we were not alone, it would have been awkward. We pulled into the airport and got out of the car but the moment still wasn't suitable. She'll say it once we're in line, I thought; but no, not there either. At the coffee shop? Nope.

Lily was taking Annie to Chicago, and we had to drug the pooch for the journey. It took some time to force the huge tranquilizer pill down that tiny dog's gullet. She fought with eerie desperation to stay awake. I-love-you had to wait until this unpleasant bit of business was done. We stuffed her slumping form into the cage and shot the lock and the airport people carted her away, still baying.

By then, Lily's flight was being announced. Time had run out—but how much time does it take to say three words? It would happen now. Lily picked up her bags. Since she had more bags than hands, I had to sling her purse over her arm. Encumbered with bags, she couldn't hug me, so we merely leaned and kissed. Last chance. She didn't speak, so I choked out a word: "Write."

She responded: "I will."

Then she walked into the jet way and was gone, and I stood there blinking. Huh? What had just happened? Was it over? This love of ours, the only time in human history that two hearts had beat so perfectly as one—had it ended? How could that be?

Not that she said it was over: neither of us had ever even broached the issue. So I wrote to her as soon as I got home to ask in writing what I had never dared to ask in person. Was it over between us? It wasn't, was it?

She wrote back twice that week. Her first letter addressed the question I had finally made explicit. Were we still together? Yes, no, maybe, was her answer. At Antioch, Lily said, she would probably have a new lover "within a month" but she wouldn't necessarily love him more than me. And if she never found anyone she loved more, then yes, we were still together. A few days later a second note arrived, a shorter one.

Tamim,

Annie got run over by a car today. I should never have brought her to Chicago. Her guts squeezed out of her ass and she's dead. It's not that I didn't love her, I did. But now I am all alone.

Lily

The Draft

My father was writing to me with disturbing frequency at this point. When my Farsi started to slip he switched to English, but I still didn't study his letters scrupulously, because they were all so similar. For one thing, government censors examined all letters coming out of Afghanistan, so people put nothing into them but the blandest platitudes.

But also, letters weren't the same sort of artifact in Afghan culture as they are in the West. People didn't use them to give detailed, heartfelt, idiosyncratic accounts of their personal lives. Letters followed a format. They started with rhetorical salutations, followed by ritual inquiries about health and school, and then a recitation of all the people who had said hello and were themselves in good health, a list that, in my father's case typically included our relatives in Kabul, a few from the wider circle, and occasionally someone from the village--as if I could place any of those folks by name anymore.

Then came any specific information the writer wanted to impart--someone had died, someone was getting married, etc. The letter finished with a series of ceremonial phrases invoking God's blessings by way of closing. Most of my father's letters more or less followed this format, and since he wrote on "aerogramme" forms, every letter he sent me by regular mail was exactly the same length. Most did have one specific bit of business my father wanted to get done, but it was always the same bit of business. By persuasion or temptation, guilt-tripping or trickery, he wanted to get me back to Afghanistan.

Sometimes he mentioned casually that so-and-so had asked when I would be coming home and what should he tell people? Sometimes he wrote bits of poetry, praising us kids. "Rebecca, flower of the pomegranate tree ... Riaz, sweet bud barely opened." I guess he thought we'd come back if only he could communicate the depth of his grief.

Sometimes he attempted subtle ploys, but I saw through them easily. "You say you want to be a writer, Tamim-boy. This is the land of stories! Consider the peculiar tale of your uncle Khan Kaka. A lifelong bachelor gets married, gets divorced, and dies-- all in the last year of his life! It's a novel! Hurry home, Tamim-jan! Here, you will find a thousand stories."

Even then, part of me recognized the authenticity of his misery, but I wanted him to stop lamenting, so that I could stop feeling guilty about leaving him. The one who leaves always wants absolution from the one who has been left. My letters to my father probably resembled Lily's letters to me.

My father never revealed the magnitude of his troubles in these letters, not to me. I was the eldest son but the second child. Only to my sister did he bare his true anxieties, and to her, only when he could send a letter by some private means—that is, when someone he knew was coming to the United States and could hand-carry a letter from him, to drop into any mailbox in America.

He told my sister his finances were tight. When he lost his post in Washington D.C. and went back to Afghanistan, he could not get a government job, the only sort of job suitable for a man of his social class. He was "on the shelf"— Kabul lingo for "unemployable on account of having fallen out of political favor." He did have a good house in a neighborhood favored by American foreign aid officials and diplomats, and if he could have found an American tenant, he would have been on easy street, because Americans paid so well and in dollars.

But American tenants were a precious resource. You couldn't get one unless you knew someone who knew someone; and my father didn't know anyone who knew *anyone*. My sister conveyed to me a vague sense of his situation, but I didn't worry for him. He was a man, I was a boy: how could *I* help *him*? Whatever my incompetence at being a grown man among men as an American, I was many times more incompetent to be a grown Afghan man among Afghan men.

And yet my father kept pleading with me to come back. He had to be crazy. The moment I stepped across the Afghan border I would be drafted into the Afghan army. Even my father acknowledged that. And if I served a single day in the Afghan army I would lose my American citizenship. My mother made sure I knew *that*. And if *that* happened, according to my mother, the Afghan royal family would never let me out of Afghanistan again. Why the royals would want to hold onto me so desperately, I never understood. I just believed it. Much later I realized that my mother's view was skewed by the fact that she had felt so trapped in Afghanistan for twenty years. But even if her fears stemmed from paranoia, there was no discounting the harsh economic reality. If I went back, I'd end up working for Afghan-level wages and would never be able to save enough to fly back to America. Plus, I would certainly have to do a couple of years in the Afghan army, and that would be no laughing matter for a boy with my light skin, my John Lennon glasses, my foreign look, my soft sensibilities, and my *farangi* mother—in the barracks with a bunch of rural recruits, I could certainly expect some bullying from my fellow soldiers. Some raping, perhaps. In fact, chances were pretty good I'd end up as some big bearded rural bastard's bitch.

On the other hand, the draft posed a problem right here in the United States. In 1970, the Vietnam War was peaking. Graduating from college ended my student deferment. I was now reclassified 1-A and would be drafted if my lottery number came up, no excuses. I had long been trying to figure out what made America's involvement in Vietnam so necessary, but I couldn't fathom it. Why did we care which side won another country's civil war?

The public explanation—that we wanted to give the Vietnamese people the blessings of democracy—sounded like puff. Lots of countries didn't have democracy—Afghanistan, for example. Why had we picked the Vietnamese to set free?

Conservatives generally said we had to be in Vietnam because so many Americans had already suffered and died there; pulling out now would mean their sacrifices had been for naught. We had to be in Vietnam in order not to disrespect the memory of our martyrs. But that explanation seemed circular to me, since it meant we would keep generating more martyrs, making it ever (and endlessly) more necessary to stay there and keep fighting.

Some lefties, boiling with indignation, told me, "It's all about rubber." I looked around to see what was made of rubber, and all I could spot were erasers, those little pink nipples at the ends of pencils. Jesus! Was I going to have to go kill people on order from men like Calley so that Americans could have pencil erasers? That just seemed so wrong! Others said the war was about tin, but what the hell was made of tin? Even tin cans were made of aluminum. A few said rice, but I hardly knew any Americans who even *liked* rice.

The awful truth seemed to be that we were in Vietnam for no reason. Some fool had made a bad decision long ago, and after that no one had ever been in a position to admit the mistake without inviting blame upon themselves; and so each new set of leaders sent more people over to there to kill and die.

Every young guy I knew was working some angle to stay out of this evil insanity. Anyone who had connections was using them to secure a coveted spot in the national guard or the coast guard, but that avenue was closed to anonymous nobodies like me. Anyone with the slightest hint of a disability was busy getting it certified and exaggerated by a doctor. One guy I knew got a letter from a psychiatrist attesting to his "homosexual tendencies." Another was laying a basis for claiming he was subject to migraines.

My only potential disability was my weight. I was only thirteen pounds over the Army's minimum. If I lost fourteen pounds by the time I went in for my pre-induction physical, I might be classified unfit for duty. But losing fourteen pounds wasn't as easy as it sounded. At one point (against all advice) I limited my diet to a single hardboiled egg a day and waited to see the pounds drop away. But what dropped away were not pounds, only ounces, and one day, walking past Manning's Coffeeshop, I smelled a doughnut. When I became conscious of my surroundings again, I was surrounded by the wreckage of cheap desserts, and that evening I found I had gained back everything I had lost plus some. Dieting didn't look to be my ticket out of Vietnam.

Lots of stories were making the rounds about people who took more extreme action. One guy shot off his big toe. Another guy drank his own urine at his physical to convince his draft board he was crazy. Others were refusing induction and going to prison, which sounded too much like getting drafted into the Afghan army.

Do nothing, then? Just go to Vietnam if called, like my friend Ralph? Ralph whose letters from the jungle were now sounding downright unhinged? That was the least tenable choice of all. The prospect of turning into one of William Calley's men, or worse, into a new incarnation of Calley himself, kept me awake at night. At least this part of the horror, I might avoid, I was told, by signing up as a medic after induction. I began exploring crash courses in first aid, only to learn that you couldn't just tell the army you would like to be a medic, please. The army would decide—except in the case of conscientious objectors.

To be absolutely certain of a medical assignment (and possibly avoid the war altogether) I would have to declare myself a conscientious objector and see if anyone believed me. This would be a more difficult case to make for a Muslim than, say, for a Quaker; although surely I was more of a conscientious objector than that famous Quaker Richard Nixon.

Actually, I myself did not know if my contention would be truth or fiction. A visceral abhorrence of violence? Check. But what if I saw a guy raping my sister and I had a gun: would I shoot him? If my answer was yes, I wasn't a conscientious objector. But was my answer yes? I didn't know.

In any case, I filed a CO application before graduation and sent out a call for letters supporting my contention. I hardly knew anyone in America whose testimony would be worth anything, so I had asked my father for help: would any of our old family friends testify that I had shown pacifist tendencies as a child? The day after I got the note about Annie, I found a letter from my father in my mailbox. It was not an aerogramme form mailed from Kabul, but a fat envelope, hand-carried to America, and mailed from Washington D.C., a whole sheaf of testimonials from my father's friends and from motley other folks such as the headmaster of my old elementary school. All these people had come through with letters that fulfilled the highest requirements of Afghan rhetoric.

Unfortunately, by Afghan rhetorical standards, in a situation like this, the appearance of authenticity had no value. Anyone can fake sincerity. Those who want to prove their true devotion to a cause must go for passionate excess. Accordingly, the letters collected by my father said things like: "Even in his cradle, a light shone around Tamim's head." And: "Many times we have seen how he flung himself upon the dirt in tears, wailing aloud because he had stepped on an ant. Yes, even the death of one ant was too much of a blow to this great soul." Or my personal favorite: "Though small in stature, Tamim was a spiritual giant." I could just picture my draft board—old white guys in suits—pondering these letters.

But all was not lost. I had one more request floating out there. Carleton College professor Arnold Gottlieb might come through with something. Gottlieb taught literature courses at Carleton College and had run a creative writing workshop I attended. He was a gentle, civilized man who looked like Mr. Magoo. About a dozen of us students used to go to his house on Sunday afternoons to pass out mimeographed copies of our fiction and trade feedback under Gottlieb's gruff but kindly direction. Dr. Gottlieb didn't really know me, but he was an excellent writer. Maybe he would write me a letter so good, I would need no other testimonial.

Get a Job

I had one further anxiety that summer. I had no money, no source of money, and no idea how a person made money. I had graduated from one of the country's finest small colleges, but all I had studied there were ideas, all I knew how to do was think, and all I knew how to be was a student.

At being-a-student I had been quite good. I won honors and awards at Reed and was nominated for prestigious fellowships. Every element of my life was yelling at me to go to graduate school, get an advanced degree in critical theory or some such, and enter academia. But the existential absurdity of this course gave me twinges of despair. What was the point of going to school to become a college professor, who could teach others what they needed to know to become college professors, who would then teach others how to become college professors… ? How was this not a Ponzi scheme? I had to get out of academia and do something "real."

But after six years in America, the only professionals I had seen up close were college professors. I had no idea what anyone did for a living in the "real world." Writing was my passion, but the only paid work I knew of that involved writing was journalism.

I was no journalist, but I wrote to the Oregonian and asked if they would hire me, and some editor invited me in for a chat, but it wasn't a job interview. He just wanted to give me some sage advice.

He told me there were no openings at the Oregonian for a guy like me. To get a job at such an important paper, I would have to clock a few years at a smaller place "getting my feet wet". In fact, he knew of a place that might hire me right now. Then he looked guilty, and I knew his suggestion was going to make me cringe.

"The nuclear reactor at Mount St. Helens is looking for someone to help them with public relations—if you're interested."

Work as a flak for the nuclear power industry? Had I fallen so low that I would make my living telling lies for Satan?

"Not for me," I said politely.

"Well then," he said, "contact some small town newspapers. There's one in The Dalles that might give you a shot, if you don't mind starting at the bottom."

The Dalles was a small town sixty miles east of Portland, surrounded by ranches. I pictured the cowboys roping me like a steer so they could cut off my hair. No thanks.

That left jobs in Portland. I pored through the classified ads every day. I called, I wrote, and I went out, but I couldn't find a job. I don't mean "a job in my field." What field? I had been a literature student. I was looking for "any job." It never occurred to me to look for work that might require a college degree. I figured jobs like that would be too hard to get, since everybody would want them. When people asked what kind of work I was looking for, I said "anything," the theory being that the least picky were the most employable. Actually, since "anything" is a job for which "anyone" qualifies, the competition for such jobs tends to be intense, especially in hard times like the recession of 1970. The odds of getting a job that only a few people can do is better—for those few who can do it.

But in the summer of 1970, this logic eluded me, so I applied to sell life insurance, file papers, haul boxes. All turned me down. I applied to work at a pickle factory but the manager felt I was not pickle-factory material. I tried to get work at a garment factory, a furniture plant, a junkyard. No go. I applied for day laborer jobs: digging sewer lines, for example. I got up at the crack of dawn but scores of people had already lined up ahead of me and anyone who looked more muscular than me—which was "anyone"—always got the nod.

So I went to an employment agency. They had me fill out a form and sit in a waiting room for a couple of hours. Finally a counselor agreed to see me. I made my way to a cubicle of a room and took a seat across a desk from a blond woman in a red polyester suit. She had hair styled into a fashionable wedge and hairsprayed into place. She wore nylons and lipstick and earrings. I was aware that in some universe of aesthetics quite alien to me, this platinum-headed creature would be labeled "attractive." Her body language told me she was certain of her own allure. But being so close to such a creature in real life made me uneasy. I was nervous about the possible cancer-causing effects of the chemicals so obviously caked onto her face and possibly her body. She smelled of sprays, deodorants, colognes and other noxious industrial products.

Wriggling uncomfortably on her pantyhosed bottom, she studied the form I had filled out. "So...you went to... ?" She squinted and looked closer. "Reed College, it says here...? Is that a junior college"

"It's a four-year college."

"I see. Four years! What did you study there? Says here literature. What is that, like literature from the different companies? How to write literature for different companies?"

"Not so much how to write it. Not companies. More, the great literature of the past. How to read it. How to appreciate it. Authors."

"Authors!" She had no handle for that word. "Well, what companies' literature have you...studied?"

"No, not the literature of companies. We studied real literature, like *War and Peace*, Dostoevsky, George Elliot, people like that. You know."

"Uh huh. Okay, well, you must have studied some business English."

"Business English?" I never knew business people spoke a different kind of English? Was it a dialect? "No."

"Accounting?"

"No."

"Shorthand?"

"No."

"What about bookkeeping?'

"No."

"Let me see if I've got this straight," she said. "You went to four years of college, you didn't pick up any accounting, no bookkeeping, and you can't even spell—"

"I can spell!" (I was sort of lying there.)

"But you don't have any background in business English."

"Well--"

"Mr. Ansary." She leaned forward and fixed me with her carefully-penciled eyes: "Did it ever occur to you that you just wasted four years of your life?"

I was at a loss. Had I just wasted four years of my life? That question only makes sense if you have a goal. If you do, you can measure how much closer you've gotten to it each year. But like the little boy in Celine's *Death on the Installment Plan*, I was just trying to stay alive and happy each day. From that perspective, my last four years had been a triumph. I had explored fascinating ideas with some of the brightest minds in America, smoked a lot of dope , taken a lot of acid, and enjoyed transcendent love for the last eight months. As for staying alive, I was still alive. But now that those years were over, did it matter that they had ever been? Of all that I had gained in those four years, what did I still possess except life?

Fortunately, just when I got down to my last few dollars, Nick and Abby came to town. Nick Durham was one of the New York guys who had lived upstairs from me at the Ivan Street House in the summer of 1969, the summer I hitched across Canada and just barely missed Woodstock. When I first moved in with those guys, I saw them as lean-mean street rats from the world's biggest city. Actually, my Ivan Street roommates were middle-class kids who had dropped out of middle-class American society, intent on crafting a full-scale alternative to their parents' mainstream middle-class way of life.

After our Ivan Street summer, Nick had gone back to New York and met a school-teacher named Abby Clark. He'd convinced her that Portland, Oregon, was the countercultural promised land, so here they were. Abby was a pretty woman of crackling intellectual intensity, devoted to poetry, theater, and cultural criticism. Her favorite poet was San Francisco wild man Michael McClure, and she had a passion for Polish director Grotowsky and his vision of a "poor theater" (whatever that meant). For all her charisma, however, there was something vulnerable about Abby. An early bout of polio had left her with a slight limp, and the limp was now as much psychic as physical. Nick and Abby had rented the top flat of a house in Albina, Portland's miniature African-American ghetto, and had found good jobs.

By "good jobs," I mean "jobs". Abby was a salad chef at l'Auberge, Portland's only French bistro, and Nick worked there as a late-night dishwasher. Our mutual friend Paul Matthews waited tables at L'Auberge. Nick and Abby had an extra room and invited me to move in with them: I would not have to pay rent until I found work.

They saved my life, this generous couple. I still spent whole days beating the pavements for work, but I had a refuge to come back to at night. A handful of other ex-Reedies moved into houses in our neighborhood. Nathan Cooper, another of those New York guys from the Ivan Street House, came back and crashed in our living room. He was on the run from some emotional disaster of his own, and we had a good time smoking cigarettes and discussing politics.

I still didn't have a job, I didn't have money, and most of all I didn't have Lily; I still felt guilty about my father and confused about cutting my ties with Afghanistan; I still lived in fear of being drafted and sent to Vietnam and still had no idea how I would fit into America if I stayed; but at least I had a group of friends and the rudiments of a community. I figured I was fine. I was wrong.

The Void

On the night of July 12th, 1970. Crosby, Stills, Nash, and Young were playing at the Portland Coliseum, and I couldn't afford to go--which was okay, I never particularly liked that band, but all my friends were going—Nick and Abby, Paul Matthews, all the six or seven people I knew in Portland. All were going, and all were planning to take LSD, standard practice for potentially mind-blowing musical events. And I wouldn't be one of them.

Acid, however, was cheap, so I could get in on that part of the festivities, and by golly I was going to. The acid we had found for this fateful night was designer LSD handcrafted by a master chemist. It had such a great reputation, it was known by its own colorful brand name: orange sunshine. It was said to be so strong that a third of a tab would take you anywhere you wanted and even to some places you didn't. Ha ha. Someone joked that on the street it went by another brand-name: Angel-of-Death. That's how strong it was. We all tittered. A third of a tab is how much my concert-bound friends were planning to take. Everyone said that would be plenty.

But I was staying home, so I felt I deserved a bit more. Two-thirds of a tab would be about right for me, I thought; and my friends agreed, even though I had chipped in no extra money. Acid, after all, was cheap.

We clustered in a ritual LSD circle, cut the tabs carefully with razor blades, and laughingly prepared our glasses of water. Then we each downed our portion of the drug with sacramental solemnity. The others piled out of the house, chittering and chattering and away they drove. Once the echoes of their hilarity died away, I was alone.

And boy, did I ever *feel* alone! How sordid to be so poor! How squalid to have no job. How shameful that I couldn't pay my share of the rent. How bleak to be at home when all my friends were at a gala concert. What would become of me? A liberal arts degree from Reed College, a Phi Beta Kappa key, a summa cum laude certificate, a nomination for a Woodrow Wilson fellowship, not to mention, son of the one-time Deputy Minister of the Interior of Afghanistan, even if that post had only lasted a couple of months--but not a single course in Business English.

I thought about rooting around in Lily's letters for comfort but some survival reflex told me no, listen to music instead. Achieve sublime elation the old-fashioned way.

Odd thing, though. An hour had passed since I swallowed that acid and I was feeling nothing yet. "We got cheated," crossed my mind. Maybe the acid was mixed unevenly into the tab. Perhaps, my two-thirds of a tab was all filler and the good stuff was all in that last third, which was still in the freezer. So I downed that too, though not without a qualm, because acid is so irrevocable. Once you swallow it, you're in for the full ride, wherever it's going.

But the minutes passed and still I felt nothing. Maybe smoke a joint to prime the high? I rolled a fat one.

Just then, someone rang the doorbell.

Ours was a poor neighborhood. We lived in Portland's ghetto, what there was of it, and we had some tough neighbors. Recently, there had been some home-invasion robberies on our very street. It was seven o'clock on a Saturday evening, and all my friends had gone to the Portland Coliseum. Who could be ringing our doorbell on this night at this time? I trudged downstairs.

It was the mailman. What brought him to my door at this hour? Well, the post office offered a service called "special delivery" back then. When a "special delivery" letter arrived at the local post office, a mail carrier delivered it by hand immediately to the addressee.

This mailman handed me a letter from Arnold Gottlieb, my one-time creative writing teacher at Carleton College. Here was the last of the letters I had solicited to support my conscientious objector application. And here is an exact transcript of the letter Gottlieb had written to my draft board. And to me.

To Whom It May Concern:

Mr. Tamim Ansary has asked me to write a statement to accompany his application to be considered as a conscientious objector to the military forces of the United States. My remarks will have to be very personal. If Tamim had ever asked me for specific advice on a course of action in the present circumstances, I would not have advised him to make the application I am now supporting. But he never asked me. I am glad. It is a rare person who can advise another these days. Rather, these are days of lonely searching of one's own life, conscience, hopes, fears, and practical circumstances. These are days of trying to find one's own true relationship to one's beliefs, friends, family, and country. I am as much involved in this as Tamim is, and so are you, whoever I am addressing. There is no gap between the generations in the ordeal of living in this century. Given my age, my experiences, my conviction that the human spirit lives in a fitful and essentially lonely communion with itself, I would probably, if required, go back into the army, fight in a self-destructive and imbecilic war, and hope I could cast out remorse when it was all over and live my life, not purely and without taint, but as a member of that ever-increasing community of the shafted. Eventually, one way or another, that is the community to which we all belong.

That was the whole letter, and even as I read it, I wondered at the malevolence of chance. If only it had come the following morning. Staring at the phrase "ever-increasing community of the shafted," I heard a groan and since I was alone, I knew it must have come from me.

Dr. Gottlieb had put it perfectly: the human spirit lives in lonely communion with itself.   He was only echoing what I had been realizing for weeks, what even the world's smallest dog had intuited the night of those fireworks: every one of us is alone. With trembling fingers, I stuffed the letter back into its envelope. This I didn't need. Not tonight damn it. Tonight I was going to break into the presence of God. Why else had I taken thrice as much acid as my friends? And where was this damned acid anyway? Why was I feeling nothing?

Then I remembered: I was going to smoke a joint. Here was the stogie I had rolled. There were the headphones. The music I had chosen was already playing: Buffalo Springfield, that great second album.

I lit my joint, donned the headphones, took a long toke, and relaxed into the sound. One song—Neil Young's *Broken Arrow*—has a place where the chorus ends, a cacophony of voices breaks out, and then the instruments come together for a rich orchestral chord that holds for a long interval before sliding into an instrumental break. This time the familiar chord held for longer than I remembered,   swelling in richness and significance, swelling in -- hey! — swelling —what the hell?— SWELLING— oh my God SWELLING—too long, too huge, swelling to engulf the world, gobbling suns and galaxies, expanding beyond all light and warmth—

Abruptly, I was standing in our living room, the headphones torn off, the joint stubbed out. My heart was booming but the world was silent. Outside, a tinkle of children's voices sounded. The world was absolutely normal. No trace of psychedelic sensations.   No trace of any LSD-distorted perceptions. I wasn't even stoned.

Sure.

I knew then that I was in trouble. The world was only as normal as I could keep it. I jumped to my feet, put my hands in my pockets, and started walking to keep from tripping out too fast. "Great acid," I said aloud to test my voice. In an effort to shape my mood, I then said, "Yes sir, this is going to be interesting after it's peaked." Next, I chuckled, because chuckling would mean I was enjoying myself.

But it wasn't working. I was keeping the trip bottled up but I could feel it inside, fighting to expand. If only Lily were here, everything would be okay. But everywhere I looked, there she wasn't. I went to my room and took out my box of letters from Lily, hoping to evoke her presence. The letters wriggled and squiggled and dissolved but I managed to decipher a few lines of the page I had plucked out at random—*Annie got run over by a car today. Her guts squeezed out of her ass*—Ouch! Wrong letter! I flung it back into the shoebox.

Hundreds of voices were chattering away in my head now at different mental levels, some almost inaudible, others closer to the surface, louder. "Yes sir-ee-Bob, this sure is good acid." "What time is it?" "...the interesting problem of the night brain..." "Maybe I've already peaked." "Getting rougher."

I hurried to the kitchen to look at the clock. Maybe such a lot of time had passed that I was on my way down now. The clock was dissolving, but I compiled enough data to determine that the time was—7:15.

Holy shit! Only fifteen minutes had passed since Gottlieb's letter arrived? So this trip wasn't ending, it was just beginning. The leash holding fear in check pulled taut. Somebody's heartbeat became a drum solo. A voice said, "Find a safe place to let go and just let go."

I went to the attic and huddled next to the dormer window up there, the most secluded part of the house. But the window gaped into the enormity of the universe. The street was melting, melting. Centuries of terror passed. Fortunately, acid peaks after about four hours. At last I figured that I *must* be coming down by now. I'd go look at the clock again.

The steps were dissolving under someone's feet. I could see someone's hands on the banisters far below. Tamim got to the bottom of the stairs. There was his body in the kitchen doorway looking at the clock, hoping to glean the good news that this trip was almost over. "Toddle Time," said the clock. Tick tock tick tock. The little hand was pointing toward seven, the big hand toward four. The time was now 7:19.

Whoa! Only four minutes had passed. Not four hours! Help! Oh how *big* the world was! Every one of us is the smallest dog in the universe. Annie's guts squeezed out of her ass. It was getting hard not to think about Lily. I must not think about sad things. Must not stare at anything too long. Must stop noticing street sounds, too scary. Ignore heartbeat, ignore the sound and feel of blood, the muscle-actions involved in breathing. But there was no way to stop the thousands of voices chattering in my head, no stopping the images flaring everywhere, touching off fireworks of mental activity that shot in myriad directions, sparking explosions of new images along every path. "Lily!" voices yowled. "Lily!" they shrieked. Something was cold. Was I catching pneumonia? Negative thought. Eruptions everywhere. Time no longer moving, yet voices piling up. Lily! Lily! Tiger loose in the kindergarten, unleashed terror running amok. Cacophony. All voices blending into a single chord that grew and swelled and gobbled galaxies—

And then—

I pause here to set off what happened next. Because, for me, the thing that happened next divided time into Before and After for years It was here that my slide toward the abyss began. What happened next was this:

The last veil of hallucinations vanished and I saw what was really out there: nothing.

Well, "saw" is a misnomer here, and so is "nothing." Words don't work for what I want to get across. What lay beyond the last veil was not the mere absence of something but the *presence* of *nothing:* I "saw" the Void.

One glimpse was all it took. One glimpse and I was falling, not just down but up, not just up but out, falling in every direction: vertigo multiplied by infinity.

One glimpse of the Void reduced me to a single imperative: shrink from it. Wipe out what was seen. Do not *ever* have looked. The Void left no option but flight. Flight was impossible, so long as awareness (of the Void) persisted, so from that moment onward all energy had to go into not-knowing/never-having-seen. But I *did* know, I *had* seen, which left no tactic but amnesia. Forget was the one imperative. Forget so thoroughly that NOTHING would be erased from past as well as present.

Forgetting the unforgettable, however, is impossible so *pretending* to have forgotten remained the only gambit. From that moment on, pretending became my entire occupation. Time passed, the acid peaked, and the drug effect began to recede, but I was not aware of it. I was too busy pretending *not* to be aware of the Void. Pretending *never* to have been aware of it.

Eons later, something existed, a hallucinated something, to be sure, but "I" clung to it. Hard pretending turned the hallucination into a bubble of "somethingness" surrounding me, although the Void remained ubiquitous outside, above, below, and on every side of the bubble.

At some point, I was shocked to see Nick and Abby, Paul Matthews and Gracie Barnes come up the stairs like creatures from a nostalgic dream about some place I had visited long ago. It hit me that I must be down now. This must be how "down" was going to feel from now on. The others were babbling about the concert. At any moment, they would ask how my trip went and I'd have to say, "Pretty good" because I couldn't blurt the awful truth, that they would cease to exist the moment I stopped imagining them. That nothing existed except an infinitesimal dot of consciousness suspended in endless emptiness. I could not tell them, because to speak of the Void was to remember the Void, to remember the Void was to know the Void, to know the Void was to be the Void.

By the time the guests left, Nick and Abby knew I was in trouble, but they knew not to ask. Instead, they did the only thing that could have helped. They took me to Portland's gigantic, beautiful Washington Park. Dawn had arrived and I walked along a path, gawking at dewdrops hanging off spider webs and at sunlight glinting through green leaves. God was busy waking up the world and I felt the sweep of his creation across sidereal spaces, from here to Mars to the sun to stars and galaxies vast beyond imagination—but I now knew something terrible about all this creation. It didn't exist.

The next day, I was back to acting like my old self, and I'm sure no one could tell I was just pretending. With strenuous pretending, I held reality together while I looked for work. Eventually I got a job sorting mail at the post office. My draft board never got back to me, never said yes or no to my CO application, never contacted me again, as if I had never existed, but I scarcely noticed. The Christmas rush was just beginning and my hours kept increasing until I was working thirteen hours a day, seven days a week, the graveyard shift, leaving home in darkness, coming back in darkness.

At the post office we sorters sat in a huge windowless room in a dozen rows of thirty, facing matrices of pigeonholes, each of us with a box full of envelopes next to him or her. We picked the envelopes up one at a time and put each one into its correct pigeonhole, and as soon as one box was emptied, a full box took its place. When you're a pinpoint of consciousness in the Void, there is nothing outside you except what you can make real at each moment by imagining it. For me, an acid casualty working the graveyard shift at the post office, nothing existed but the infinite matrix of pigeonholes and the repetitive task I was charged with endlessly doing.

Every time I came home, I felt a premonition that Lily would be there in the living room to greet me: she'd come back, I'd wake up, the nightmare would be over. But she was never there.

Meanwhile weird things were happening in my house. Nick and Abby and I were getting very close, *very* close. A few sympatico souls were accumulating in houses around ours. Somebody brought an archetypal sixties science-fiction book into our lives, about groups of people on some other planet, who got so intensely close to one another they broke through the barriers of material separation and developed telepathic connections, each person retaining an individual consciousness but all partaking of a group consciousness as well, whereupon they became a biologically new type of organism, something that the characters in the book called a "snowflake."

Abby was the first to say it. "Maybe we're a snowflake being born." A few days later, Nick made a similar observation. Then Dusty said it, then others. Soon we were all getting so intimate we were actually turning telepathic. Late nights in one of "our" houses, deeply immersed in heavy conversations about cosmic topics in rooms lit only by scented candles and permeated by the aroma of incense, while Jackie Lomax was weaving intricate layers of acid-music in the background...our boundaries began dissolving...we could feel ourselves blending into a single breathing organism. And suddenly we'd all be dancing. That's what I mean about telepathy. No one said, "Let's dance." The spark jolted through us and suddenly we were all just doing it.

At home in the privacy of our fortress, or together in some isolated spot in the woods near a waterfall or a stream, it was natural to be naked together, no different than being naked alone. We were, after all, practically a single person—a snowflake. As a snowflake, we felt normal rolling around on the floor hugging, or sitting in a circle playing "sensitivity games"—sharing all, revealing all ... At the end of a long night of emotional intensity it was never a given who would end up sleeping with whom,. Coming into "this thing"—whatever "this thing" was—some of us had been couples. Nick and Abby... George and Dusty... But the couple-identities dissolved into the group identity of the snowflake, a new "us" permeated by sexuality.

I was getting all this in *tiny* droplets. The others had part-time jobs or no jobs at all. Whatever the nascent "us" was doing, they were the ones doing it, mostly. I was at the post office. But when I did eke out a few minutes to be with the private snowflake "us", the others included me as if I were always there.   My membership in the "snowflake" came with a crucial caveat, however. The others were in the room where the snowflake-event was taking place; I was outside, clinging to the window of a skyscraper floating in nothingness, peering in. If I lost my grip, I would fall away in every direction because the Void is everywhere.   Only by faking absorption in the imaginary drama visible through that eye-shaped window could I keep us all from disappearing.   Sometimes the emotional intensity drew me in enough to forget that none of this was real, the way at a movie theater, when you get totally absorbed in a film, you forget you're sitting in darkness surrounded by strangers, and you start imagining that you really are in a ballroom lit by chandeliers, with a band playing, and a lovely woman in your arms.

In the middle of all this I got a letter from my father, informing me that he was in America for a conference and would come to Portland for two days, to see me. I went to the airport to get him. The man who got off the plane was a dead ringer for my father, but older. I was wearing my usual threads: purple bellbottomed pants,   a tie-dyed T-shirt, a colorful bandana-style headband keeping my shoulder length hair under control, and a few strings of beads.   My father made his way out of the jetway with the crowds wearing a slightly over-sized suit, no tie, and a white shirt casually unbuttoned at the neck. When he spotted me coming, alarm fluttered through his eyes, and he glanced around for possible escape routes, then realized that this hairy creature was his son. We hugged awkwardly. I said, "You didn't recognize me."

 He said, "Of course I did. I was only joking with you."

But the moment felt false. I took him home and introduced him to Nick and Abby and other members of the Snowflake, without of course telling him we were a snowflake. Abby made a delicious meal, and my father gave everyone gifts, all of them suspiciously appropriate—but then they would be, if my imagination had invented him, for I knew Nick and Abby well: I had invented them too.

We spoke in English, so as not to exclude the others, but also because, as we already knew from letters, I could no longer communicate with him in Farsi. The next day, I drove him around to show him my town. During that drive, he suddenly asked, "What is this LSD, Tamim-boy? Do you ever take this LSD?"

"Yes," I said. I knew I would never take it again but "No" would have felt dishonest.

"Why do you take it?" my father asked. "Is it for the kicks?"

I had to laugh at that one. "No," I said. "LSD doesn't really give you 'kicks'. It opens your eyes. It shows you how the world actually is."

"And how is the world actually?" he said.

"Not good."

My father sighed. "For this, I don't need LSD, my boy. I already know the world is not so good. The hell with it, Tamim, don't take these drugs. Why don't you drink whiskey instead? Just one small glass after dinner."

"Whiskey dulls the mind. I don't want whiskey."

"*Kho*," he shrugged. "You know best." After a moment he said, "What about *namaz*? Do you ever say *namaz*?" He was referring to the elaborate Muslim prayer ritual.

"I don't know how."

"You should learn," he advised me. "It's meditation, really."

He did not suggest how I might go about learning the Muslim prayer ritual there in Portland, but it didn't matter. I had no interest in *namaz*. When we went home, he showed me pictures from Afghanistan, and told me all about "our" house in Kabul, "our" lands in the village, "our" relatives in the village, and "our" family friends: the Tarakis, Kayeums, Shalizis, and others. I remembered these people because I had full access to all the memories of my former self, they just didn't feel like mine anymore: they felt like biographical data about some other guy. The acid trip had divided time into Before and After, and these folks all belonged to Before.

Then my father started singing his usual song: I should come back to Afghanistan. The land of stories! A lifetime of material for novels! He joked that the family would find me a good wife. I joked that I would think about it. He joked that he was only sorta' joking. He idly mentioned some girls in our circles who were now grown up, beautiful, and "educated." He just wanted me to know the possibilities. I responded with noncommittal nods. The poor guy had no idea that the prospect of an "educated" wife secured for me by the Ansary clan would never, ever, *ever* lure me back to Afghanistan. Anyone they found would have one catastrophic flaw: she wouldn't be Lily. The next day, my father got on a plane and vanished from my life, and I was left wondering: did that really happen?

At one point, someone calling herself Lily came to Portland— to do a six-month internship, she said, and "give our relationship a chance." She was an alien-imposter wearing Lily's body. The six months passed in a blur of anxious sentiments and fuzzy memories. When her internship finally ended, and she flew back to whatever hell she'd come out of, I was happy to see her go, but the moment she was gone, I started craving Lily again. Since there was no Lily except the one I had just put on a plane, the question did arise: whom was I craving? It had to be some miraculous lover Lily had merely foreshadowed, as John the Baptist foreshadowed Christ. They say that after a terrible earthquake, rumors spread wildly about an even worse quake soon to come. Sociologists say such rumors arise to justify the anxiety people are already feeling. I'm guessing that an agonizingly intense in-love feeling with no actual person as its object triggers the same mechanism. The imagination invents a mythic someone to explain the feeling one already has. And so I started waiting for The One.

Somewhere in there, I moved, to a three-story communal mansion of long standing known as E-Street (This was long before anyone had heard of Springsteen.) Anywhere from fifteen to thirty people lived there at any given time. They didn't all have bedrooms. Many tucked into habitable nooks and crannies throughout the house. One guy fixed up a place for himself in the basement, behind the furnace. My old friend Ralph Garner moved into the house as soon as he came home from Vietnam—where he never fired a gun, it was the first thing he told everyone he met— and found an alcove big enough to accommodate a mattress off the hallway on the third story. Some people just crashed in our living room for a few days, then drifted on.

The pillar of the household was Karl Friedrich, our friendly community dope dealer, a country boy with thick, amiable features and a haircut that made him look like Prince Valiant. He might never have finished high school, but he could smoke ten different kinds of marijuana and tell whether the tenth one was stronger or weaker than the first, an awesome skill. Karl sold only to people he knew, and to people they knew, but he knew hundreds of people, and they each knew hundreds, so the house saw constant traffic.

I got a new job too. The Genoa, a brand new Northern Italian restaurant hired me to wait tables. The entire staff consisted of former Reed students and professors. The work called upon me to be intensely sociable in the shallowest possible way, which a pinpoint of consciousness floating in an imaginary world surrounded by the Void could manage and even enjoy. I brought my tips home in cash and stuck the bills between the pages of books in my bookcase. Working a couple of nights a week made me so rich, I never thought about money. But waiting tables was only my job. Waiting for The One was my full-time vocation, my obsession.

Every night that I wasn't working, I knocked about with herds of acquaintances from tavern to tavern or house to house until we pooled up somewhere and became a party. My senses were on hyper-alert for The One, but she never showed. Sometimes we tumbled stoned and drunk into venerable Rose's across the street from E-Street, the oldest Jewish deli north of San Francisco, a place with vinyl faux leather seats and gooey slices of cake the size of bricks. I remember dancing at the White Eagle, a bar in a neighborhood of warehouses and railroad tracks, guarded by a bouncer named Tony, who looked like Popeye's Bluto, a man with enormous arms bulging like sausages out of striped T-shirts. Those who got past Tony squeezed into a room more jam-packed than any subway car at rush hour except that here all the bodies were jiggling and writhing against one another, and not a one of them was Lily. It was torture. And ecstasy. And torture.

The Eagle was at its best when Puddle City was playing. Puddle City featured guitar god Peter Langston, whose Portland Zoo was seared into my heart forever as the soundtrack to the night I fell in love with Lily. I never missed Puddle City night at the Eagle. I knew one of the guitar players in the band, a guy named Chris Montague: he was a friend of my friend Paul Matthews. Montague of course didn't know me. He was a rock star under the lights onstage, I an anonymous stoner in the crowd.

To all outward appearances, I was living an ideal life now. I had a job I liked, all the dough I needed, a secure place to live, free dope, and lots of people to hang out with. But appearances can be deceiving. The thing is, the acid trip had never ended. I spent the whole first day after the trip, pretending to be normal. When I woke up on the second morning, I found that sleep had given me fresh strength to hold the illusion of reality together, but the effort remained as necessary as ever, because the illusion wasn't going to hold together by itself. When yours are the only eyes in the universe, you can't blink. All day, every day, I pretended that other people existed, that I was listening to music, that I was wandering in a forest, dancing in a club, waiting tables... It never occurred to me to seek therapy. Nothing was wrong with *me*. My problem was, I had seen the truth. The Void exists. Nothing else does. What needed fixing was the universe. Pretending, however, is like any skill, you get better at it with practice. Eventually, I could go days and days without noticing I was pretending.

Sometimes I toyed with going back to Afghanistan; maybe pretending would be easier there, since the moment I stepped off the plane, I would have a complete, prefabricated identity held in place from the outside by countless Ansaries and by the society around our clan. I would be the son of Mir Sahib, I would have a house. I would have an instant set of cousin-friends—Mazar, Najib, the whole gang. On the other hand, I would have to get fluent in Farsi again, internalize Islam, and accept the one thing I found so intolerably abhorrent about Muslim Afghan society, the sequestration of women and their subservience to men... If I could only do those things, I would be Somebody, and Somebody would soon have a wife, and Somebody and his wife would soon have children... and they'd be glad, because Afghans love children: and with luck, all the children would be boys...

But even as I was trying to decide if this alienating Somebody could actually be me, an improbable thing happened. I stumbled into a relationship with a girl. Improbable because every minute of my day was spent waiting for The One. And if she wasn't Lily, I had no idea what she'd look like or what her name would be, I just knew I couldn't get involved with anyone while I was waiting because what if The One came along just then and saw me with another girl? No, until The One showed up, my job was to *keep the wrong girlfriend out.* Yet somehow, I got involved with Natty.

Natty was an heiress, of all things, the daughter of a local steel magnate. The words "Portland" and "steel magnate" probably don't seem to go together, and maybe Portland didn't have *many* steel magnates, but it did have this one. The family lived in a distant suburb where people couldn't see their neighbors because each mansion was surrounded by so much wooded land. Natty was home for the summer from some fancy East Coast college. In her world, teenage girls were known as debutantes and when they reached a certain age they had "coming out" parties reported by the newspapers with photographs showing what gowns the girls had worn. But Natty scoffed at such rituals. She came down to the mud flats where the real folks lived and got herself a summer job, a job she didn't even need, as a bus girl at the Genoa, where I was waiting tables.

She came home with me one night and stayed till morning, but we did not make love because, she told me, she couldn't cross that line in the same municipal district as her parents. I pointed out that her parent's suburb was technically in a different city, but she said we were all in Multnomah County. The county was the thing. Could I understand?

I could, I would, I did. This was good actually. So long as we didn't cross the sex line, it wouldn't matter that Natty wasn't The One. And so that summer we fell into an innocent, lust-flavored relationship such as I'd always imagined American high school kids having. Sometimes she slept over, and we cuddled and played till we fell asleep, and daytimes we tooled around as affectionate pals to movies and parties, dance clubs and scenic country spots. Hanging out with her was a relief precisely because we weren't "in love." She didn't have to win a contest with Lily. I liked her, she liked me back, and that was good enough.

The Edge

Strange to say, however, even though I knew Lily didn't really exist, I had never stopped writing to her; and the imposter Lily never stopped writing back. My letters to her remained ludicrously passionate just as if she were the real Lily. Hers to me remained mundane social notes. A new letter from this "Lily" never failed to jangle my week. "My mother had a birthday party..." "I bought a new coat..." "I'm smoking cherry-flavored Tiparillos now..." I pored over such details the way religious fanatics study lines of scripture, looking for deeper meaning.

Then came a letter from her that contained, buried among its mundane details, two casual sentences: "After all this time, I think I've fallen in love again, Tamim. His name is Ted."

It didn't bother me. Two years had passed. Why should it bother me? Ted. Why should I care what his name was? That August, Lily breezed through Portland with her new boyfriend, and I didn't even care. I was waiting for the One, and she wasn't the One, so why should it upset me that Lily was here with this Ted-fellow? I showed them around town like any other mere acquaintances. I even scored tickets to a Grateful Dead concert in Corvallis. I can't remember if Natty was with us. Who sees the milky way when the sun is shining? We suffered through three hours of Jerry Garcia's interminable guitar solos. It wasn't fun, but I wasn't upset. Why should it bother me that I was next to Lily's body and she was Ted's girlfriend? It didn't. Not at all. They said goodbye and drove away.

I congratulated myself on my rock-solid stability. It was like the early hours of the bad acid trip. Everything felt hyper-normal. Life went on. Art and dope and work and dancing and music and nature... September came, and Natty headed back to college. I was not crushed, because it wasn't like we were having some great love affair. We never even had sex. She was fun, and mere fun can be relinquished without emotional catastrophe.

Then one day, as I was coming home from Reed, where I was reading up on the pre-Socratic philosophers, who interested me because one of them thought the only underlying reality was "the Void", the sidewalk went soft. Like most acid casualties, I had endured "flashbacks" after my bad trip. They usually started with the visible scene dissolving into a churning screen of psychedelic squiggles. I could make the squiggling stop by blinking and shaking my head, and if that didn't work, I had other tricks. But one or two of those early flashbacks took a more worrisome form: I'd be walking along and the sidewalk would go soft. You might wonder what was so terrifying about that. Did it hurt? No. Did it end? Always had. So what was the big deal?

The big deal was this: "solid" is the *least trivial* feature of material reality. If a sidewalk can dissolve, anything can dissolve. And now as I waded through concrete, the whispering of the wind in the trees turned into voices. By the time I reached E-Street, I was wading through material reality up to my knees. I could not think for terror because here in the light of day, on a full night's rest, reality was dissolving and I couldn't make it congeal again. I got myself to my room and huddled under the covers, trying not to notice the Void surrounding my shroud of nightmares.

The experience was less extreme than the original acid trip, but that time I could cling to the idea that I'd be fine once the drug wore off. This time, there was no drug from which to anticipate coming down. By afternoon, I had managed to restore illusion enough to go downstairs and pretend to socialize with my imaginary friends. By five o'clock I was in good enough shape to head for work, but I was 100% back to pretending. Nothing *looked* different than it had yesterday, but everything *was* different. The world was illusory again, and the moment I stopped pretending, it would stop existing.

It's true I had never stopped pushing to keep the Void at bay, but in the two-plus years since the acid trip, I thought I had at least moved the line of scrimmage. Now suddenly I had lost every inch of ground gained. That day, another friendly note arrived from Lily, and her casual words fell on my consciousness like drops of carbolic acid. As I filed the letter with all the other ones I had gotten from her, I became conscious of a fog surrounding me. It was everywhere except wherever I was looking at any given moment. So I couldn't actually see it, but it was there. It was everywhere.

It was not necessarily outside me, this fog; but are outside and inside really so distinct? Scientists agree that perceptions of an outside world boil down to private neural events. They would say the inner events correlate exactly to an outer world; it's as good as being out there. But that's faith, not fact. We can't really know there is any such thing as "out there." And if "seeing" and "hearing" are events transpiring inside a person, how are they different from "thinking" and "feeling"?

Whatever this fog was, it became as constant as a cancer. Slowly, it revealed itself to be an autonomous organism with a will of its own. I went outside hoping to dispel it with fresh air. I walked for miles in the thickening twilight, through the quiet rich-people streets of the Portland Hills, up through Washington Park and back down to 23rd Street, and I couldn't keep my heart from racing. The mother of all panic attacks had me in its grip, and trying to sort out the many strands of fears was like trying to sort living spaghetti.

I lay down and tried to sleep but six hours later my heart was still a Gene Krupa solo: I could not even count my pulse. The day passed, and the night too. No sleep. My heart should have sent me to the hospital except that I couldn't tell anyone what was happening. The one imperative was to look normal, look normal. No one must guess I was in trouble. Not that anyone would have noticed—no one was focusing on me. But I was focusing on no one other than me, so I didn't notice no one noticing me. Another day passed. I went to work, I went to bed, I didn't sleep, morning came, another day passed, another night fell, and still I could not fall asleep because sleep would mean surrendering to the Void.

I still had time, money, and friends, all the things people covet, but so what? I went to a party at Nick and Abby's house, and I wanted to tell Abby I was in trouble, but it was hard to get the news out while obeying the categorical imperative to look normal. And what good would it have done anyway? Nothing was real except for a single infinitesimal dot of consciousness within the Void. Finally, however, behind a couple of beers, I managed to choke out, "Abby. I'm afraid I might kill myself."

She looked into my eyes for a long, soulful moment, and then said, "It's always about you, isn't it? This isn't exactly a great time in my life either, you know." So we conversed for a while about Abby's troubles.

That night, I worried about the words that had come out of my mouth. When I spoke them, I wasn't saying I wanted to kill myself. What "I" wanted was to get back to normal and be happy. The utterance meant that "I" was not in control, what "I" wanted might not matter, "I" scarcely even existed. The fog was gaining power, it might use "me" to get what it wanted, and what it wanted was a quick exit: oblivion. And it could get what it wanted by putting out that dot of consciousness.

Then Natty called from Bryn Mawr. "Tamiiiiiim," she lamented. "I am going crazy. Will you pleeeeease come here and help me strangle some people?"

Standard Natty. "What's going on?" I asked, sounding perfectly normal. She told me about some professor who was making petty demands and some obscure Victorian-era painter she was forced to research, and how she didn't even like his stupid watercolors.

The conversation was wonderfully quotidian! And how was I doing, she wondered. So I complained about an altercation with one of the chefs at the Genoa and some ridiculous thing a roommate of mine had done, as if these trivia constituted the sum of my problems.

"You should come here, T. Right now," Natty urged. "Don't think about it, buddy-boy, just jump in a car and come to me, mister. You hear? I need someone to laugh with, and you *need* to get out of Portland. Come to me, Tam. It'll be fun."

Come here right now.

It never occurred to me that Natty's invitation might not be serious. I only knew I was coming to the end of my rope and couldn't fathom what would happen when the last shreds of it slipped through my grip. By the next afternoon, after much stewing, the committee of the mental interior had made its decision. My orders were to head east immediately and get Natty into bed. If the One existed and Natty was she, I needed to know. If not, I needed to know that too. Right away

I called the Genoa and talked to our manager, Will McPherson, a former Reed philosophy professor. "Will, I've got to leave town."

"Okay," he said. "I'll get Jan to cover for you. Starting next Wednesday, shall we say?"

"No!" I shouted. "I have to leave town *right now.* "

I never said I was about to blow, but my voice must have telegraphed something. Will said gently: "Okay, Tamim. Don't worry. You go do whatever you have to do."

You-go-do-whatever-you-have-to-do were the eight kindest words ever spoken to me, but I didn't notice the kindness. I knew only that I had been released, and so I was on to the next thing, which was: "call drive-away companies". Within twenty minutes, I found a company desperate to have a car delivered to Cleveland in four days. I said, "I'm your man."

After that I went to Portland State to look at the bulletin board where people wanting rides posted notices. Now that I was executing a plan, I felt less crazed. By five o'clock I had found four people willing to go east with me the next morning.

On the Run

The car we got was a brand-new Buick Riviera with cruise control. You got out on the highway in that baby, and man you were tooling. Cruise control reduced driving to steering, and we all agreed this was a bad thing because it robbed you of connection to the road, yet we rarely turned off the cruise control. Over the Cascades we went, across the Blue Mountains, into the Bitterroot Range and beyond, not driving, just steering.

We had a few near misses but never hit anything. We never stopped except to get gas and once or twice a day to stretch our legs. We bought groceries and made sandwiches in the car. We drove all day and drove all night: those were the rules I set when I recruited these partners: I'd pay all expenses, their only job was the keep the car moving. Suicide was off the table so long as I was going somewhere. Anyone who needed sleep, catch the next car, wimp.

I don't remember who else was in that vehicle. At the time, I had no doubt we five were forging an intense, life-changing connection because all of us were on a journey from night to light. Today I can't recall a single name or visualize a single face. Some of my fellow travelers were females, I believe, but I can't be sure, I was not registering details at that level of subtlety.

The only vivid image I retain is of Kansas: that great blue bell of Kansas sky! At one point, I just had to pull over. "What's wrong?" my road-mates said.

"Nothing. I just want to gawk."

So we all got out and gawked. Surrounding us were fields and "above us only sky." There were no houses to be seen, no cities, no dips, no rises, no hollows, no bumps in the unspoiled flatness of the world. And that sky was the biggest I had seen since Lashkargah. So blue! The sky, of course, does not actually exist. Science tells us the blue dissolves as one approaches, into air, thinning out at last to a black emptiness. The Void.

But that day in Kansas, the sky was such an amazing, imposing blue, it felt as solid as a ceiling, which made me feel ever so slightly safer. Hafiz has a line in one of his poems about seeking out the Magus, whom he finds in a tavern, gazing into a glass filled with wonders. "Master," the poet exclaims, "*when* did you get this all-world-seeing glass?" (Odd question, really--why should he care *when?*) The Magus laughs: "I got it on the day the dome was painted blue." That' from the great song that begins, "*Years out of mind I sought the grail of King Jamshed... From others I demanded what my heart already had. The pearl which is impervious to space and time, I solicited from the lost ones at the river's edge ...*"

Whenever it was light enough and I wasn't driving or sleeping, I was reading. Just before leaving Portland, I had bought a book at Fred Meyer, Oregon's prophetic version of Walmart, the store that sells anything you can name or imagine, so long as you're not too imaginative. The book was *Endless Love* by Scott Spenser, and I must say I am pleased that Spenser made a lot of money off that novel (if he did), because there has never been a greater piece of literature marketed so relentlessly as trash. And if there is a more sweeping sentence in the English language than the opener of *Endless Love,* I have yet to hear it. Listen.

When I was seventeen and in full obedience to my heart's most urgent commands, I stepped far from the pathways of normal life and in a moment's time ruined everything I loved—I loved so deeply, and when that love was interrupted, when the incorporeal body of love shrank back in terror and my own body was locked away, it was hard for others to believe that a life so new could suffer so irrevocably.

Endless Love is about love as a hunger that won't quit, as a fire that consumes everything in its compass, love as an illness: the Romeo-and-Juliet disorder. In that novel, a boy takes up with a girl. They're teenagers, and the ferocity of their sexual craving leaves no one near them unaffected. The parents at first try to take a liberal attitude, even let the boy stay over in their house and sleep with the girl under their roof; but teenage sexual hunger, a force as terrible as a storm, shakes them, warps them, scars them, blows them all off life's normal course like cars blown off a highway by a hurricane.

At times that novel poked up a turmoil I recognized from older days. Spenser seemed to be talking about Lily and me. *Spenser knew!* The cosmos must have sent him. I'm talking about a proliferation of those mystical coincidences that signal the imminence of a universe-cracking breakthrough. The boy in *Endless Love* falls in love with a girl who lives in Chicago. Can you beat it? Lily hailed from Chicago! The parents of the girl in *Endless Love* are liberals who live in Hyde Park. Why—so did Lily's family! The father in *Endless Love* is some kind of mental health professional. Unbelievable—ditto again. The girl in *Endless Love* has two siblings—oh my God, I was getting the chills!

The sense of cosmic signals bombarding my senses echoed the remembered intensity of that moment at Mallory Street when one note kept swelling past all possible limits, acid pushing at the door, Professor Gottlieb's letter burning in the background (*try to live out my life in the ever- growing community of the shafted...*) This time I couldn't tear off the headphones. Then again, this time the sensation growing in my head was not horror but elation of some kind. And all I could do was keep reading.

When I was 17 and in full obedience to my heart's must urgent commands. Oh man   Can words really sink through flesh and bone this way?   Far from the pathways of normal life... *Yea, though I have walked in the shadow of the valley of death* ...and in a moment's time ruined everything ...Osage City, better stop for gas... and when the incorporeal body of love shrank back in terror ... Anybody hungry? ... get a cheeseburger to go... *that a life so new could suffer so irrevocably...*

I read that book like a speed freak ingesting meth, and it lingered in me as dream images linger, probably because I kept falling asleep while reading, snuggled against strangers whose names and faces I've long since forgotten.   And in that Buick Riviera, sleep did come, because in that Buick somehow I was able to believe that once I reached Natty, everything would be okay. I was the guy who has bought a lottery ticket and in the brief interval before the numbers are announced, he's a millionaire.

Everyone pitched in to keep us going because all of us had reasons to hurry.   The others were headed for various destinations, but I was happy to drop all of them exactly where they wanted, so we did some zigging and some zagging across the plains, and one by one the passengers dropped away until I was alone. It was my job finally to deliver the car.   The address took me to a place east of the city, to a lush suburb called Something-or-other Heights.   I pulled up to an imposing house.   A slender pretty woman took delivery. Her hair looked permed, her clothes store-bought. She was about my age but seemed indefinably older, probably because she was in that other bracket of society: one of the ones who had *not* strayed "far from the pathways of normal life."   This woman had no doubt gotten married just out of college and had children, and her husband made good money and supported her. This big house and this nice yard in this classy suburb was her life. She didn't work, not even keeping up the house: she had maids for that. She was nice though, and perfectly cordial to the scruffy guy with patched jeans and ass-length hair who had driven her car across the continent.

"Where can I drop you?" she inquired.

"The bus station."

"Hmm." This failed to thrill her. The bus station was downtown in a bad neighborhood. Not that she minded going down there in the daytime, but she did want me to realize that, "Cleveland is actually very nice. You should see some of the nicer parts." So she took the long way to the bus station, winding through the Cleveland she knew, lovely glens of suburban greenery, elegant mansions set among picturesque shrubbery: living postcards. Very *very* nice...but to me—irrelevant. I was never going to live in a house like any of those.

Bryn Mawr

She was right about the Cleveland bus station, though. It was sordid. But the bus came quickly, and after much meandering dropped me off in the little fairy tale town of Bryn Mawr, where the bus station was anything but sordid. When I called Natty, she seemed taken aback. "What are you doing here, Mr. T?"

"Don't you remember? You wanted someone to laugh with."

"Oh … Okay... " she stammered. "Let me think about this." In a few moments she recovered her aplomb and gave me directions. The campus was only two blocks from the station, and I had nothing to carry but a backpack, so I walked. Natty met me on the sidewalk, pigtailed and pretty. We hugged, but her hug was tentative. There was a problem, she told me.

Bryn Mawr was a girls' school. I knew this, but I didn't know that the Bryn Mawr dorms were citadels to feminine modesty: no boys allowed. Natty had figured out what to do, however. She got a few of her friends to stand guard at a succession of points and they moved me furtively into the garrison like operatives in a spy movie. I made it past the reception desk, the barricades, the proctors and the monitors, and up the stairs to Natty's room. She had no roommates, thank God, so I was safe there!

The door closed, and we were alone with each other. Arrival in this town had been like a grenade blast. Now the roar was subsiding, and the flashbang was fading into ordinary light. I don't know what I thought would happen. Sex was the default assumption, I suppose, but I had not driven 3,000 miles in three days to get my rocks off. What I wanted was a certain moment. What I wanted was that moment three years ago, when Lily stepped out of the airport van at the Hilton Hotel, and our eyes met and history stopped. I wanted history to stop again, like it did in that moment. I didn't want a moment like that moment. I wanted that moment.

That moment didn't happen. There was no foundation for it. As soon as the door closed, Natty and I moved into each other's arms, but when we moved apart from our brief hug and bit of kissing, what I saw before me was not a magical creature from the Planet Wonderful but a pretty girl whom I sorta' knew but only sorta'. I was glad to see her, and she was glad to see me, but all this gladness lacked an erotic flavor. She was my friend, sure; but my girlfriend? Not so clear. Could we fling off our clothes and plunge into hot, heaving sex? Good heavens no. We'd have to get to know each other first.

"So." Natty cleared her throat. "What are you doing here, T?"

I told her as best I could. "I was going crazy in Portland. I thought I'd come and see if you could make me feel sane."

I don't know what she heard. What she *didn't* hear, clearly, was crisis. "How'm I doing so far?" she joshed.

Though she asked lightly I answered her seriously. "I feel better."

It was a modest evaluation but true. I didn't feel the skies splitting asunder or the angels commencing to sing. It was more as if a fever had broken and I had woken up. The events of the past few weeks seemed like fragments from a dream. To a sane fellow, surely, the expectation that the skies will open and the angels sing sounds foolish, and foolish was exactly how those expectations sounded to me right then, which had to mean I was a sane fellow.

I peered around at my surroundings, blinking like a sleepwalker who has woken up in a place he's never seen. The room was long and narrow, with walls so solid I might have been inside a castle. Here was a dresser, there were a few bookshelves, and over there a desk. I glanced at Natty's neatly made bed and saw a few girl's garments—a sweater, a bra. Little pots of makeup sat on a table with a mirror. A record player in one corner. An armload of records on the floor. There was nothing remotely surreal about the scene. This was a college girl's dorm room, no different from any other. The only thing that didn't belong in this picture was me. I was the single surreal detail.

"Um, Tam," said Natty, "I don't know what you were expecting... "

"I just want a good night's sleep."

"I knew you'd understand."

"I haven't slept for days. Before I left Portland, I was hallucinating."

"That'll happen if you don't get enough sleep, buddy-boy. Let's get you into bed and we'll talk in the morning."

I spoke of Will McPherson's eight kind words. Let me now heap a bit of praise on Natty Pierce. When I showed up on her doorstep with my eyeballs spinning, she could have freaked out. It would have been quite natural. And for me, that response would have been catastrophic. But instead, Natty let me into her life as if this was nothing more than just a little awkward. Only one response could have kept me out of the abyss right then, and hers was it. I climbed into Natty's bed and drifted off with James Taylor singing in my head: *winter spring summer or fall...* Taylor was right. I had a friend.

Strangely enough, Natty quickly shrank to the least of my concerns at Bryn Mawr. Even though I had stormed east fixated on her, I hardly remember what she and I did in our private time together. I was the only guy living in a dormful of college girls, and coping with that weirdness took everything I had. It was like dropping out of a plane onto a log in the middle of a log-rolling contest where the stakes were life or death. Every minute took fancy footwork, full concentration, and undivided attention.

I had assumed that Bryn Mawr would be like Reed., where boys and girls hung out in each others' dorms routinely. Hell, I was living in Lily's room half my senior year. It's true that girls' dorms were locked at midnight, but that only meant boys had to get inside early. Whenever I was late, I just tapped on my lover's window and she let me climb in.

Bryn Mawr was not like that. Apparently, no man had ever been seen in those dorms. I was the first in living memory, and I assure you, if there had to be a first man in those girl's dorms, I was the perfect pioneer: so well-behaved, so utterly housebroken, the soul of tact. A credit to my gender. No running up and down the halls playing grab-ass like some guys reading this probably think they would have done. No. I stayed in Natty's room until we were both going somewhere. I went to the bathroom only with an escort, who stood guard outside the door to protect my dignity and save other girls from the embarrassment of coming upon me unawares. When I moved through the public spaces, one girl ran ahead to warn that the Man was coming, the Man was coming! My life at Bryn Mawr probably resembled my mother's life in Afghanistan in those early years when she was the only American woman in a male-dominated, gender-divided world.

The girls saw me as a curiosity, or a sort of exotic pet. They borrowed me to make a fourth at a game of hearts or to listen to their papers. No one could figure out what the hell I was doing there, least of all me. But none of the girls disapproved of my presence, as far as I know, because they didn't categorize me as a man, exactly. They saw me in some category outside of male or female. This again, reminded me of my mother: Afghan society had allowed her to break the rules for women, not by altering the rules but by redefining her as something outside the normal pigeonholes of gender. Once, I overheard two girls talking about me, and (somewhat to my dismay) one assured the other, "He's sort of sexless, in a good way."

Meanwhile, instead of moving toward becoming lovers, Natty and I locked into a weird and ever more heated argument about which was the better school, her Bryn Mawr or my Reed. And it wasn't just Natty; all the Bryn Mawr girls held Reed in light regard and sometimes pretended for humorous effect to have forgotten its name. What was that school again? Stem College? Cattail College? I indignantly contrasted the imaginative daring of a Reed education with the dogged scholasticism of Bryn Mawr's. If Da Vinci were alive today, he'd have been at Reed. This sent the girls into gales of laughter.

Epiphanies

Finally, craving a break from the condescension of the Ivy Leaguers, I headed to New York to see a couple of Nick's childhood friends. Nathan and Aaron were political guys I had met when they visited Portland. They were "red diaper babies." Their parents had been union organizer types, had been hauled in for interrogation by HUAC—the works. Nathan and Aaron had witnessed all the big political events of the sixties. They had riveting stories to tell about the police riots at the Democratic Convention in Chicago in 1968, about the Mobilization March Against the War in Washington D.C., about registering Black voters in the south at the height of the Civil Rights movement, about working for magazines like RAT while living in roach-infested apartments on the Lower East Side...This was the milieu I longed to steep in for a few days, as a corrective to Bryn Mawr.

That week, I had three pivotal epiphanies, one on the way to New York, one in New York, and one after I got back to Bryn Mawr. In order to catch a train to New York, I had to take a commuter line into Philadelphia and as I travelled this stretch of rail, landscape turned into an allegory of dreamlike power. At first, we were rolling through a land of mansions barely visible in the distance... then past large stone houses covered with ivy ... then past good-size brick buildings with porticos ... then past largish houses with small but pretty yards... then past smaller houses packed close together ... then past row houses without yards... which gave way to brick apartment buildings ... which gave way to grimy poured-concrete housing projects ... which gave way to looming hulks of smoke-blackened buildings, whole neighborhoods that looked bombed out. It was a palpable descent through concentric rings of diminishing elitism, each ring less luxurious, less inviting, and more cramped. Along that course, the color of the people changed like a relentless parallel metaphor, from white to mixed to black.

I didn't know where to transfer once the train reached the core of Philadelphia. The information was written on a slip of paper I had left on Natty's desk, so I got out at some random stop to call her for directions. But all the pay phones in the station were broken. How eerie! I went upstairs, hoping to find one on the street, but all the payphones up there were broken too. What the hell...? At ground level, every window I saw had bars on it. The gutters were filled with litter. Not one leaf nor one single blade of grass greeted the eye. There were no white folks here, no Asians, and no one with Mediterranean features. Every face I saw was African American.

The walls were covered with graffiti, and some of this graffiti was lettering, but the letters were not from the English alphabet and the words they spelled were unintelligible. A lot of the "graffiti" was art: jagged shapes, mostly abstract and strangely rune-like, rendered in fierce colors. Some of it was beautiful, but when I envisioned the kids who must have done this work, I could only picture prisoners screaming "I exist!" But no one would hear the screaming unless they were right at this spot. Twenty-something miles away, beyond many rings of increasing privilege and wealth, Natty was writing a paper about some obscure British water-colorist who had died a hundred years ago.

When I finally found a phone, Natty shrieked, "You're where? Get out of there, T! You're going to get killed!" Alarmed, I looked around but no one I saw seemed actually interested in killing me. In fact no one was even taking notice of me. People were shopping, tanking up on gas, strolling places on errands. Three guys on a bus bench outside a barbershop were talking about a boxing match coming up between Ken Norton and Henry Clark. So why was adrenaline stropping my senses to a razor's edge? There could be only one reason: everybody here was black, and I was not.

I had not been black this morning, either, but this morning not-being-black had been a meaningless factoid. Now it was my whole identity. How could that be? Nothing had changed inside me. Nothing was different except for what was *outside* of me. At that moment I felt the intractable reality of an outside world. My imagination did not create it and my imagination could not alter it. Something existed out there, in spite not because of me.

The second epiphany came during a conversation around the dinner table at Aaron's house on my last night in New York. Talk had turned to British psychotherapist R. D. Laing, who was creating a buzz just then, with his novel theory that schizophrenia was not an illness inside a person but a tangle outside the person, a tangle of contradictions in his or her social context. Madness was external.

"But Laing doesn't go far enough," Nathan declared. "He claims there is no such thing as mental illness, but then he goes ahead and tries to cure people."

"What's wrong with curing people?" I burst out. "What's wrong with making misery go away, if it can be done?"

"Misery is not insanity," Nathan pontificated. "Defining unhappiness as insane and then trying to cure it—that's a political act. The oppressor would like nothing better than for me to blame myself. As long as I'm focusing inward, I don't look out and see *him*. My only options are then to feel crazy or get cured. And 'cured' means accepting oppression as 'normal.'"

I had never heard such outlandish tripe. "To me," I said, "crazy means you're so fucked up, you can't even bargain. You have to accept anybody's terms. Healthy means you have the strength to make your own choices."

"Your own choices?"Aaron laughed. "What does that even mean? What you want and know—it's all given to you from birth. You pick it up from your society. You're molded into a member of your class. You're born into a stream of history. Society doesn't just tell you what to see, it gives you the eyes you see with. Nothing's inside you that wasn't already outside you. We're all coming from somewhere. Choice has nothing to do with it."

I went back to Bryn Mawr and the third pivotal incident occurred. A bunch of us were passing time in a coffeehouse that catered to students. We did a lot of socializing at such bistros and the Bryn Mawr/Haverford kids thought nothing of ordering the most expensive items on the menu, which was getting a bit awkward for me because some one person usually picked up the bill, and in order to keep up appearances, I had to be that one person at least occasionally; but each time I paid, the tab walloped me. I had left Portland feeling as rich as anyone ever needed to be, but the money was draining away fast.

That day, our group included several Haverford guys, two of whom were African American—Mike and Howie. The chatter drifted from Nixon's re-election and his "secret plan" for ending the war—safe topics among college students of that day (consensus could be counted upon)—to gossip about who was dating whom, whereupon, all of a sudden, consensus wasn't so certain. When the two black guys started joking about how tough "today's girls" were to "control," tension prickled up.

Howie was a man of wiry build and smooth features, with a delicate nose and skin so dark it looked glossy. His eyes had a glisten to them, as if he were constantly on the verge of tears, and his mouth seemed forever clenched. His friend Mike, sitting on my side of the table, was a big, easy-going athletic-looking fellow with a bushy afro and a handsome scowl. His green Haverford sweat shirt announced that he played basketball.

Mike was dating a Bryn Mawr girl, but she was not at the table because some friction had flared up between them earlier. Apparently Mike had set his hand on his girlfriend—maybe in a way that boyfriends normally do with girlfriends—but maybe in a demonstration of possession that crossed a line. It was a matter of interpretation. Anyway, she had pushed his hand off—or had she slapped it away? Open to dispute. And where exactly had he touched her? On the knee? The thigh? The arm? Had he transgressed? Did she over-react? Opinions differed.

Whatever happened was over in seconds and seemed hardly worth discussing, but now that the topic had come up at our table, the discussion would not stop, because opinions *did* differ, even where people agreed on the facts. Natty's friend Susan wanted to know where the girlfriend was now.

"I sent her home," Mike shrugged.

"*Sent* her?" Susan bristled. "Is it your *place* to send her anywhere?"

"My *place*?" Mike's eyes darkened at the phrase. "She's my woman."

"*Your* woman? Do you think one human being can *own* another?"

Spectacularly ill-chosen words. Mike's scowl deepened. "Times like these, a man has got to be a man." I still remember that utterance so clearly—how it reeked of emasculated desperation.

Howie, shifting in his seat, aching to support his friend, burst out, "Amen! Times like these a man's got to *BE* a man!"

Just like that two bristling sides had formed, the white kids, both girls and boys, against the black kids: race and class this time trumping gender. Glancing across the table, I locked eyes with Howie and that brief glance jolted me like a spark from a live electric wire. I remembered how I had felt as the only non-black person in that endless Phillie ghetto. Here, Howie and Mike were the only black faces in a sea of white.   How must Howie feel, sitting here? The urge to blend in is ferocious. I know. But for Howie, blending in with *this* group would require adopting the attitudes of this group—which would mean despising himself. How must that feel?

It struck me that Howie and Mike might be scholarship students. If so, we had something in common. I was in America only because I had gotten a scholarship to attend a private high school in Colorado. It's true that I wasn't a student anymore, so not getting any money, but "scholarship student" isn't about what-you're-getting, it's a who-you-are kinda' thing. Of the hundred or so kids at that high school, three of us were on the full ride: a black girl from Atlanta, a Navajo boy from a reservation, and me from Afghanistan. Each of us had been plucked out of our context and plopped among the privileged, but background doesn't shed like cellophane. History trails along.   We all come from somewhere.

After that day, my argument with the girls about Reed and Bryn Mawr changed character. It wasn't really an argument about this school versus that school,   old-fashioned versus modern, classical versus romantic, stuffy versus daring.   It was about class. The Bryn Mawr girls' condescension didn't come *from* them, but through them. It wasn't them looking down on me but their whole class looking down on my whole class.   They couldn't   help themselves.

Which raised the question: what was my class? Foreign? Muslim? Third World? Poor? Well, sure but none of that was the crux of it.   When two sides formed in the coffeehouse, I did not instinctually line up with Howie and Mike. Why not?

Well, my American mother, for one thing. A fervent product of American democracy, she was intensely *anti*-class conscious: She declared that every notion of higher and lower was artificial. People differed only in their talents.   Such was the creed she transmitted to us children. When I took that fateful tab of acid, it was easy for me to believe that "I" was a featureless point of consciousness deep inside my skull and that everything else—my thoughts, my opinions, my values, my judgments—were like garments I could put on or take off.

Now, however, as I looked into my own history, a brutal truth stared back: "I" took shape in a country where blood counts inordinately. I was an Ansary. The most primeval swamps of my upbringing brimmed with the knowledge that Ansary means "of the helpers," that the name "Ansar" was given to the brothers who *helped* the Prophet (peace be upon him) escape from Mecca to Medina, the men who helped precipitate the Hegira, that key moment in Islamic history, the event from which the calendar is dated—in short (from the Muslim perspective) the pivotal event in all of human history.

I felt more at home in Bryn Mawr than in the ghetto because I too was an upper-class man. I had never noticed this growing up, because in Afghanistan there was a class far more "upper" than we, the royal family, the royal clan.

But the king and his relatives were in fact only the top aristocrats. Every ethnic group had its tribes, every tribe had its chieftains, all those chieftains had families, and all those families were aristocrats in their milieu. We Ansaries had no military prowess, nor did we have spectacular wealth, but we did have religious and cultural credentials, and in Muslim Afghanistan those badges mattered every bit as much as guns and gold. I was an aristocrat. I didn't ask to be, I didn't choose to be, but choice had nothing to do with it.

It didn't matter that I came from the upper strata of the lowest strata. When it comes to attitudes, upper is upper. And upper-class exists only by virtue of lower-class. The condescension I felt at Bryn Mawr, someone must have felt from me at some point. I did not know who, because I had never noticed myself condescending to anyone, but it must have happened, because the class thing permeates reality. In the end Nathan and Aaron were right: the outside world was inside me—in fct, the outside world *was* me.

Thanksgiving

Emotional memory tells me I stayed at Bryn Mawr for about two years, but the calendar says two weeks. The Sunday before Thanksgiving, my mother and brother arrived by prior arrangement to take me back to Silver Spring for the holiday. As long as they were in town, my mother insisted on taking all of us out to lunch. Natty was on her best and cutest behavior, and she charmed my mother with her vivacious chatter, but the glint in her eyes told me she was barely squelching an urge to poke fun. I knew it was my mother's "choice" of restaurant that made her so merry: a Howard Johnson's for God's sake... how crass can you get? Natty didn't realize that taking four people out to lunch, even for hamburgers, was a huge economic strain for my mother; Hojo's was not an aesthetic decision for her but an economic one. A class decision. Not a choice at all, really.

After lunch, we took Natty back to campus, where she and I hugged and parted ways, never to set eyes on each other again. No sooner had she vanished from the rearview mirror, then my mother turned to me with shining eyes and uttered the words she'd been bursting to say: "Oh, Tamim! I *like* her. Is it serious?"

I turned away from the roguish twinkle of hope in her eyes. "It's over."

I left Bryn Mawr with clenched gut because after Thanksgiving, I would have to get back to Portland, and I didn't how I was going to do it. Bryn Mawr had emptied my wallet. I didn't have enough money left to fly back to the West Coast. And now that winter was setting in, I couldn't hitch. Most of all, I couldn't hit up my mother for cash. She was poor herself, but if she knew I was in trouble, she'd gladly sink herself into deeper trouble to help me out. I couldn't let that happen.

My brother Riaz was still a teenager living with my mother; my sister Rebecca came in from Kentucky for the holiday. It was the first Thanksgiving we four had spent together. One night, while Riaz was out on a date, my mother, my sister, and I sat around sipping wine and chatting. My mother did most of the talking; and she talked mostly about the trivia of her everyday life because one thing human beings need desperately is to talk about the trivia of their everyday life, and my mother had no other adult to talk to normally. Much of what she told us that night, I already knew. She taught fifth grade at Oak View elementary school, and what's there to say about teaching, right? It just grinds on. Yet somehow, taking in her small stories that night, I found myself impressed by the difficulties my mother faced and the nobility of her response. Her bureaucratic superiors brutalized her; parents yelled at her; people threatened to sue her; the media blared contempt for teachers; Pink Floyd sang "Teacher! Leave them kids alone!" But she soldiered on because she cared about them kids. Years later, when I asked her what she thought made for great teaching, she said she thought the key was to make every child feel like the only child.

Then my mother drifted into reminiscences about her girlhood, growing up in Chicago between the wars: how it was, looking out at American society through the bars of her Finnish immigrant family, her teenage social life restricted to a single outlet—the Finnish-American Hall, which sponsored ballroom dancing on Saturday nights. There, she could *dance* with boys, but *only* there, and *only* dance. She couldn't date. Caged by her tyrannical father, she idolized the smart, well-educated American kids she saw at school, especially the artistic ones, the Bohemians; she longed to be one of them. Only then did I realize how much my mother had invested in raising us kids to be the people she had idolized as a teenager. How could I have thought I invented myself? I was shaped by currents flowing not just from Kabul but from many places, from her, through her from the Finnish-American Hall, from Chicago, from Finland... countless places I had never seen or thought about...

Growing up outside mainstream American society had planted a longing in the girl who became my mother for a great transformative adventure, but until she met the lanky Afghan student she would end up marrying, the biggest adventure she had managed was to move out of her parent's home and liberate herself (just barely) from her domineering papa, Robert Palm. The moment she married my father, the Afghan Government cancelled his scholarship and ordered him home. My mother said she would gladly go with him, gladly be the first and only American woman in Afghanistan.

My father laid out very frankly what a tough life she would face. Could she get used to shitting in an outhouse? Yes! What about cooking over an open fire? She looked forward to it! And the bitter winters in those Hindu Kush mountains? Piece of cake, Chicago was cold too.

My father also mentioned the restricted role of women in Afghan society. He was very open about it, she gave him that to the end, but she did not fully understand what "restricted" meant in Afghanistan, and perhaps he couldn't see it, the way a fish can't tell how water feels.

World War II had just ended. Traveling from America to Afghanistan took at least a month, and it was a great adventure at first. Trains, ocean liners, airplanes! Heady stuff for a girl who had hardly ever left Chicago. But after Cairo, she began to get a little nervous. And by the time they reached Pakistan, she realized oh my God this is real.

It was then that my father went to the bazaar and got her a *chad'ri*—the garment that in the West is so famously called a *burqa*. "Incidentally," he explained, "Once we're in Afghanistan, you'll have to wear this when we're in public."

My mother put it on, tore it off, and yelled, "I'll never wear that thing!" And she never did. For the next twenty years, my father shouldered whatever consequences accrued to a man whose woman insisted on leaving the house with her face all naked. Shortly after they arrived, the prime minister called my father to the palace and told him the government would blacklist him until he got rid of the foreign woman. The family met to discuss the Ansary position. All my father's brothers and important male relatives came to the meeting, including some from the village. Even Dada Gul was there, a half-brother of my father's, born to one of my grandfather's other wives, an illiterate, jobless dependant living in my eldest uncle's household—even his views were solicited, respected.

But not my mother's. She was not invited. In a matter this serious, a woman's opinion did not count. Boy-children scuttling back and forth between the men's council and the women's quarters kept my mother informed.

I already knew this story but I felt the lash of it that night. I knew the rest of it too: how, after much deliberation, the clan decided to reject the royals' order, come what may—an astounding decision in a country where the royal family held the power of life or death over all their subjects. What a brave bunch we were, we Ansaries. But there were dark threads in all this bravery. And this too was me. We're all, as Aaron said, coming from somewhere. And where I was coming from we had millennia of debt to repay to women.

Solo

Thanksgiving ended, my sister headed back to Kentucky, my mother and brother got ready for school and I had to confront my problem. How the hell was I going to get back to Portland? To my mother, however, I minimized my plight. Get back to Portland? Piece of cake: I'd do it the same way I came: sign up with a drive-away company. Hell, I had more than enough money for gas (just barely but I downplayed that.) I looked in the Washington Post, and sure enough, the classifieds had a whole section for driveways. One company needed a car delivered to San Francisco within a week. I took a bus downtown and picked it up that day.

Then—oops—I realized a hitch. When I came east, five of us were splitting driving duties, so we could drive nonstop. I needed people to share the ride with me. In Portland, I had rounded them up in a couple of hours by checking hippie/student bulletin boards.

I had no idea where to find any such boards in suburban Maryland or any other way to get riders.

And time was short. The car had to be in San Francisco in a week. So I decided oh, what the hell: I'll line up places to crash along the way and do it solo. I called Portland and tapped my networks—the great thing was, I now *had* networks: the E-Street crowd, the restaurant I worked at, contacts from the Snowflake days. Nick took it upon himself to act as my switchboard, and a couple of hours later he called back with three possibles.

The first was in Newton, Iowa: Ben Van Dorn's mother. Ben had been my roommate at Carleton freshman year, but he lived in Portland now, and he told Nick I was more than welcome to stay with his mom. This felt a bit iffy. Who stays with a friend's *mother?* And Ben wasn't actually a *close* friend. We'd been buddies as roommates, but that was six years ago and honestly, we rarely got together anymore.

Still, I had at least met his mother. Ben and I had once hitchhiked to Grinnell to hear Marshall McLuhan and Buckminster Fuller, two semi-forgotten pop-philosophers

of that time. Grinnell being just a stone's throw from Newton, we had stayed with Ben's mother. Her husband had died when Ben was a child, so she lived alone.

Newton's only claim to fame was the Maytag Appliance Company. The one time I visited Newton, a cousin of Ben's had just invented a machine for extruding plastic tubing. That weekend, a bunch of us sat around in Mrs. Van Dorn's living room and watched him demonstrate his device. First, he extruded a plastic tube one inch in diameter. We clapped. Then he extruded a tube that was half an inch around. We cheered. Then came a two-inch tube, then three-quarters. Whatever size of tube you wanted, he could extrude it, and each time we clapped and cheered. I went away thinking of Newton as the kind of town where a celebrity was someone who could extrude plastic tubing. But hey, a place to crash was a place to crash. I jotted down Mrs. Van Dorn's phone number and address. "What's next?"

Next was oldest-friend Ralph's uncle Jim, in Laramie, Wyoming. I didn't know him, but Ralph was practically like a brother to me, because his father was an eccentric inventor who spent most of his career in Afghanistan. Our family had known their family forever. Back in the old days, when we were children, Rebecca and I used to play Fry-the-Bacon and Kick-the-Can with the Garner kids in their yard at the end of the alley in our neighborhood of Dehbouri. Claire was officially my girlfriend then, and Ralph was officially Rebecca's boyfriend, whatever that means to six year olds. Ralph's sister Claire was still in Kabul, working as a nurse. I knew Ralph's father as Uncle Roy and his mother as Aunt Mary: that's how tight our families were. Ralph's relatives were practically my relatives. Cousin Jim, as Ralph called him, was either Uncle Roy's brother or Aunt Mary's. I couldn't remember which, but it didn't matter. This was family, they'd shelter me, I wouldn't even feel awkward about imposing.

But Laramie was a long way from Newton, Iowa. Didn't anyone have a friend in Nebraska?

"Sorry," said Nick. "Nothing in Nebraska."

It figured. From previous journeys, I had an impression of Nebraska as a featureless plain that existed only to be crossed. Oh well. "And after Laramie?"

"Then in Salt Lake City you've got Montague."

"Who's Montague?"

"Chris Montague. Paul Matthews's friend."

"The guitar player from Puddle City? He doesn't know me from Adam."

"Well, he knows Paul, and Paul knows you, so I think he might let you crash for a night. I bet he won't mind."

"I think" and "I bet" and "he might" didn't make me feel very secure. Back when Montague played in Paul's basement band, I was one of the crowd hanging out but gee, Chris Montague wouldn't know me from *there*. Later, when he played with Peter Langston at the White Eagle as part of Puddle City, I was a regular, but Montague *certainly* wouldn't know me from *there*.

He was a star hunched over his guitar on that bright stage. I was just another drunk in the crowd, dancing if I could stay on my feet. One time, in fact, I was slumped at one of those teeny-tiny café tables with my eyes closed, grooving to the Puddle City roar, when I realized that some of the thumping didn't fit the rhythm. I worked out that it was someone thumping at my skull. I looked up and standing over me was the sandy-haired, big-cheeked, friendly-looking, busty, blond barmaid I had seen every few nights for months and secretly lusted for and never said a word to. There she was in her cute little apron, saying something to *me!* Well, actually, not so much saying as barking: "Hey! Get up! No nodding out here! Come on now! Get up!"

"I wasn't nodding out," I protested. "I was achieving nirvana."

"Jes' pick up your head," she snarled, "Or I'm going to have Big Tony throw your butt outa' here and yew can score your nirvana out on the railroad tracks."

That exchange, my first and last with the hot barmaid, took place right under the stage where Chris Montague and his band-mates were playing. Chris and I might even have crossed glances at that moment. If he knew me at all, he knew me from that moment. Could I really knock on his door and say, "Remember me?" Might he not say, "Step the fuck away from my door before I get Big Tony to crush you like a flea?"

Beggars, however, can't be choosers, so I wrote down Chris Montague's contact information and that's what I ended up with: 3,000 miles to cross, three places to crash, and only one that I could really count on.

Yellow Springs

Next morning, I left early, but commuter traffic slowed me down, and Pennsylvania was long; by the time I tooled into Ohio, daylight was waning and Newton, Iowa was still at least ten hours away. Showing up at the Widow Van Dorn's house at four a.m. would be totally uncool. I should pull over somewhere for the night, but it was too cold to sleep in the car. I did have a *little* extra money, which I had been planning to use for food, but maybe I should find a low-end motel instead. Oh hey, here was a seedy-looking one now. Ouch, 15 bucks a night, the sign said. I didn't have *that* much!

Okay, then: get off the highway and drive a few random miles to some small burg that never got any traffic. Maybe there I'd find a super-cheap Bates Motel. It might be worth putting up with a knife-wielding psychopath dressed as an old woman to save a few bucks. Just don't get lost, I told myself.

I filled the tank and studied the map. Dayton thirty miles to the west was too big. Springfield, to the north—also too big. Tremont... hmm, sounded small but it was kind of far. What about heading south on highway 72 to "Green Township" which sounded so wonderfully obscure? Or take the next turnoff, onto Yellow Springs Road, and go—

Wait a minute. Holy shit.

Yellow Springs? Where Antioch College was located? Was I indeed a skip and a heartbeat from Lily? Was this truly accidental—or had I planned this all along without knowing it?

A tremor ran through me. Lily and Ted. Well, when I saw them in August, they did say, "If you're ever in Yellow Springs..." I should take them at their word—anything less would disrespect their integrity.

Anyway, why on earth would I *not* stop with Lily? Just because of that old relationship we once had, that sex thing? That obsolete old girlfriend/boyfriend thing we used to have? It seemed quaint to even consider that factor now. Her address was in my little book, and her phone number too. I could give her a call and just make sure she was open to a visit from a random old friend, but then I thought naah: just show up. She'll be so surprised. What a merry prank.

I drove through yellowing corn fields and reddening orchards. Oh my God, what was I doing? Was this a bad idea? Lily. What the hell could come of this? But some little devil of a voice kept whispering, "Place to crash. Save twenty bucks... She is your

friend, isn't she?... What's wrong with a friend visiting a friend?"
I did, after all, need a place to crash. I should have thought of Lily
earlier.   When it came to calculating closeness, how could the
Widow Van Dorn compare?   Or Chris Montague?   Or even
Cousin Jim?   I had not even been inside those people houses,
much less inside their bodies. Not to mention inside their very
souls.

The final turnoff came up. I slowed down to study the sign and
then took the little road that meandered into Yellow Springs. Lily
and Ted lived in a place of their own off campus. I drove up and
down the quiet streets, looking for their address, and it wasn't
hard to find. The town wasn't huge. I parked the car and strolled
across a pleasant little yard. A smell of apples filled the air. The
formal walkway to the front door looked unused... Friends
probably went around to the back. I followed the well-worn little
snake of a path around the house. Should I have called ahead after
all?

In the back, two small steps led to a door that opened directly
into the kitchen. The door was open, and Lily was just inside,
making bread. She was hardly the bread making type, but on any
given day, anyone might be doing anything. At the rustle of my
arrival, she looked up and her eyebrows arched.   "Tamim!
What...?"

How unpleasant I myself find such surprises nowadays! God
save us all from unannounced drop-ins.   "Just passing by.
Thought I'd stop and say hello."

"Oh. Well...hello!"   Her nose crinkled with genial good
humor.   God, she looked beautiful.   "You always were
spontaneous."   Shaking her head at my zany spontaneity, she
opened the door wider, "Come in....come in... Ted will be home
soon." If she saw me as a possible destabilizing monkey wrench
wrecking the clockworks of her life, she showed no sign of it.

I sat on a skinny little chair in her kitchen as she went on
preparing dinner. I told her I had been visiting a girlfriend at Bryn
Mawr, and had spent Thanksgiving with my family, and was now

on my way back to Portland, delivering a drive-away, and I needed a place to crash. She said I had come to the right place. Then she talked about her life. School was going fine, she and Ted were both majoring in psychology, this being her last year, she was exploring careers in mental health... She had a possible internship lined up for next semester. She still liked dance as an art but didn't do much of it anymore—life could get so hectic. We chatted on as if this were our relationship: trading bits of news about trivial markers on the separate paths of our very different journeys. The conversation felt remarkably free of trauma.

Then Ted came home.

What the hell you doing here? You still after my woman? Goddamn it, you son-of-a-bitch, can't you get it through your thick head? It's over! She's mine now! Get the fuck outa' here before I call Tony the Bouncer to come in and stomp your ass flat as a bus pass!

Those were the words Ted didn't say. He didn't say anything like those words. He didn't seem to even think them. In fact, Ted was cordial and made cordial look easy. "Hey, Tamim! Good to see you, man. What are you doing here?"

Ted and I then traded bits of personal news, more or less the same conversation I had just conducted with Lily, as if my relationship with him was much the same as my relationship with her.

That night the three of us shared the dinner Lily had cooked and passed the evening in low-keyed, sociable warmth. There was chatting and drinking, eating and storytelling. Music playing softly in the background. I puzzled over the mystery of this unexceptional, slightly overweight Ted. Lily could have had her pick of men, in my opinion. Your Marilyn Monroes and your Liz Taylors came in a distant second to her allure. Why on Earth had she chosen this genial pudge?

Maybe she just liked him. Three years ago she could have chosen anyone and instead she picked me. Maybe she and Ted just clicked...as she and I had clicked... once upon a time ...

Ted took out a little pipe and we smoked some hash together. Then Lily wanted me to sample *her* favorite new drug, Boone's Farm Apple wine. It was sweet and tasted truly awful and we had a great good time drinking it. Lily and I may have exchanged a few words that night, but mostly I conversed with Ted, maintaining the polite pretense that I had veered off course for this one-night stopover in Yellow Springs mainly just to crash with a couple of friends, not to see Ted's girlfriend. All three of us maintained this fiction. It seemed socially necessary.

But as the night wore on, it also started to feel true. Whatever Lily and I had been to each other didn't seem to matter anymore. Ted and I were the guys and she was his girlfriend: that was the equation now.

It came to me then. Yes it did: Lily was part of a story I had been telling myself relentlessly ever since Reed. We fell in love ... I lost her ... I went crazy... But it was not a story we invented. It was one that our society was constantly telling and retelling. Lily and I merely plugged into a socially created myth that existed fully formed before we came along. We just emoted along grooves our society had laid down for its own purposes: the Myth of Romantic Love was a mechanism for creating nuclear units; and nuclear units had a larger social function. Had I grown up in tribal Afghanistan *without* an American mother, I would never have had a Lily in my life, nor lost her, nor gone on a haunted quest for a One and Only. I would still have emoted, of course, but along different grooves. Leila and Majnun were not Romeo and Juliet.

Lily eventually went to bed, but Ted and I stayed up for a couple of hours, talking. Good guy. If we'd overlapped in college, we might have been friends. And when he finally trundled off to the bedroom, I crawled into my sleeping bag and drifted easily into a pleasant dreamless sleep. The fact that Ted and Lily were cuddled up together in the next room didn't keep me awake nor even cross my mind.

The next morning, Lily got up to see me off. In the cold light of dawn, we had a cup of coffee together. I thanked her for the hospitality and asked her to convey my fond farewells to Ted, then flung my backpack into the car. Outwardly, every detail of our parting conformed to last night's fiction: I was just an old friend passing through. But it didn't feel fictional. I turned the key, and the engine turned over. The car sounded good. Crisp leaves twinkled and shimmered in a slight breeze: gold and green and red and yellow on the branches. More red and yellow on the ground, leaves chased by wind, flurrying and fluttering across sere lawns. The empty hills in the distance evinced the thousand subtle gradations of colors that I had never noticed until I smoked dope for the first time at Carleton and had never stopped noticing since then.

I pulled away from the curb, just a visitor moving on.

What happened to all the trauma between Lily and me? What happened to my obsession? Lily was still as beautiful as ever. My eyes could see it, but my heart said: so what? I'd seen scores of beautiful women just that month. I was living in a whole dormful of them a few weeks ago. Lily was a former lover of mine, but so what? So was Marcy. So were Dusty, Abby, Sharon …

Lily was different, though, wasn't she? I had been in *love* with Lily.

But what did in-love mean? I had no idea why she really left Reed or what was troubling her when she came back to Portland. I didn't know anything about her life; I knew her only as someone in *my* life. We used to sleep together; now some other guy was sleeping with her. What had I been so crazy about? My heart couldn't remember.

And that gave me a pang. My heart felt nostalgic for the pain it wasn't feeling. My heart wanted to be capable of hurting like that again. But I already knew it was not to be. That emotion was gone and I would never feel it again.

Mebbe That's the Answer

Newton being my next stop, my thoughts turned now to my one-time roommate Ben Van Dorn. He was a likeable guy with prominent front teeth and a frank Midwestern way about him. We used to call him VD for short, poor fellow, or sometimes BVD, which wasn't much better—nothing personal, we were boys, we couldn't resist such acronyms. He tolerated the humor, knowing we all liked him. Before we met, I wouldn't have described a guy like him as my kinda' guy, but freshmen did not get to choose their own roommates, they got whoever the college put them with. I got Van Dorn, and we got along fine.

But the closer I came to Newton, the more anxieties bubbled to the surface. What if Ben had never actually called his mom? What if he'd called and she'd said no to my visit but Ben just hadn't had the heart to tell me? My own house had always been open to drop-in travelers, but only to those who belonged to the quasi-Masonic band of young-people-in-the-know. Also, I was still somewhat steeped in the ethos of Afghanistan, where travelers could count on hospitality from strangers with or without any personal or ideological connections, so long as they were in trouble and far away from home, an easy standard for travelers to meet.

But this wasn't Afghanistan, this was Iowa. And Mrs. Van Dorn wasn't a 20-something hipster, she was my former roommate's *mother*. A couple of hours out of Newton, I called her from a payphone, trepidation twisting my innards.

But the moment she answered, she disarmed my fears. The Widow Van Dorn knew I was coming and eagerly anticipated my visit. Her only question was, did I want spaghetti for dinner or hamburgers?

I pulled into her driveway at quite a respectable hour, and she greeted me at the door, a nice lady in a dowdy housedress, with fluffy slippers on her feet and her hair in curlers, looking very much the generic middle-American Somebody's Mother.

She took me directly to Ben's room to show me where I would be sleeping. Ben's clean, well dusted, room felt like a shrine. Clearly, nothing had been disturbed in here for years. With the bed made, the sports equipment shelved, and the books and papers all in place, it had a neatness no boy's room exhibits when he's still living in it.   This room was ready for a boy who no longer existed to move back in.

Then a huge collage caught my eye. It was constructed of headlines, photographs, old newspaper articles gone yellow with age, record jackets, ads, banners, decals, and other cultural detritus and it covered most of the wall facing the door, a single work of art that Ben must have put together before he left home, his view of the world at one moment in time, frozen forever

"Oh, he worked hard on that one," his mother beamed.

Ben had gone off to college in 1966 and it was now 1972, so the montage was at least six years old: How poignant to see this tableau preserved by his mother on a bedroom wall that hardly anyone ever saw. The collage centered around the front page of a Newton newspaper from October of 1963. It proclaimed in massive type that the Newton Prairie Dogs (or whatever the Newton football team was called) had won a big game against their arch-rivals, the hated Smalltown Bugs (or whatever.) Ben didn't play football, and this game had no significance outside of Newton: it wasn't even a championship game in whatever league these teams belonged to.   This was merely a game in which the home town team had beaten a traditional rival from another nearby town, yet for Ben the event had loomed so large that he had put it smack dab in the middle of his memorial to the year 1963 as a whole.

Scraps of further trivia surrounded that front page news item: an announcement about the crowning of some blond as the Homecoming Queen—she wasn't Ben's girl; he must have loved her from afar.   An announcement about a new drive-through hamburger joint that had opened in a town ten miles down the highway from Newton. The jackets for various number one A.M. radio hit singles of that moment: "My Boyfriend's Back." "He's So Fine." "Breaking Up Is Hard to Do."

Then I spotted one last clipping in the lower left hand corner: an event just big enough to win a place on this wall but not big enough to merit any prominence:

KENNEDY SHOT IN DALLAS.

How flabbergasting: the Prairie Dog's victory over the Smalltown Bugs had loomed 50 times larger for Ben than the assassination of President Kennedy. I didn't say anything to Ben's mom, who was busy carting sheets and towels into the room. She didn't notice me gawking at the collage in surreptitious wonder.

But *then* I saw the capper. A one-line label, maybe 5 inches wide, taped below the whole display.

1963 as seen by Frank Johnson

Suddenly the whole display made sense. This was not a snapshot of Ben Van Dorn's world view just before he left Newton. This was Ben Van Dorn's sardonic commentary about some asshole named Frank Johnson. The pathos of the whole display vanished.

And then came flooding back, because, when a guy devotes one quarter of his daily environment *from 1964 to 1966!* to a single mocking comment about some other fellow, one has to wonder: did this other fellow ever see Ben's wall? Did Frank Johnson ever feel the sting of Ben's sarcasm? Did he even know Ben existed?

I returned to the kitchen where the widow Van Dorn was making spaghetti. She didn't seem to feel awkward about having me around.   Any friend of Ben's was a friend of hers. Conversation came easily. How did Ben seem these days, she asked. Was he happy, was he dating? Did he still play tennis? Who was this Laura he sometimes mentioned? Unfortunately, I hardly ever saw Ben anymore, and not being able to tell this mother much about her son made me feel I was here under false pretences.

But Mrs. Van Dorn did not think the less of me for my ignorance. Her hospitality had no quid pro quo. She was happy to host me, no matter what I could tell her about Ben. She did touch on the old days when Ben and I were roommates at Carleton. That time the two of us came to stay with her—did I remember? I did; and now that she brought up that occasion, I remembered plenty more about those days.

There was never an awkward lull after that. Sometime in the course of dinner, I lost all sense of "making conversation." During that evening, it stopped mattering that she was maybe 30 years my senior, that she had her hair in curlers in preparation for tomorrow, that we were sitting in a pre-fab house in a bleak little town in Iowa; and that I was a cross between a pampered non-royal semi-aristocrat from Afghanistan and a penniless intellectual Bohemian dope-smoking acid casualty from the West Coast. The idea that these differences might make a difference never seemed to occur to the Widow Van Dorn, so they dropped off my screen too.

We ate our spaghetti on a Formica table in the kitchen and drank red wine poured from a gallon jug, just two human beings talking about our lives. Incredibly enough, I found myself telling the Widow Van Dorn the whole story of my obsession with Lily and the psychic devastation I had suffered upon losing her, and the remarkably unremarkable time I had just spent with her and her boyfriend. Pouring out this intimate story to my one-time roommate's *mother* seemed perfectly normal.

Then the Widow Van Dorn told me her story, and hers was about Mr. Van Dorn. She was young, she said, and he was young, when they met and that was oh so long ago. She loved him so much, she said. They got married, she got pregnant, and Ben was born, and she could picture the life she was going to live, all of it ahead of her, and it seemed so good. Then her husband got sick and died, and she was a single widow with an infant child.

I had assumed, like any self-respecting egotist, that no one had ever loved as I had loved or suffered a disappointment like mine. Sure, others had loved and lost, but they hadn't lost Lily, so what were they whining about? That night, hanging out with the

Widow Van Dorn, I realized there were stories of love and loss far exceeding mine. I didn't have to be convinced about the precious greatness of the late Mr. Van Dorn to appreciate what this woman lost when he died. She didn't weep about her story, she didn't lose control, she never even lost the hearty buck-toothed rabbit-like Midwestern goodness she effused when she found me on her doorstep and remembered me as a friend of Ben's. She never moved from clunky to cool. She only showed me that you don't have to be cool to suffer profoundly.

And I thought about my father, then. He expressed himself in purple rhetoric, but his emotional suffering must have been every bit as real as mine. I had lost Lily? He'd lost his whole family, and all because he fell in love with my mother, and she was American, and he was Afghan. The outside world sure as goddamn hell exists.

Hard in the middle of that conversation, I remembered one thing I did know about her son Ben, and I told her. He had just started working for a do-gooder organization called OSPIRG.

What the Widow Van Dorn said to me in reply was not a witty epigram worthy of Shakespeare or even a thought I had not heard before. It was a platitude plainly stated, but it hit me with all the force of a Hadith to a believer. This is what she said:

"He'ping others—mebbe that's the answer."

She went on to tell me that after her husband died, she could see no way out of grief. A new romance didn't look like the answer.   She couldn't breathe. She felt like she was dying. Nothing looked like the answer. Then one day she realized what was killing her, and it wasn't the loss of her husband. It was self-pity.

What she really needed, she realized, was not a way out of grief but a way out of self-pity. And she could think of no way to escape self-pity except to immerse herself in the troubles of others. So she went to work in a hospital as a volunteer. She became a "candy striper' and devoted the rest of her life to cheering up the sick and dying, while raising her only son.

Blizzard

It was autumn when I left Lily's house, but by the time I pulled out of Mrs. Van Dorn's driveway, full-on winter had arrived. I remembered Midwestern winters as cold but clear--light without heat. But the day I left Newton the sky was gray and the wind was beginning to howl.

In Nebraska, snow started to fall. Periodically I saw trucks that had slid off the highway. Deep banks of snow were piling up along both sides of the road. The radio was talking about a storm that stretched from Buffalo to Wyoming. Tons of disabled private cars lined the highway too. Why disabled, I wondered. Could cold alone stop a car dead? For my sake, I hoped not. Thank God, my car was damned near new, a Dodge Colt that had only 500 miles on it when I left Washington.

I passed another semi lying on its side like a dead elephant. The people gathered around it looked helpless. The snow banks were closing in. I kept arriving where no plow had yet arrived. For a while, cars were tamping the snow into mush, keeping two middle lanes clear but after a while, not completely clear. And a while after that, we were all driving on a few inches of slush. And then the banks had piled up high enough and had closed in enough to squeeze westbound traffic into a single lane flanked by white walls.

Night fell, but I kept driving, because I couldn't afford a motel and had no one to crash with. The next time I slept in a bed would have to be in Laramie, with Cousin Jim's family. Unfortunately, Laramie was in Wyoming and I was still in Nebraska.

I was driving at top speed because arriving in Laramie in the middle of the night would not have felt polite, even though Ralph's relatives were practically like my own. But driving at top speed didn't feel wise either, because cars were sliding off the road by the dozens. I saw another one in the ditch every few miles, and I thought man oh man, I cannot afford for that to happen to me.

Darkness fell and the road started getting icy, but another hour would get me out of Nebraska, if I kept the needle at 60. I couldn't just keep going, though. I needed fuel. A gas station sign loomed up, so I got off at the exit, swung down a steep incline, turned left, went under the freeway, and made my way down an even steeper ramp, into a Standard station. The sign had been visible for miles, but for some reason it was out now. Eerie. And the station? Closed. I got out and made my way to the office to peer through the windows--uh oh: more than closed, more than dark: this place looked boarded up and abandoned. How unsettling. I hurried back to the car because the temperature had dropped in just those few minutes. It was now the kind of cold that hurts the face. Bits of ice were swirling in the wind like glass shrapnel. I was so glad to get back into the car and shut the door, so eager to get back on the road. I checked my watch—yikes! Ten o'clock, already.

I turned the key. A red light went on, but nothing else happened. There was no engine sound, not even the click-click of the starter motor. For some reason, the car was dead. The wind was keening and I could see nothing of the outside. This little Dodge Colt was no place to spend the night, but here I was and here I would have to stay. Back in Carleton days, I heard stories about fools who went out in Minnesota blizzards and walked in circles for hours, trying to find their way back. They didn't know they were walking in circles because by the time they got to their own footprints, the snow had filled in the hollows. People sometimes froze to death within ten feet of their own front doors. I knew from such stories that getting out of the car was the one thing I must not do.

The car was made of thin metal and was flimsily insulated, but I did have an alpine sleeping bag and thank God I hadn't put it in the trunk. Camping equipment was about the only thing I spent money on without stint, so this wasn't a cheap model like the car but a goose down mummy bag suitable for Arctic camping. I unrolled it, wiggled into it fully clothed, zipped it shut, and tightened the drawstring at the top so that only the smallest hole remained to let in air. Inside, I tried to keep my body from making contact with the sides of the car, because those parts were colder than the interior of a freezer box.   Snuggled in the darkness, I remembered Riaz and my mother and Rebecca, and wondered what Natty was doing now, and thought about my friends back in Portland, and about E-Street, and about cozy nights on big pillows in dimly lit rooms, listening to the Mahavishnu Orchestra.

I guess I fell asleep because eventually I woke up, or rather, a loud banging *woke* me up. I poked my head out of the sleeping bag and found the car interior no longer dark, although not exactly bright, either, because the windows were caked with a thick layer of ice. Outside, ten or twelve voices chattered with excitement. I could barely make out what they were saying, but it sounded like, "Over here! Found another one!"

Someone started whacking at the ice on the side window— whump—whump! These idiots were about to break the glass in the brand new car for which I was responsible.

"Hey!" I unrolled the window and just in time, because the guy outside had a hammer, and on the next swing, the window being down, he crashed his hammer through the ice, exploding shards of it against my face. Through the jagged hole, a state trooper stared at me, looking even more astonished than I felt.

"This one's alive," he said.

I squirmed out of my sleeping bag, opened the door, and staggered out. The blizzard was over, and Nebraska was back to bright and cold, the way a Midwestern winter is supposed to be. The troopers—there were two of them—told me that last night's blizzard had dropped the temperature 30 degrees in a matter of minutes, immobilizing vast numbers of cars along the interstate. Within a few miles of me, up the road and back the way I'd come, a number of people had frozen to death in their cars during the night.

"You're damned lucky," the trooper said

I told the troopers my car wouldn't start and one of them said, "There's a gas station just the other side of the freeway."

"It's open?"

"Twenty four hours."

"It was open last night?"

"All night, every night."

Oh. The bright sign I had seen from the freeway must have been theirs. If I had turned right instead of left at the bottom of the ramp, I would have ended up in a warm, inhabited gas station instead of at this deserted one. How ironic if I had frozen to death within a few hundred yards of hot coffee. The troopers, those good fellows, helped push my car to the other gas station free of charge. There, a mechanic looked under the hood and said, "Well, got some good news and some bad news."

The good news turned out to be, the problem was minor. The vacuum release valve on my intake manifold just had a broken clip at the end of the u-spring. I'm making up those terms: I don't remember the exact (or even approximate) name of the part I needed, only that it was trivial. "Four or five bucks'll get you a new one."

"Excellent! What's the bad news?'

"We don't have one. This here's just a roadside service station. We could get one from North Platte by tomorrow...or we could get the car started for you, and as long as you keep driving and never let the engine die, you'll be good. Where you headed?"

"Laramie, Wyoming."

"You might could make it on one tank of gas, you fill up here. Shops in Laramie'll have what you need. They've even got a Dodge dealer there. How many miles you got on this baby--3,000? That valve shouldn't have give out on you. Might be this car's a lemon. Too bad, 'cuz with a lemon, you just never know what'll go next. Well, like I say, just keep the motor running and you should be fine."

I fueled up and headed for Laramie. Just keep the motor running, the guy said. Well, as long as I didn't stop to eat, drink, or go to the bathroom, and as long as I didn't hit the brakes suddenly and kill the engine or slide off the road...

On the map, Laramie was marked as a city, but on the ground it looked like a small town that just went on and on. Back in 1972, you didn't get off the highway to enter it. The highway shrank into a city street that ran between single-family houses spaced well apart. I came to an intersection with a stoplight and there, set a hundred feet back from the road, was a garage consisting of several sheds separated by wide strips of weed-choked land. Between the road and the sheds stretched an expanse of gravel and snow. In front of the sheds were a couple of islands, each with a couple of widely spaced gas pumps. In the cities I'm used to, land is so precious, every inch of it is put to use. In Laramie, apparently, land was so abundant, nothing needed to be crowded up against anything.

I stopped at a pump, set the brake, and jumped out, leaving the engine running.

"Hey," barked one of the mechanics, "turn it off, buddy. We got fumes here."

But I explained my problem and showed him the name of the part I needed. "Got one of these?"

"We could get one from AutoZone, if you don't mind waiting a couple of hours."

"I'll wait." I drove the car into an empty bay. "Got a phone?"

He pointed across the highway to a motel complex, two rows of bungalows and a stand-alone hut for an office. I walked over there with trembling legs, like a landlubber who'd been at sea for years and was finally back on dry land where he belonged. Internally, my body was still rolling as if to accommodate rough waves, but the ground felt solid enough. I had made it. I was with family now, or at least with Ralph's family. For this one night, I was safe.

The Kindness of Strangers

The motel porch was glazed with ice. I dropped coins into the wall-mounted payphone and stamped my feet to keep warm as I stood listening to the phone ring and ring. The wind subsided to a frigid breeze, but even this cut through my jeans.   Finally someone picked up. "Hello?"

What a relief. "Hi. Is Jim there?"

"This's Jim."

"Oh man, am I glad to hear your voice! This is Tamim!"

"Who?"

"Tamim Ansary, Ralph's friend. From Afghanistan?"

"Ralph who?'

"Ralph. Your nephew Ralph Garner. Uncle Roy and Aunt Mary's son?"

"Oh. Mary's kid. Uh huh."

"Did Ralph talk to you?"

"Um... just a minute." I heard him shouting to someone in the background. "Nancy! You talked to Ralph recently?" A pause. "Mary's kid. Mary! My *sister* Mary."

Another pause.

Then he spoke into the phone. "Um, yeah... we might have—uh—haven't, uh...heard from Ralph in a while. Um. Anyways. What can I do you fer.... Tamin?"

"Oh—I thought he called ahead. I was wondering if I could stay with you guys tonight. I'm just passing through. I had car trouble and—"

"Well, we're kind of full up here, Tamin—"

"Tamim—"

"Tam - een. I don't see where we could 'comodate you."

A long silence. I didn't know how to explain to this guy that we were practically related. He didn't seem to know that relatives had obligations. "You know Mary and Roy Garner, right? You know Ralph?"

"My sister Mary. Yeah. Listen, I gotta' go now—"

"Wait. You know they were in Afghanistan, right? Most of their lives—"

"We're busy this weekend."

"I'll be gone by the weekend. Just tonight—"

"And we've got things to do tonight—"

"Ralph's my best friend!"

"We got guests coming in, heck, we got a full house here—kids 'n all."

"In your garage," I blurted desperately. "I'm sorry. It's just that I've had car trouble. I've been driving for hours, I got caught in that blizzard—"

"I gotta' go now, TAM-in."

"What if I just park in your driveway?" I bleated. "What if—"

Click. Dial tone.

"Well, thanks anyway," I said into the dead receiver and dragged myself back to the car, heavy with humiliation, hoping to stay warm until the mechanics got that little part installed. Cousin Jim had touched the raw nerve-ending of my worst fear: that in the end, if you need help, you'd better have something to trade.

The motel looked like crap but even there a single cost $25, and besides they didn't have a vacancy. I would have to drive on to Salt Lake City and hope that Chris Montague would give me shelter. But if Ralph's cousins wouldn't let me near their house, what could I expect from Montague? With him I could hardly claim any connection at all. He was hitting a peak of artistic achievement just as I was getting slapped in the head by a cocktail waitress—that was our shared moment. Not quite the sort of life-changing connection that creates a timeless friendship.

It was 400 miles to Salt Lake City, give or take. As I drove, I tried to rehearse what to say to Chris, but hunger and tension jangled my internal dialog.   Sleet still blurred the air, ugly clouds still hunkered on the surrounding peaks, and the radio kept advising drivers to turn back if they didn't have chains. I had no chains but also had no "back" to turn to. I figured if I could just make it to Salt Lake City, I'd call Mr. Gordon at the drive-away company and get him to front me the money. Chains were his responsibility, after all. Yes, they were, I insisted in my mind. I could picture Mr. Gordon precisely, pompous in his checked suit, his belly too big for his shirt.   I could picture him shaking his head. I found myself trembling with anger. I pictured myself getting tough. You want your car in San Francisco by Monday? You better fuckin' pony up, then, Mr. Gordon, because I'm not risking my life, I'll abandon your fucking car in a ditch, how 'bout that?

I pulled into Salt Lake before the sun had even set, and my anger subsided. Now that the storm had let up, the city looked bright and white with its broad boulevards. Chris's neighborhood had small bungalows with large yards. Interspersed among the houses were meadows and empty lots. I came to the address I had, a yellow-frame house facing a field covered with the stubble of last summer's harvested alfalfa.

A scruffy stranger answered to my knock. "Wussup, man?"

"I'm looking for Chris Montague? I'm ..." The obvious words—*a friend of his*—wouldn't leave my craw. "Friend" was the word that stuck. "I'm from Portland," I hedged, "...passing through—"

"Chris isn't here right now. Come in, I'll give him a buzz. He's prob'ly over at Daphne's. You know Daff?"

I shook my head, but failed to take this opportunity to explain that I didn't actually even know Chris, really.

"Well, come in anyways, I'll call him for you."

Shyness reared up and panic scattered my resolve. "Never mind, I'll just come back later."

"Naw, he might not come back later unless he knows you're here. I better give him a ring. What'd you say your name was?"

"I'm from Portland..." I didn't dare to say I *knew* Chris Montague from Portland. Even that would have felt like an egregious claim.

Besides, the man was already dialing. I stepped gingerly into a home that looked rather like E-street: overstuffed couches and armchairs. Big speakers mounted to the corners of the room Wooden-slate grocery crates full of records stacked on the floor. A threadbare rug covered with dog fur. A few posters hanging on the wall: Jean Paul Belmondo, Marilyn Monroe.

"Hey—" The guy was speaking into the phone now. "Montague? … Hey! A friend of yours from Portland just showed up, he wants to talk to you."

He waggled his finger at me, and my reluctant feet dragged me across the room. I took the receiver from him and I was on.

"Chris Montague…? This is Tamim Ansary—I, uh—hello— I'm—" I was all primed to bang into my speech: "I'm a friend of Paul Matthews, he plays bass, you and him were in a band once, you used to jam on 48th street, I was one of those people that used to hang around in the basement—and then later, when you were in Puddle City and you guys were playing at the White Eagle—" but I didn't get any of that out. Montague cut me off at hello.

"Tamim! Great to hear from you, man. What're you doing in Salt Lake?"

What? I *existed* for this guy? I didn't have to trace our connection? How could this be? "I was on the east coast, just driving back—"

"Can you spend a day or two in town? Where are you staying? You could crash at my place."

"I can?"

"Sure! I'm over here at Daffy's most nights, no one's using that bed. Listen, why don't you park your stuff and come over here if you've got wheels. You met my roommate Rick? He'll tell you how to get here."

I stood with the phone pressed to my ears, feeling dazed. How strange that Chris Montague knew me. It wasn't the fact that *Chris Montague* knew me, actually. It could have been anyone. The fact that I existed on somebody's map unbeknownst to myself—this was huge. If I existed for this guy, I probably existed for God-only-knew how many other people. "I" existed in places I knew not of. Yes, this really was huge. It meant Aaron and Nathan—and R.D. Laing—were right: the self is not a miniscule pinpoint deep inside a body. It's a nexus in a network of relationships that exists *out there in the world.* Come to think of it, Chris existed on my map too and my impressions of him constituted some part of who *he* was. I was constructing him. He was constructing me. All of us in this world were constructing one another.

I tossed my backpack and sleeping bag into Montague's room and followed his roommate's directions to his girlfriend's house. How spectacularly pristine the fields looked, covered with snow. It was as if someone had taken a squeegee to my eyeballs and cleaned off a film of grease. I was reminded of the first time I got glasses, at the age of eleven: standing on a street in Quetta, Pakistan, I parked those glasses on my nose and looked through them at a tree, and oh my God. I could see every leaf. Was *this* how trees looked normally to most people? Now, on my way to Montague's girlfriend's house, I thought: is this how the world feels to most people? This good? This *normal*?

It might have been at this moment that the Void vanished from my life. I was driving through Salt Lake City without making any effort to shut out awareness of it. No such effort was needed. These roads and houses and fields, those snow capped mountains, that sky—none of it was a hologram. Above the sky was not the Void but more sky. Below the ground was not the Void but more ground. The universe contained no emptiness, only plenitude. If I were to wink out of existence, all this would still exist. Which was good. What counted, what really mattered was not "I" but "all this."

Montague looked just as I remembered him: thin and pale, with soft blond hair and intelligent eyes behind wire-rimmed spectacles. The house was crowded. People were drinking beer, and I had a beer. People were playing music and Montague was one of them. His guitar work had that familiar fragile sweetness to it. Even in this room, he tended to turn sideways to the listeners, just as he used to do at the White Eagle. He seemed uncomfortable with applause, but his musicianship was wrenching.

Later, Chris gave me the keys to his house and I drove "home" through slick, quiet streets. That night, lying in the darkness feeling unusually relaxed, I got to thinking that life was just as surprisingly good as it was surprisingly bad. Both extremes. Everything positive one could say about the world was true; so was everything negative. Life is short and then you die? True. Love is real and you have friends? True. Some of the people you trust the most will betray you? Uh huh. Some people you hardly know will shower you with kindness, even reach out and make sacrifices on your behalf? Yes. They will. Is life worth living? You can't go by the evidence. The evidence goes both ways. The evidence will *always* go both ways. In the end, you have to choose. And you *can* choose. You *do.*

Donner Pass

The next day, I went to an auto parts store and priced a set of chains, then called the drive-away company and got right through to Mr. Gordon.

"Tamim!" he boomed. "Made it to San Francisco, eh? Good man!"

"Actually, no. I'm calling from Salt Lake. I'm going to need some chains—"

"Why's that?" Mr. Gordon was fascinated by my problem in an abstract way. "Salt Lake City—you're over the Rockies, son. You've made it through the worst."

"Not really. There's still the Sierras." The Rockies have the reputation, but the Sierras are the real Himalayas of North America. Low passes do cut through the Rockies, but over the Sierras, there is no avoiding Donner, where a group of 19th century pioneers got stuck in a blizzard and had to eat some of their own party to survive. "This time of year, the Sierras can be pretty dangerous," I said. "I can't go over without chains. I don't want to try." My pulse was racing, my was voice rising.

"Well, when you put it that way," Mr. Gordon interrupted, "go ahead and buy some chains. Safety first, I always say."

"You'll pay for them?"

"Absolutely. Equipment's on us, my friend. Let me talk to the clerk."

I felt like I had just set down a fifty-pound suitcase. When I said goodbye to Chris Montague and his girlfriend the next day, I thanked them warmly, but there was no way I could tell Chris what he'd done for me. It would only have embarrassed us both. I never saw him again, just as I never saw the widow Van Dorn again. I'm sure neither of them knew they had played such a key role in some stranger's drama. I only hope I have been that guy for someone else a few times.

It wasn't over, though. I still had the Sierras to get over. Eight hours got me to Reno, "the Biggest Little City in the World," where Johnny Cash sang that he killed a man just to watch him die. This close to the end of the journey, I could splurge on one night's lodging. After checking into Reno's cheapest hotel, which was very cheap indeed, I went out for a stroll.

Reno is said to be Las Vegas writ small, but not small enough. Reno at night had all the appearance of fun: neon lights running like waterfalls through glowing tubes flashing Food! Music! Joy! But that was just a veneer. Flushing money down a toilet a.k.a. gambling was the only actual "fun" on offer. Even the public bathrooms had slot machines mounted above the urinals. It was easy to see why Islam forbids gambling, though few Muslims I've known seem to care about that proscription. I went back to my hotel, ignored the slot machine mounted above the TV, and went to sleep. Warm bed, dry room, sleep—now *that's* entertainment.

The moment I opened my eyes the next morning, I could tell snow was coming down and I was in trouble again. I jumped out of bed thinking that if I left at once I could get over the pass before I had to put on chains. But the snow was already six inches deep outside and coming down in a hypnotizing whirl of monotony. When I stopped for gas I had to pump my own. The attendant wouldn't come out until I was ready to pay and even then he chuffed into his cupped hands before reaching for my money.

"What do you hear about the pass," I asked. "Can a guy still get over without chains?"

"Without chains?" He dragged his sleeve across his dripping nostrils. "Buddy! You'll be lucky to get over at all."

Crap. Reluctantly, I took out my brand new chains and after many bewildered, frozen-fingered attempts, got them on. I just hoped that I had done it right and they wouldn't fall off. West of Reno, the snow was swirling even harder. A couple of highway patrol cars were parked on the shoulder ahead, their lights flashing. The cops stood in the middle of the road, directing traffic. One cop strolled out to block my way.

"I've got chains," I protested.

"I see that. Pull over."

"I've *got* chains."

"I see that. Pull over to the side of the road. We haven't decided if we're letting any more through today."

I pulled over. Three cars were parked ahead of me, and the drivers of those cars kept peering back, looking impatient. Behind me, the line of parked cars kept lengthening. In the distance. I could see the troopers conferring. From time to time, one of their radios let out a burst of static-riddled chatter.

Then—all three of the cars ahead of me pulled out in unison. Did they get clearance to go? Did they just decide to flout the cops? Were they a convoy connected by walkie talkies? If they could go, why not me? I hit the gas to catch up with the last of them. In the rear-view mirror I could see that no one else had moved. The cops were busy stopping cars and had not noticed us departing. In another few moments, I couldn't see them and they couldn't see me. The thickening curtain of snow hid us from each other. I'd gotten away with it. Yay! You'll never catch me, coppers! California here I come!

The car ahead remained visible, so I kept following it at a steady pace of 25 miles an hour or so. Eventually the radio blurred into static so I turned it off. After that the snow muffled every sound except the hiss of my own wheels.

The road was tilting steeply upward. The car ahead of me diminished to a faint glow of tail lights in the ever-thickening snow. I stepped on the gas and felt acceleration but the car ahead nonetheless vanished into the white swirl.

Thank God, that gizmo under the hood had broken in Nebraska, not here. Thank God my car was new and reliable...unless it was a lemon. Hey, what if the road curved just here? I let up on the gas and peered hard but my headlights penetrated only a few feet into the shimmering opacity. The silence was appalling.

I had no choice but to stop, get out, and see how close I was to the edge. If another car was coming, it would plow right into me, but that was a chance I would have to take. Scuffing at the snow with my shoe, I exposed enough asphalt to see that my wheels were still three feet from the edge. Not bad. And now, standing outside the car, I noticed a metal pole sticking up by the side of the road. Fastened to the top was an orange plastic reflector disk, such as bicycles have: a marker for travelers in just these circumstances. I got back into the car. No one had come up from behind. Perhaps mine was the last car to start over the pass.

When I pushed the gas pedal, the tires found traction, and the car moved. Good old chains! The orange disk gave me something to steer toward. After I passed it I was driving blind for a while but eventually another reflector disk came into view. And then..after a longer interval... another...

I could move no faster than a toddler crawls. Sometimes, I had to open the door and stare at the road as I crept forward, to make sure I was still on pavement.

Hours of tremendous solitude passed this way, just me and the blizzard. Not once did I berate myself for embarking on this crossing, because berating myself would have required attention, of which I had none to spare. I had to focus on the task at hand.

Yesterday ceased to exist. This morning vanished. The future did not intrude. There was no "tonight." My entire life became the growl of the motor and the tortuous struggle to move one more inch forward. I experienced no fear, because in each "this-moment" I had a destination to try for and a next move that I could make. Instead of frightened, I felt fully absorbed.

Lots of people think happiness is winning the lottery so you can wake up every day without obligations and spend the whole day drinking pina coladas on a beach. I used to think some such thing myself. But that day on Donner Pass, I came to realize that the two indispensable ingredients of happiness are a destination to try for and at least one next move you can make. If you have those two things it doesn't matter what else you've got. If you lack those two things, it doesn't matter what else you've got.

Gradually, the intervals of driving blindly between orange disks grew shorter. A time came when I didn't have to keep opening the door to check the pavement. The tilt of the car shifted subtly from up to down. The air grew less opaque, the snow thinned out to flurries, black tracks appeared where earlier cars had worn through to pavement. I was coming out of the mountains.

Another hour and I was driving through rain. Another half hour and I saw an inn beside the road, the first place to stop coming down. No one who had made it over the pass had skipped this joint. The parking lot was jammed. Inside, the place was crammed with people in a mood of hilarity. None of them was sitting demurely at a table. People were singing. Strangers had their arms around each other. This was no longer just a bar but a public party. Even those who weren't drinking were acting drunk.

After chugging some hot chocolate and hugging a few strangers, I traveled on. The further downhill I went, the greener the world looked. The jagged black-and-white landscapes east of the Sierras receded into memory as I descended into the lusciously rounded, feminine hills of California. I delivered that tin-can of a Dodge to a shipping company at Pier 12 right on time and hitched to Portland the next day.

"He'ping others—mebbe that's the answer." I remembered those words when I got back to E-Street. Once I settled in again, I decided to start volunteering at Crash Crew, a crisis hotline, one of several services provided by a free clinic called Outside-In. What we did was man an all-night phone line that people could call if they needed to talk to someone in those dark hours when despair is hardest to hold at bay. Ultimately, our mission was said to be suicide prevention. We were trained in first aid, which is not enough to prevent a determined suicide, but we had a doctor on call, and if a real emergency looked imminent, a whole team of us went out.

But we didn't go out much in my time there. Mostly, we just answered the phone. One night a week from 8 pm to 7 a.m., every week for the next two years, I sat in a ratty room furnished out of a thrift store and listened to anonymous voices telling me their stories. I don't know how many of the people I talked to were really suicidal. All of them were unhappy though, and over the course of those years, I learned that Tolstoy was right: unhappy people are all unhappy in different ways.

Some are unhappy because they stepped on a land mine in Korea and now they're housebound, wheel-chair-ridden, and addicted to pain medications. Some are unhappy because they're young and new in town, and lonely and horny. Some are unhappy because they're gay and everyone they've ever known has tried to make them feel ashamed of their desires. Some are unhappy because they're a middle-aged woman with two kids living in a nice house in the suburbs and they never thought life would turn out this way.

No one I talked to was unhappy in quite the same way, and none were unhappy for the same reasons as I had been; so I didn't actually have anything useful to tell anyone. In fact, I hardly told anyone anything. Mostly I just listened: all those disembodied voices lamenting over the phone in the wee hours before dawn. All I did was listen, and the only life I'm sure I saved was my own.

The End of Civilization as We Know It

At the tail end of 1974, I climbed into a car with a woman named Shay and left Portland without a destination or a schedule. Our plan was to head east and roam wherever whim took us. If we found a place with home-like resonance, we might just stop there and sink down roots. If not, we'd come back to Portland. We put our stuff in storage and gave up the rooms we were renting so that once we hit the road, we'd have nothing to come back to.

We were taking nothing more than we could pack into my Volkswagen bug. To maximize the car's carrying capacity, we replaced the back seat with a piece of plywood and a thin foam pad, thus turning the bug into a micro-mini-station wagon. We stuffed the cabin to the ceiling with sleeping bags, ice chest, clothing, bedding, art supplies, camping gear, books, staples, and whatever else would fit. The remaining space, our two seats up front, felt as cozily enclosed and functional as a cockpit.

This was only fitting because we took this trip to restore a cozy closeness we had lost. Too many people had been yammering at us from the outskirts of our relationship, compromising our intimacy so severely that Shay and I could scarcely hear each other think. So we decided to leave friends and obligations behind and hit the road and just go and go and go, sharing many months of adventure with no one but each other.

Money was no object. I don't remember why, I just know it wasn't. We certainly had people to crash with all over the country, and I guess we both had savings. If we had to hole up in a motel, we could afford it. If we had to eat on the road we could make sandwiches, although I don't remember that we ever did: when we weren't with friends, relatives, or acquaintances, we ate at restaurants.

In outward form, this was the closest thing to a classic beatnik road trip I ever did. Kerouac and Cassidy, move over. Huckleberry Finn, you too. Here come Tamim and Shay, lighting out for the territories.

To give the trip a narrative throughline, we came up with a zany idea. On the day we left Portland, we would each start a journal. At the end of the road trip—wherever and whenever that turned out to be—we would trade journals and discover what the other had been thinking all that time. Sounds cool, huh?

Or perhaps you see the trouble built into that scenario. We didn't.

Vast Communal Project

If a road trip includes what leads to leaving, the story of this trip begins soon after I came back from Bryn Mawr. I landed in Portland feeling like a changed man because finally, finally, I had learned the single most important truth. Gotta' tell you, it's exhilarating to stumble on the single most important truth. And what was this epiphany? Simply that the world exists. The outside

world, I'm talking about. In fact, nothing exists *except* the outside
world. This was my new understanding. Interior selves are
constructed entirely of what's out there. Working on one's own
self was pointless. The key to happiness was to work on what was
out there. Take care of the outside and the inside will take care of
itself. Not that I thought I could "change the system" or any such
grandiose delusion. It's only that I saw participation as the key. If
you want to be happy for the rest of your life, join the vast
communal project of making the world work.

True to this epiphany, I plunged into one social project after
another and oh my God, life did open up. This is when I joined
Crash Crew and tried to steer desperate people away from the
abyss. One of my fellow-volunteers there was a beautiful woman
named Mary Phillips, and if "beautiful" brings Raquel Welch to
mind, I'm using the right word. Mary was volunteering at Crash
Crew because she'd broken out of a bad marriage and was trying
to reclaim her own identity. One Saturday afternoon, she and I
found ourselves in bed and it was delicious.

Mary had a two-year-old son and he's the crucial figure in a
striking image I retain from my days with her. One afternoon, the
three of us were strolling through the quiet tree-lined streets that
formed the campus of Portland State University. It was spring, and
the trees had blossomed, and we were scuffing along ankle-deep in
petals. In those park blocks stood an enormous abstract sculpture
made of black metal. It looked ponderous, but unbeknownst to the
casual passerby, it was poised on a single pin-sized point and
rigged to pivot if pushed. It was tiny Timmy who discovered this
feature. He started chortling, Mary and I looked up from each
other, and there he was, this toddler, pushing ten tons of metal
around and around. It felt symbolic.

A few weeks after this, Mary told me an old friend of hers
from high school days had looked her up and confessed that he'd
wanted her for years, and now that her husband was out of the
picture he couldn't help but declare himself, whereupon she

realized he had always been The One. She hoped? That I...? Could I? Understand? She didn't want to hurt me but... ?

Hurt me! Was she kidding? How could I be hurt? I was delighted for her! If, on top of all the fun we'd had, this woman whom I cherished had found true love—holy smokes! This was inspiring! "Go," I exulted. "Go where the river takes you. Have a fabulous life with this guy. I'll never forget you." (And I never have.) After she was gone, I marveled at this latest revelation: that love and sex did not have to entail obsession and pain! In fact, love was easy and letting go was a cinch. Who knew?

Anything was possible, because it was 1973, and a new era had just dawned. I had felt this new time coming on New Year's Day of that year. A bunch of us had gone out to some guy's ranch in Estacada, about twenty miles outside the city and I remember the occasion as vividly as a lucid dream, even though nothing in particular happened. I remember that the air was wet and cool out there. Ambling about the ranch, I walked past some motorcycle parts, scrupulously cleaned and oiled and arrayed on a dry cloth. Beyond them, in an open corral, a bunch of horses were stamping and snorting, blowing out white plumes of breath. Patches of crusted snow covered the ground, but where the snow had worn away, green blades of grass were poking through. Winter and spring sharing the same flat field. Horses and motorcycles living side by side. I looked back the way I'd come and suddenly the people I was with that day looked like ghosts to me, all those dopers and bikers and layabouts and do-nothings. We were enjoying ourselves, sure, but it came to me that mere enjoyment could never redeem a day, except as a reward for *getting something done*. And in order to get something done, you had to be doing something. Ideally something big. And that's when I felt the new thing coming, like the wind out of a subway tunnel, when a train is approaching, even though the train is still too far away to see or hear. A new era.

Sure enough, for no explicable reason, I began meeting new people as if some invisible force was operating among us. Friends

I knew connected me to friends they knew. Through Nick I connected with Thor, and through Thor with his friend Moses, and through Moses, others and more others, and still more others. The networks kept expanding, and new networks kept appearing as mysteriously as crop circles.

Feminism was surging at that moment in history, and it felt like the leading edge of a wave we were riding: here was that one big social project that just might fix the world. Anyone who could be part of that project was splashing in the fountainhead of true satisfaction. But how could we men take part in the quest? It wasn't clear, but at the very least we could wake up to who we were as human beings, beyond arbitrary categories of feminine and masculine imposed on us by a corrupt, dying society.

And so it was that four of us human-beings-who-happened-to-be-guys decided to *consciously* form a men's household. "Conscious" being the key word: we made a deliberate decision to be four guys living together. We committed to making our house a home of the kind that took skills guys normally consider the domain of womenfolk. We would cook and clean and decorate and nurture and occasionally (in moderation) express our feelings.

Nick's good friend Thor had a lover named Harriet and she formed a "conscious" women's household ten or twenty blocks from ours. Of course, we men got to know them women quite well, since we had much in common: we were all doing "the conscious" thing. In fact, one of us men got sweet on one of them women. Really, I should capitalize Man and Woman here to emphasize that we were thinking in archetypes: we were the founding figures of some future civilization. The two in question happened to be Nick and Harriet.

Now, this was interesting, since Harriet was already "in a relationship" with Thor. She wasn't Thor's "girlfriend," though. "Girlfriend" would imply that Thor owned her. A pox on such thinking. No human could own another human. If Harriet and Nick were drawn to each other, why should Thor have a say in whether they got intimate? We had to get beyond the oppressive ideology that turned individuals into halves of couples who owned each other just because they were sexually involved. Each of us was a sovereign being. And so it was that Nick—who was still sexually involved with Abby, incidentally—began moving toward an involvement with Harriet. We all leaned in to see where this would go. One thing no one doubted was the nobility of the experiment. It was certainly the right thing to do.

In our community, everyone knew the thing I had come to realize at Bryn Mawr: coupledom in any form was just society's mechanism for creating the fundamental economic unit of industrial capitalism: the nuclear family. Others might have thought of it in different words, but such was the gist of it for us all.

Unlike my friends, however, I knew of another whole system— I had grown up in a tribal society, wherein married couples weren't autonomous units living by themselves and earning their separate sustenance, but were parts of larger networks in which the women had as much to do with each other communally as each woman had to do with her wedded husband. Not that I thought the Afghan/Muslim social system was the answer. Not at all. I despised the Afghan/Muslim social system's assignment of gender roles. It's just that, given my upbringing, I knew there were systems other than the one based on the nuclear couple, which to me meant that all cultural systems were provisional—all. None had an absolute legitimacy ordained by nature. The verities and values that held a society together were decisions people had knowingly or unknowingly made in common, and whatever people had decided, people could un-decide.

Attractions like Nick's to Harriet and Harriet's to Thor and (for that matter) Thor's to Elise (and on and on) bled into the atmosphere, flavoring every interaction with a certain effervescence that was--oh, let's go ahead and say it: *erotic*. Anything was possible. Feelings I had barely glimpsed in the days of the snowflake infused my whole world now. Whatever it was, this "thing," it was no longer limited to some little cluster of friends jammed into adjacent houses. It was a far-flung organism, new in the world, indefinable but pulsing, growing.

Lest I leave a misimpression, let me note: we are *not* talking about a cult here. We're talking about a culture. Cults are like cells: they have a membrane separating them from their surroundings, and they have a nucleus, a leader. We had no center because none of us followed any of us, we were all leaders without followers. We could not be closed off, because there was no "we," and no one to close the gates, and no gates to close, since no one could define where "we" ended, or what line distinguished the inside from the outside. How many people were "insiders?" No one knew. Thousands certainly, but how many thousands? Tens? Surely. Hundreds of thousands? Maybe. We only knew this wasn't a mere world but a universe; and like the universe of the physicists, it was expanding.

An Australian mime who had studied with Etienne Decroux came to town around then and started teaching classes, and dozens of us signed up and got busy learning to juggle and "find our clowns." My pal Nick started taking tai chi, and I joined him, and soon that enthusiasm swept the community. We herded to pickup soccer games and volleyball games and made expeditions to the coast and the Columbia gorge, and our friend Thor directed some of us in a play, while others of us were rebuilding the engines of our cars, or solemnly smoking pipes at round robin communal chess games.

And there were bands like Upepo, which played in bars around town but really came into their own in the back yards of communal houses in southeast Portland, surrounded by 40 or 50 or a 100 people, all tapping on improvised percussive devices as they listened or danced, the boundary between audience and band blurred or nonexistent.

On Mondays, some of us got together to play writing games. We called ourselves the Acme Lit Club in homage to Scrooge McDuck. Our evenings always featured fine food, good wine, and superb dope. Our writing centered around endless variations of

Exquisite Corpse, the game invented by the surrealists, in which one person writes a word, the next person adds a word, the next adds another, and so on until a sentence or even a story has taken shape.

In the classic version of the game, the players follow certain grammatical rules, such as that the first word must be a noun, the second a preposition, the third an adjective, and so on; but we didn't believe in arbitrary rules, we departed from the basics to elaborate numerous new forms of communal writing. Some were quite complex: pass a dictionary around and let each person find an interesting word at random. If there are twelve in the group, you end up with twelve words. Then each person writes a twelve-sentence story in which each sentence uses one of the words.

Others were simple. Write half a proverb, throw it into a pile, pull another one out, and complete what you find. *A penny earned* IS A PENNY SPENT. My personal favorite was the simplest of all: keep a sentence going as long as possible, each person adding one word. Forty years later, I still remember one of those:

Feet
stepping
cautiously
impede
underwater
missionaries
who
often
swim
self-consciously
alone
in
the
ponds
just
off
shore.

Some evenings, we'd flock to a house with a TV set—there were only a few such houses, so there were always a lot of us watching—to take in the only show any of us watched. It was called *The Watergate Hearings*.

Oh, man, what great theater that show was! Week after week, they hauled the most colorful real-life scoundrels into Congress and forced them to stammer out their lies while cameras filmed their sweat. I remember Sam Ervin, senator from North Carolina, glowering like an Old Testament prophet as he thundered imprecations at oily hatchet men such as Bob "Buzzcut" Haldeman and goons like the infamous G. Gordon Liddy.

Once in a while, we got a special treat: the Dark Knight of American politics, the Hunchback of San Clemente, President Richard Nixon himself would shamble under the klieg lights to deny everything in a villainous rumble. Everyone knew the government was full of rats and cutthroats and murderers and snakes and bagmen, but who ever thought they would be dragged into the light like this?

In fact, the mainstream world seemed to be coming apart. It was so gratifying. Frank Church's senate committee was exposing the CIA. And the truth was coming out about the slave camps that were America's prisons, where virtually all the inmates were black. White people were beginning to fathom what black people knew only too well, the tragedy of the slave trade that had shaped America's social structure. And all of us were coming to know of the genocidal destruction of Native Americans, and the devastation of nature by megapowerful faceless corporations, and the corporate manipulation of puppet states around the world. Before our time, none of this had been common knowledge. Now, all the secrets were coming to light in the dance-macabre that was the beginning of the end of civilization as we knew it.

Fitzie

I still worked at the Genoa, which had evolved into one hub of that ever-proliferating web of communal social networks. My fellow workers and I enjoyed our work, but one day a bunch of us decided to break away and start our own restaurant because, after all, we were the talent here, why should Talent work for The Man?

The Man, in this case, was a failed folksinger who had given up music to build gourmet restaurants. He wasn't exactly the Denny's Corporation, but he was a boss and we wanted out from under bosses, so we quit the Genoa to found our own place. Macondo, we planned to call it.

Macondo would not merely be a business. It would embody a noble ideal. That was the crucial point. At Macondo, no one would have a fixed wage. Every worker would get a share of the profits. The only formula for sharing would be time: if you put in more hours, you got a bigger share, simple as that, whether you were bussing tables or planning menus. No work would be valued above any other, since each of us was a human being, the value of which could not be quantified.

Also, no one would be the boss. The "boss" idea violated our principles ipso facto. All decisions would be made collectively, no one would have the authority to tell anyone else what to do, everyone would decide their own schedule, and all conflicts would be resolved with a negotiated agreement between equals.

Step one in starting such a business was obvious: make a T-Shirt. (It was gorgeous; I kept mine for 20 years.) The second crucial task was obvious too: write a manifesto. Lots of people in our vast band of siblings contributed to the 50-page document explaining our enterprise and why it was so important, but the main co-authors were a woman named Fitzie and I.

Frankly, I don't remember how I met Fitzie. It was not like it had been with Lily, spotting her across a crowded room and all the rest of the world receding into background. With Fitzie, there was no moment. By the time I was aware of her, I had already known her for such a long while I couldn't remember a beginning. I might have met her at the Women's Household up the street from our Men's Household; she was part of their penumbra. Perhaps she was there the day Nick and I dropped in, tripping on peyote. Or perhaps it was somewhere else. What did it matter?

Fitzie was fun. The better I got to know her, the more I liked her. She was easy to hang out with, a boon-companion type of person, solidly smart, an enthusiastic reader, you could talk about books and movies and music with her; an unpretentious cheerful soul, always up for a trip to a tavern to quaff a few beers, a witty presence at the Acme Literary Club--every time a communally written story went through her fingers it came out funnier, more compelling, more mysterious. Everything she touched she improved.

Earlier, I mentioned the movie star beauty of Mary Phillips; evaluations of this kind never occurred to me with Fitzie. It's not that she wasn't beautiful, it's more that the question wasn't relevant. We weren't going there, which made me proud of my non-sexism. Fitzie and I were two human beings. Hanging out together wasn't man-woman fun, it was human-human fun. How evolved we were!

Such deeply satisfying fun that at parties and other festive gatherings, I often found myself gravitating to her vicinity. We'd linger near the chips, immersed in deep discussions. I found her life story so compelling. She had spent her formative teenage years in Salt Lake City but her family was Catholic, not Mormon; which made for an odd childhood. Her father had been a flight controller, a job so tense he died of a stress-induced heart attack when Fitzie was on the verge of adolescence—she was there when he died. She said being on the threshold of sexuality when her father died had messed with her head in ways she'd long been struggling to understand. Yeah: just like that, standing around a chip bowl, this woman was telling me about her sexuality. We were that comfortable with each other. And I told her about my long obsession with Lily, and how I broke it by understanding that romantic love was a fantasy created to serve a dying social system.

Once, a bunch of us were at the Villanova Pizza in North Portland, just down the street from a porno theater that was, on

that night, showing a movie called *A Hard Man Is Good to Find*.
I was there with friends, Fitzie was there with friends; some of us
knew some of them, so our groups mingled into a single bigger
group, turning that public place into a private party, which
happened a lot in our Portland, the secret Portland inhabited by our
Community.

Fitzie and I played some pool together. Neither of us was
much good, but we strutted around the table like sharks, bending
over our pool cues for long moments to consider shots that we
usually ended up missing. But who was counting? We were
chatting about a book called *Combat in the Erogenous Zone* by
Ingrid Bengis. I checked that book out of the library recently, just
to see what had floored me so totally back then—and was
surprised to see that the first chapter is titled *Man Hating*. Hmm.

Bengis said a woman's core experience in this society was the
threat of rape, and Fitzie told me this was in fact exactly what a
girl, any girl, experienced in this society, anywhere, anytime, in
any city, walking down any sidewalk among strangers.

I came from a society in which women hardly ever walked
down a sidewalk among strangers, and when they did they were
covered from head to foot in those body bags known today as
burqas. What their experience of being in public was, I had no
clue, but I did know what Bengis was talking about, because in
Afghanistan, where women were sequestered and men dominated
all public spaces, young *boys* had that experience outside the
safety of their homes. I never got raped, but when I was in
Afghanistan I often felt like I might—not in the compound among
my clan, certainly, but out in the public world, on the bus, for
example, going to school... stray fingers poking, prodding,
exploring...Every Afghan boy knows the anxiety of which Bengis
spoke...

We felt close that night, Fitzie and I, but never did it strike me
that we were feeling close in *that* way, because ours wasn't *that*
kind of relationship. We were outside the realm where women feel
the threat of rape and men have to wonder if their arousal is an

urge for which they ought to apologize. We talked about our own past relationships, and what made relationships so difficult. "Timing," was Fitzie's theory. "Timing is everything." And I remember another aphorism she tossed out that night: "All feelings are mutual and obvious." Then she added some caveats: "Eventually. Unless someone is fooling themselves." But the caveats felt minor. The core maxim seemed so profound, I never stopped to wonder if it was true.

Macondo kept us busy for a year. Many joined our great quest during that time and many dropped away. We scouted locations and collected donations. We planned menus and cooked sumptuous sample meals and had long discussions about policy: should friends get free meals? What was the limit? Who counted as a free-meal level friend? What were the criteria?

But starting a restaurant turned out to be harder than we dreamed. We had to deal with the city, meet countless codes, and get all sorts of friggin' permits. And you couldn't just lay in a supply of wine, you needed a "liquor license", to get which you needed to know someone who knew someone, all of which confirmed the picture we already had of the mainstream world: it was a rot-riddled edifice about to crumble.

We never did get Macondo started, but we handed all of our documents and discoveries over to a lesbian collective even more committed than we to building an agora, and they succeeded in opening a community place called Mountain Moving Cafe, which lasted for years. They didn't have to specify which community they were talking about. If you had to ask, you weren't part of it

Mountain Moving Cafe was just one more nexus in the growing web of collectives and cooperatives that constituted our community. Collectives and cooperatives which, I might mention, dealt with every aspect of social and economic life. I mentioned Outside-In, where doctors worked as volunteers to provide free medical care; and there was KBOO, our radio station; and there were farm collectives out in the wet green countryside; and trucking collectives (really, just guys with trucks) hauling produce into town; and there was the People's Food Store, where the food was local and fresh and cheap, but if you wanted to shop there, you had to volunteer there, which is why every so often I woke up at the crack of dawn and spent a couple of hours unloading boxes from a truck. It was exactly the same kind of work I had done in my first job during college, at an alienating stationery warehouse except that here there was nothing alienating or unlikable about the work; here no one told me how to look busy without getting anything done; here we *wanted* to get things done, because this was our food store. Why on earth would we cheat ourselves?

I had long been planning a trip to the Ashland Shakespeare Festival with a couple of women I knew. Abby was a former I-don't-know-what-to-call-her. "Girlfriend" wouldn't be correct, but we had been in that posture with each other as members of the snowflake. The other was Maggie who lived around the corner from me, and whom I found insanely attractive, probably because of her eerie similarity to Lily. (Yeah, I'd defeated that fantasy, but traces of it still wriggled in my psyche.) Anyway, the three of us had picked our plays, bought our tickets, and found a campsite to stay at, and I felt tremulous about the trip, fantasizing what might happen between the gorgeous Maggie and me around the campfire on one of those nights...

At the last minute, however, Maggie dropped out. Something came up. She was distraught because she'd already bought tickets and now she'd have to swallow the loss: but Fitzie stepped in with a noble offer to take the tickets off Maggie's hands. The swap disappointed me, but only a little. Okay, so this wasn't going to be a romantic adventure, but doing the Ashland Shakespeare festival with a couple of good friends would be totally fine. Removing the possibility of sex from the equation might even eliminate some awkward discomfort, leaving us free to just enjoy.

And we did enjoy. Ashland was a fairy tale town for the likes of us, with its Elizabethan-looking main street, and its many restaurants that sold alfalfa sprout sandwiches on 9-grain bread, and vegetarian grocery stores vending organic avocadoes, and taverns with sawdust on the floors and blues-rock bands that knew how to lay down a 4/4 beat—combining the blues and the bard. Man! It doesn't *get* any better! We hit those taverns, danced till late, strolled the sidewalks, window shopped the countless stores that offered arts and crafts of the kind we ourselves did, and saw our plays: Becket's *Waiting for Godot, The Merry Wives of Windsor,* and a third one I've forgotten.

And then each night, we went back to our campsite some ten miles east of town, up in the green, quiet hills, and sat around a fire surrounded by darkness, smoking dope and sharing deep thoughts. What deep thoughts? No clue. Funny how the feeling of profound conversations lingers long after the content of them is gone. In any case, it was there around the campfire, on those three nights, that my friendship with Fitzie deepened to the borders of romance.

I wasn't aware it was happening, however. I thought a good friend was becoming a *really* good friend, was all. It wasn't until we were back in Portland a bit later that we crossed the final frontier. A bunch of us were herding around one night, from tavern to tavern, and the amateurs gradually dropped away until the herd was down to Fitzie and me. We went to an apartment she was crashing at. Whoever lived there was moving and boxes were stacked everywhere, giving the place a warehouse feel. The only furnishing was Fitzie's sleeping bag, so we sat on the floor and she read me a poem by Sylvia Plath called *Finistere,* and then a few poems of her own, including one she had written at Short Sands, my favorite place on the Oregon coast. There, looking down from the tip of a cliff, you could see waves crashing into a blowhole, each time pumping out a plume of spray, hundreds of feet high.

Fitzie's poem didn't focus on that spray but on the sea itself, which she compared to an old man flinging his white fingers onto the sand, trying to pull himself up onto the land, only to be dragged back by the tides. There was something lonesome about the poem, something that made me want to comfort her. A bit later, somehow, we were making love, a shock to me, because whoa! Was this done? Did one have sex with a friend? Wasn't this a little bit, I don't know, kinky? Kinda' wrong? Fucking a good friend?

Turned out, when you're having sex with your best friend, you can share thoughts you never shared with anyone, and you can follow up on them. I had grown up with the impression that raw animal sex was something men wanted and women went along with in exchange for the pleasures *they* wanted, which had to do with candles, flowers, and romantic dancing. Men's gut desires were inevitable but shameful.

Fitzie let me in on the great secret: girls had gut desires not so different from ours. They too could feel and appreciate the best thing about sex, its dark, transgressive mystery.

Conscious Man

Meanwhile, the Macondo project had foundered, and I had joined the Scribe, a collectively owned and operated 32 page weekly tabloid that billed itself as the community newspaper. It was the media version of Macondo and it was (but of course) one more iconic institution of our community.

Joining the Scribe was like finding water and discovering that I had always been a fish. It wasn't just that, here, I could cut loose and write and thousands of people would read me every week. That was fine, of course, but the most surprising thing I discovered, working at the Scribe, was that I had a skill I never even knew existed.

I was good at doing meetings.

Yes, this was a skill, a highly specialized one in our culture. At the Scribe, no issue was too trivial to merit a policy meeting. Should we review a cafe that used white sugar in its baked goods? Better call a meeting. Was a photograph of art painted on the shoulders of a woman with her back turned to the camera sexist? Better call a meeting. Should we reject ads promoting products we didn't believe in? Well, that meant figuring out what we believed in. We sat around in big groups at all-day policy meetings discussing it. There was no guide book, because the cultural values we were trying to respect didn't exist before our discussions.

Participating in such meetings took special skill because no one was leading them. Our culture didn't believe in gatekeepers and controllers and I (it turned out) knew how to keep a discussion moving without seeming to lead and how to move it my way without appearing to push. I had an instinct for knowing when to say nothing and how to say strategic somethings without stepping on the rules of our culture. Well, not rules, we had no rules, the absence of rules *was* our culture, but we did have unspoken understandings of right and wrong, what would have been called traditional values had our "culture" not been so new we were making up our traditions as we went along, shaping them collectively in the course of wrestling with real-life issues. The process was happening everywhere, but as the community newspaper, it was our function to articulate and embody it.

Most of the world had not yet realized that the earth could run out of resources. Until now, throughout history, the only question had been who would get how much of the abundance. Even Karl Marx had bought into the idea of infinite perfectibility and unending industrial progress. But the truth was coming out now: infinite abundance was an illusion, and the industrial civilization built on this delusion was doomed. Only a few could see it yet, but we were among this happy few: our community. The Community. We were the smithy where a new culture appropriate to this truth would have to be forged.

The key principles of this new culture had to do with relationships. Relationships, improperly conducted, posed the risk of reducing people to property, which was the cardinal wrong. And in sexual relationships, the ones most vulnerable to this reduction were the women. The onus, therefore, was on us men. We had to make a *conscious* effort not to act out the macho patterns embedded in us from childhood. We had to be *conscious* of our own behavior enough to notice when we were being

possessive or domineering. The enlightened among us all aspired
to be conscious men! That became the standard term: conscious
man.

Once, some guy new to the Scribe tried to put a move on a
woman there. She told him she was open to a relationship with a
man, but not just any man: she had standards. Well, what standard
did he have to meet, the newbie wondered? What kind of man was
she looking for?

"I want," she declared, "a man who's conscious

"Conscious," he gasped. "That's all? He just has to be
conscious?"

Fitzie and I embraced the values of our culture, and our
togetherness was so tight in that springtime of our life that we
decided to take the most pioneering step of all. We were in Fitzie's
room at the Madison Street house the night we made our decision.
We had just deliciously made love and were lying in the dark,
nestled in piles of Fitzie's bedding, moist and exhausted, gazing
up at her unfinished ceiling and listening to the floorboards
creaking as people walked around up there. Then Fitzie broke the
topic open.

"I saw you talking to Maggie the other day. I could tell you
were attracted."

"Well, yes," I confessed. "There is some chemistry there."
Was I in trouble? I waited for the other shoe to drop.

"It's only natural," said Fitzie. "It's not chemistry, Tamim, it's
biology. I'm attracted to other men too."

We digested this in silence for a while. Then Fitzie said, "We
don't have to be monogamous to be what we are with each other.
We're close in a way I couldn't be with anyone else."

I lay there pondering her words, and all I could think was
"Phew!" She was right. Our sex was wonderful, but only because
our intimacy went so much deeper than sex. There was no one on
Earth I trusted or had ever trusted more than this woman.

"Having other relationships won't change what you and I have," she asserted solemnly. "You're my primary relationship."

"And you're mine," I declared fervently. "Nothing will change that."

Primary relationship! It sounds so unromantic now, but in 1974, in that warm basement room, listening to my lover assuring me that nothing I did could ever make her jealous or erode our bond, *primary relationship* sounded like the most loving term ever invented by human imagination. In that moment, I confess I thought about Maggie: could my fantasies about her come true after all? Without damaging this precious thing I had with Fitzie?

We discussed what the rules would be, but we couldn't think of any. Well, other than total honesty of course—we'd tell each other everything. By no means were we breaking up: just the opposite. This was a tribute to our deep connection. Only the closest and most trusting of lovers could say to each other, go ahead, make love with other people if the spirit moves you, I won't be jealous. Nothing more needed to be said, then. We had cast off from all convention and were sailing into uncharted waters, two trailblazing adventurers side by side on the prow of a ship heading into the unknown, our hair blown back by the wind, our eyes fixed (as Plath put it in *Finisterre*) on the beautiful formlessness of the sea.

Fate of the Universe at Stake

In 1973, the price of gas had started to rise--from 25 cents to 30 to 35 to a shocking 40! Then in 1974, around the time Fitzie and I decided to go all multiple-relationship on each other,   the shortages began. Suddenly gasoline was not just expensive but un-friggin'-available! Yes, yes, this time it could be explained: oil embargo, Arabs and Israelis, petroleum corporations, yadda, yadda. This time the crisis was manufactured, but the oil really was finite, and it really would run out. What we were seeing now was a preview of days to come.

The state of Oregon imposed gas rationing. Cars were authorized to buy gas only every other day. On our designated days, we had to get up at dawn, by which time the line at the gas station usually stretched around the block. It took hours to get to the pump and by then the gas was all too often gone. It was then that bicycles became noble.

Those were scary days for most folks, but exhilarating for us because we alone understood the signs, and we alone were getting ready. The only thing anyone could know about the world to come was that nothing could be known about the world to come. The only relevant skill anyone could develop now was adaptability. The mainstreamers surrounding us were busy doing just the opposite, making themselves obsolete by acquiring specialized skills to succeed in a world that would not exist.   They were studying to become investment bankers or certified public accountants. What good would that do once the money-system collapsed? They were busy learning law. What good would that do, once nation-states and their legal systems had dissolved? They were learning to repair cars. How sorry would they be once the gas was gone?

After civilization collapsed, all the specialists would be in trouble. Only those who had specialized in adaptability would still be functional, and of those, the best adapted would be the enlightened few who had outgrown fixed social roles: man and woman, old and young, butcher, baker, and candlestick maker—all that stuff. We alone would be able to roam the world as fluid *affinity groups*, a phrase I coined for an article in the Scribe, 30 or 40 of us to a tribal band, shape-shifting to meet ever-changing circumstances, perfectly adapted to a money-less world in which every person was a full-time volunteer.

The first time Fitzie told me she had slept with some other guy, I knew which guy: I had met him briefly. He was a hitchhiker passing through town on his way to Alaska to work on the pipeline. He met someone in Fitzie's communal house, and accepted an offer to crash there. Several of us were sitting around the table into the wee hours that night, smoking weed and chatting about the Patty Hearst case. Then I went home because I had a ton of work to get done for a special issue of the Scribe—I was co-editing the religion issue (The tagline was going to be "Yes, we have no nirvanas"). The next day, Fitzie told me that she and this hitchhiker guy had stayed up after everyone else was gone, and things had drifted into sex. "You know how it is." She gazed into my face looking for reassurance.

I did know how it was. It should have been fine. After all, it wasn't as if I had felt a great disturbance in the force the moment their two bodies joined. If she had not told me, I would never have known, which meant that our theories were correct: sex really was no different than tennis. There was no reason for jealousy here. No need for the ugly beast to rear its ugly head. Not here.

Except for one little thing. The moment Fitzie *did* tell me, I felt a great disturbance in the force. The world went dim. She saw my stricken face, and her heart broke. I could see as much in her face: good God, what had she done, had she jeopardized the thing she held most dear? I had to reassure her immediately: "No, no, Fitzie, it's not you. We said we'd do this and here I am being a jerk. I'll get over it, just give me a little time. A little time to get used to this." I didn't want her to feel guilty, and she didn't want me to feel hurt: our feelings were mutual and intense. We gathered each other in for a hug. She whispered that she loved me, which I already knew. I think there might have been a tear or two shed in there, but if so, it was Fitzie who shed them, because I did not know how. I had unlearned the skill as a boy, growing up in Afghanistan, where guys who cried were dead meat in the social group. Too bad, because it would have come in handy just then. There was no backing out though. A line had been crossed, and we both knew it. We had said we'd do this thing and by God we had to do it. The only direction was forward. The only question was how to do this with pure and loving hearts.

Right around then, a guy named Jack Frost blew into town to organize an event he was planning with Ken Kesey, author of *One Flew Over the Cuckoo's Nest*. They called it the "Bend-in-the-River Conference," a weeklong meeting to alert the world to the environmental catastrophe looming for planet Earth. It would draw scientists, thinkers, artists, writers, and activists from every locale, from distant cities, and from other countries even, to Portland. Thanks to heavy media coverage, this conference was going to trigger the global shift in consciousness the world needed to avert disaster. In fact, this event would take humanity around "the bend in the river."

Frost was a lanky, tweedy guy. He would have been a poor man's Robert Redford except for his toothbrush mustache and tortoise-shell glasses. Portland State gave him a little office, which he crammed with books, papers, and statistics documenting the damage our hard-charging industrial civilization was doing. His frontline issue was water, but don't get him started on oil, he often warned us, whereupon the sound of his own voice saying "oil" generally got him started and he'd point around--"That's oil. That runs on oil. That's oil. That runs on oil—" I staggered out from one such session and all I could see was oil. Cars revving and chugging. The street itself made of tar. Men pouring out of offices, wearing suits made of oil by-products. Women with beautifully crafted hair-dos, held in place with oil derivatives. Who were we kidding? Oil was the lymphatic fluid of our lives and when the last drop was gone—as it would be soon—holy apocalypse!

As a leading member of the Scribe collective, I was well placed to help with the project and I sank into it neck-deep. I walked the neighborhoods, knocked on doors, talked to people, distributed leaflets, wrote articles. I became part of the core planning committee. I took part in endless meeting. Decisions were hard to come by due to our diversity, let me tell you. Some of us were Marxists who came to meetings only to argue that this whole "conference" approach was bourgeois bullshit. Some of us were feminists who argued that this committee squelched the voices of women and the gender issue had to be tackled before the environmental one. Others of us were tough white revolutionaries in Mao caps who demanded to know why more of us weren't black or Hispanic. Good thing one of us was me, who had a touch for keeping diverse conflicting factions moving toward consensus at a meeting.

While I was doing my bit to save the planet, Fitzie went home to visit her mother. When she came back, she told me she and some distant cousin were in a swimming pool together and sex just, you know: sorta' happened. Oh my God, talk about a brick to the gut. But why? Where was this reaction coming from? Fitzie was only following the tenets of Fritz Perls, whose "prayer" people were constantly quoting in those days:

I do my thing and you do your thing.
I am not in this world to live up to your expectations
and you are not in this world to live up to mine.
You are you, and I am I,
and if by chance we find each other,
it's beautiful...

Why was it not okay with me, what she'd done? I couldn't find a reason, so my feelings had to be invalid, and yet I had trouble breathing. "This is kinda' hard for me," I confessed.

She tried to warm me out of worrying with kisses. "We're strong. You're strong! We are! This is all so new. We'll get better at it."

Knowing how much I loved Mexican food, she took me to La Casa Del Rios, which was a funky little dive, *our* funky little dive. There, over dinner, she told me she wanted to change her name. Fitzie was short for her last name Fitzpatrick, but she wanted something more lyrical now, a more feminine name. We brainstormed variations of her first name Shannon, and I was the one who came up with Shay. It fit how beautiful she looked across the table from me that night. It's the name she goes by still.

After dinner, we went to her house and I had never felt more loved or in love than I did that night, tangled up with her body in her sheets.

That week, while I wrestled with the conference, Shay went to the coast for some contemplative time alone. From her cabin there, she sent me a mournful, troubled letter. This was going to be hard, she said, letting go of neediness without letting go of love. It was all about trusting that we wouldn't fly apart if we stopped clutching. She worried about us.

I told her not to worry: "Our relationship is good, and getting better. It's strong and getting stronger. It's myself I need to work on. Give me a wrench, and if a wrench doesn't do it, give me knife, but don't ever doubt that I love you." Let me confront, now, the word "cheating." Shay and I weren't cheating, ever, at all, period. Oh, if only we had been! It was torture to know she was with someone else and imagine what they must be doing. But we had no secrets from each other. Full disclosure was the rule. It was painful for her too. Every time she saw an attraction brewing between me and some woman, she knew this might be the night she'd start to lose me.

And me? *Did* any of these secondary attractions come to anything? Well, I made an effort. It was expected, you know. I hung out with Page from the Scribe a bit, I went to the coast with her, we spent some nights together. There was a Louise in there, and a Justine, briefly. But it was an effort, as I said, because here's the dirty little secret: I didn't want anyone but Shay. I couldn't say so, though. It would have been unfair to Shay. It would have put too much pressure on her, might have hobbled her with guilt. Shay was struggling so hard to establish her own center of gravity, poor girl. She didn't want to be a satellite in orbit around me or anyone else, and who could blame her? It was an honorable but oh so difficult quest. This was after all the era when, for the first time in known history, women were rejecting identities built around wife-hood, mother-hood, and keeping house. Out in the mainstream, careerism could plug the gap. "Outa' my way, I'm going to be a lawyer, don't tell me a woman can't." But the new culture we were forging disdained careerism, so what did that leave?

Some women defined themselves by a passion they could call their own. Abby was all about theater, as everyone knew. But Shay had always been a dabbler. She wrote poetry, but no one thought of her as The Poet. She enjoyed nature, but no one thought of her as The Naturalist. Her energies funneled mainly into relationships, and that was the problem. Relationships were the sinkhole for women, the whirlpool in which they lost themselves and became the man they were embracing. If relationships were Shay's thing, she couldn't have just one. It would have made her quest impossible.

I knew this. Even at the time, even in her presence, I sort of knew it: I didn't doubt her love. When she told me I was her primary relationship, I knew she was saying something big. To be sure, it did not make the bleeding stop. Jealousy kept gnawing at me like a beast, but at least—when it got too painful—I had a best friend I could go to for solace. I had Shay.

I told Shay I wasn't criticizing what she did. We'd agreed to put no limits on each other's relationships, but "relationships" was the key word here. It was the casual nature of her encounters that bothered me: What I felt wasn't jealousy but disappointment, I said. "You're better than that, Shay."

And she agreed sheepishly that she could have been more sensitive. She conceded that women had a responsibility to be "conscious" too. She said she'd try to do better.

Primary Relationship

Then at last the Bend-in-the-River project came to fruition. Instead of a week-long conference, we ended up throwing an event that lasted one afternoon. Instead of a vast network of meeting halls, we secured a middle-school lunchroom that was sitting idle because it was a summer weekend. Instead of scientists and thinkers from around the globe we got Jack Frost and Ken Kesey. Instead of people from all walks of life and states as distant as

Florida, we got people from all segments of "the community" and places as far away as Clackamas County. Instead of heavy coverage by every form of media, we got one correspondent from the Scribe: me.

Frost and Kesey split after the conference and I never heard from them again, so I don't know what they thought, but we locals considered the conference a great success. We didn't turn humanity around, but we got a better look at each other. We got clarity on who we meant by "the community." We were not the activists of the long-ago sixties, activists whose Days of Rage had been about fixing a world they expected to inhabit. *We,* the new breed, knew the old world could not be fixed. The dog-eat-dog capitalist civilization that had prevailed for millennia was about to self-destruct. Our job was to get out of the building before it collapsed. Our job was to build the new world that would rise from the rubble, starting now.

I explained all this in a triumphant article for the Scribe the following week. After we put that issue to bed, a bunch of us went drinking at a tavern called Ken's Afterglow, and I ended up a little tipsy. Shay's place was closer than mine, so I headed there. I mean, why would I not? She *was* my primary relationship.

She had moved recently. She had a tiny apartment of her own at this point, on the third floor of a creaky old mansion. I made my way up to her door and knocked. She didn't answer. In fact, I heard no sound at all from inside. I had not, of course, called ahead to make sure I could come over. Why would I? This was not just some acquaintance. This was *Shay,* my primary relationship.

Except that ... Come to think of it...

I descended to the street and looked up from the sidewalk and, sure enough, I saw light in her windows and shadows moving against the curtains. Shay was home all right—just not to me.

The next day, I was in my driveway, working on my car, when a blue sedan pulled up across the street and Shay got out. I had noticed a blue sedan exactly like that one parked outside her building the night before. A scraggly-bearded blond guy in a bulky army surplus jacket got out and followed Shay, hanging back a few steps, his head lowered, as if he were ashamed of himself. And I knew at once.

I didn't know how to behave. In a world where no one owned anyone, how was a guy supposed to behave with a man who'd just spent the night with his primary relationship? There was no established etiquette for this situation. This was the sort of moment we would have to figure out if we were inventing a new civilization. I wanted to call a meeting, but who would I call? Only three of us were involved and we were all here. And this meeting, I more or less blew. My capacity for courteous grace dried up. I lost the ability to be friendly. Shay introduced the man to me as Ron and the best I could muster up was a cold hello.

Shay knew how I felt about casual, meaningless sexual encounters—hadn't I explained it? She hoped and had every reason to believe this new relationship would make me proud of her, because this one wasn't casual or meaningless. She always expected the noblest reactions from me. "You're my primary relationship," she told me later, in her apartment. "But Ron," she went on, "is someone I also really care about."

"That's wonderful," I snapped.

"Are you angry?"

"No!" I barked. "Why should I be angry? You're free, I'm free. Isn't that what we said? Do whatever you want." I stomped around in rage and tore her curtain down and yelled some more.

Shay saw this as a real step forward for us. "We're learning how to express anger." She confided that she herself had a lot of pent up anger she could not seem to release. She envied my ability to let go and let it show. "I wish you and Ron could spend some time together," she proposed wistfully. "I think you'd really like each other."

But I knew that spending time with Ron was never going to be high on my to-do list. One thing I'll have to say, though. Once Ron appeared, no more random hitchhikers made their way into Shay's bed. Ron settled in as her steady secondary relationship.

Look, I wanted to like the guy, but there was something unlikable about him. Hard to pinpoint what it was, since I never spent time with him. Ron was married, as it happened, to a woman named Helga, and I didn't like her either. She didn't mind Shay sleeping with her husband because she had other lovers herself, and each of them had other lovers too. Such was our world.

The good times continued, though, with Shay. They did. We still had our warm days and our good sex and our treasured outings. It's just that petty quarrels broke out from time to time. The problem was me: any little thing could set me off. Like the time she went to see *Nashville* with Ron. How *could* she? Altman was *my* favorite director! How could she not know that?

And if by chance we find each other, it's beautiful...

Meanwhile, my stature at the Scribe kept growing.

The Road Trip Remedy

Finally, Shay came up with a proposal. What if we spent some unmitigated time together, just the two of us? How about if we did a long road trip together, just the two of us? Roam around until we felt solid again? Just the two of us?

We spread out a map of the United States and got inspired. By God. America was dotted with places we wanted to visit. If we left soon enough, we could be in Washington D.C. in time to spend Christmas with my mother and my siblings. If we played our cards right, we could hit New Orleans in time for Mardi Gras. Maybe stop in the Okefenokee Swamp on the way. Always wanted to see Pogo. And what about the Superstition Mountains? Might we find the Dutchman's lost gold mine? How about smoking dope in Disneyland? The possibilities made us swoon.

The night before we left Portland, Shay took me over to Ron and Helga's home in North Portland for dinner. I'd never really spent time with this couple, and before we left she wanted me to see how congenial we four could be. The dinner was good and the conversation not entirely unpleasant. In fact, now that we were leaving this couple behind, I even found them likable. Ron turned out to be a soft-spoken man of many interests. Helga, with her boisterous laugh, her blond hair, and her Scandinavian features had a certain kick-ass charm. My affable warmth pleased Shay, which made me even more affable, because pleasing her pleased me. Ron played his part properly, receding into the role of Shay's insignificant other. Helga took no dislike to me. She cracked rowdy jokes as she put away the wine, nudging me from to time as if there were flirtatious innuendos between us.

We ended up in their sauna. Naked, to be sure, but naked was no big deal. People like us were often casually naked with acquaintances, it didn't mean anything. Decades later a friend of mine referred to those early seventies as the era of "non-sexual nudity." Of course, in this situation, "nonsexual" was not quite as axiomatic as it might have been, given our configuration. At one point I noticed a bead of water hanging off one of Helga's nipples, but only in the way I noticed arty drops of rain hanging off tree branches after a spring shower. When I reached my hand out to let it drop into my palm, she said "Hey." But it was a coy "Hey."

In that sauna, we told Ron and Helga about our Mardi Gras plan. Helga's eyes sparkled. Why, she and Ron might just join us there in New Orleans, if she could get the time off from work. Ron wrinkled up behind his facial hair and I guessed he might be smiling. Oh wow, we all said, wouldn't that be great.

I contributed to the hilarity, and Shay took my enthusiasm at face value—and no wonder. I myself didn't recognize my qualms. Mardi Gras was still four months away, and New Orleans was thousands of miles from Portland. What were the chances, really, that we'd meet up with this couple in that distant place, in that distant future? Waxing enthusiastic about an encounter that would never take place felt perfectly safe. And since it felt safe, I let myself believe I wanted it to happen.

The next morning, we took off in the Volkswagen bug I had recently acquired from my artist friend Ralph. The car had been green originally, but Ralph had covered every inch of it with vivid, hand painted abstract-expressionist squiggles and splatters. It now looked like a poor man's Jackson Pollock in the shape of an automobile.

It was mid-November. The air was cold and still, and dusk began in mid-afternoon.   Eastern Oregon and Idaho felt mythological in a Norse kind of way. We drove south and we drove east. Oh, what a sense of freedom we enjoyed, tooling down any which highway in the work of art that was my Volkswagen bug.

We knew people in LaGrande so we stopped there. We knew someone in Moscow, Idaho, so we stopped there. We also stopped in Salt Lake City where Shay had grown up. Some high school friend of hers still lived there with his girlfriend, and we must have spent Thanksgiving with them. I remember going out with this couple and their friends one weekend night. Utah was officially a dry state, but in Salt Lake you could join a private club that served liquor. You did this by signing up at the door and paying a membership fee, which was exactly the same as a cover charge anywhere else. Once you paid, a membership card was issued to you on the spot and you walked into a "private club" that looked and felt exactly like a bar or tavern in any other city. As soon as you left, your membership expired, and when you came back, you had to "re-apply."

The club in Salt Lake was a cheerful, rowdy watering hole with a lot of healthy-looking athletic types quaffing Coors. I was having fun until I noticed Shay and her old friend trading a knowing look. A knowing look about what? Jealousy rose up roaring. As a conscious man, however, I caged that rabid beast before it could hurt anyone. So what if Shay and her friend had some private understanding that excluded me? Even if it had to do with sex, who was I to object? Of course, nothing happened between Shay and her friend, and yet I felt relieved to leave Salt Lake behind.

We washed up at Colorado Rocky Mountain School, a.k.a. CRMS, the tiny private high school that had gotten me out of Afghanistan by giving me a full scholarship, including room and board. I had been lonely at this school, mostly because popping out of Afghanistan and plopping into Colorado was a tough transition for a 15-year-old, and all the more so since my family was fragmenting and I knew I was never going back to Kabul. After graduation, however, I had replaced my real memories of CRMS with sentimental images of me and my high school friends playing in the snow, drinking hot chocolate in the lodges in Aspen, and horsing around in the dorms: I transformed my time there into a fairy tale.

The moment we pulled into the parking lot at CRMS, however, the fairy tale popped and I recollected the loneliness. Only for an instant, though, because I was not that person anymore. Now I had Shay. Loneliness was a quaint memory from a distant past. And visiting that old school offered an unexpected gratification: the teachers still remembered and liked me as if I were Someone. We stayed with Ken Hause, my former math teacher, a genius of his profession and a restless intellectual spirit. He introduced us to a landmark book he was reading, *Zen and the Art of Motorcycle Maintenance*, a philosophical journey framed as a physical road trip. He gave us a copy of it before we left. I felt especially at ease with my one-time mentors because they were now my peers and because they included Shay in their warmth. If she was their kind of person, they were my kind of people! And among those red hills and snow-splattered slopes, the issues of a non-monogamous relationship simply didn't come up: no one was hitting on anyone. I could have stayed for months.

Mutual and Obvious

Shay got restless, though, so we moved on and then moved on some more, until we entered Nebraska. You know you're having a good road trip when you can drive all the way across that state without suffering a single second of boredom. Shay and I knew not to drink and drive, but no one had ever warned us against mixing sex and driving, and even if we'd known of such a rule, we would have broken it, because driving didn't take much attention—the road ran like a ruler and traffic was sparse—and because, most importantly Nebraska—well! Nebraska was so arousing.   I'm talking about the endless fields of fertile soil stretching to the lips of a circular earth. Not aroused? Not your kind of porn?   You hadda' be there. In this season, early December, the land had been shaved, even the stubble of crops was gone, but the fields were plowed and ready, and the fecundity of the soil was so obvious, abundance seemed ready to erupt from every inch of that rich, black loam. At least, so it seemed to a couple of people immersed in sexual pleasure while driving.

Then we hit Chicago. Getting from the outer suburbs to the heart of the city took about as long as driving from one end of Nebraska to the other. Chicago was not erotic. Here, you could not even exchange one short French kiss while driving. Even when you were doing nothing wrong, someone was honking. Even when you were focusing intently, you were getting lost. We would have driven straight through except that we had someone I wanted to crash with here: my one-time beloved Lily and her new guy Ted. I had written to say we might be coming, and Lily had written back to say oh, by all means, yes, come visit.

In person, her welcome felt more muted. Lily and Ted were living in a cramped apartment in some gritty neighborhood with wide and filthy streets flanked by endless rows of buildings, five or six stories high, all of them made of bricks that might once have been orange but had grimed to grey.

With them, we mostly sat around as a foursome and made awkward conversation. Lily and Ted had jobs as social workers and came home every day beat to shit exhausted. After dinner, they put on thick, shapeless, matching robes. Each one seemed totally in charge of the other. Neither could make a move without the other one's consent. I couldn't remember ever seeing two people our age so suffocated by one another. This was the life

Shay and I had rejected, the prison cell out of which we had broken. All the travails of non-monogamy seem a small price to pay for not being this couple.

Ted aspired to greater freedom, but Lily set the rules, and her rules sent them to bed at exactly the same time each night. They had a gigantic pendulum clock in a corner of their small apartment, which bonged out the hours, every hour on the hour. Each set of bongs made me tense up in anticipation of the next set. The worst were the eleven o'clock bongs, becuase one knew the twelve clangs of midnight were coming but not for an hour: there was no chance of falling asleep in that hour. If Lily and I had stayed together, this would have been my life.

Lily and Ted wanted us to wrap up our day and go to bed when they did, but officially we were welcome to come and go as we pleased. We figured the best way to avoided disturbing our hosts was to go out every evening looking for adventure.

We had taken some dope along on this road trip—just four joints: we intended to pick four iconic moments to memorialize by getting stoned. This meant deciding beforehand whether an outing would deserve to be memorialized. We decided to make our last night in Chicago our first iconic moment. Our plan was to hit a cocktail lounge we had heard about, at the top of the recently completed John Hancock building, the tallest building in the world, taller even than the Empire State if you counted the antenna spires.

The lounge was not at the very top but damned close, and from its big plate-glass windows, we seemed to be hovering at least a mile above Chicago which stretched to the horizon in every direction, an immense black tapestry studded with sparkles. Height alone was not what made this night such a bright moment. What was it, then? Well, we were a couple of scruffy kids from Portland and this was such a sophisticated, adult thing to do. We even got dressed up for the occasion. "Dressed up" meant something different to us than it did for the bulk of the patrons at the top-of-the-world lounge. They were wearing suits and evening gowns. We were wearing gorgeous colors and feathers and rhinestone shawls and hand painted ties. I'm sure the other people thought we were circus clowns, but what did we care? Shay was very girly-girl in her vividly red and purple velvet dress, but we understood that this was a costume, not submission to a gender stereotype. She was playing a part, putting on an image, inside which she was the same feminist powerhouse I loved, a human being who could never be possessed. Just for tonight, however, to enhance the fictional feel of it all, she would let me curl her in my embrace and behave as though she were "mine" in the old fashioned sense.

A jazz combo was playing, and though we'd never heard of them, you can bet the musicians playing in the cocktail lounge on the 98th floor of the world's tallest building were not some amateur garage band. In real life we only drank beer and wine, but here in this fiction of being adults, we ordered cocktails. We didn't know from drinks, but Shay had heard of something called a "Brandy Alexander," so we ordered a couple of those, and they were so delicious, we ordered a couple more.

The capper came when people started gliding out of their seats to do something I associated with movies from the forties: they danced. I don't mean the kind of dancing we did back home in Portland, where dancing meant each person twisted, jerked, and writhed on their own in time to the music. Here at the top of the John Hancock, people were doing the waltz! Yes, men were holding women in their arms and twirling gracefully around the floor, each couple making much the same moves as all the others.

As it happened, my mother had insisted on teaching me ballroom dancing when I was a kid, one of several ways she thought to keep me connected to her culture. So I knew how to waltz, foxtrot, polka, you name it. Shay didn't, but she could follow, so I held her in my arms and we waltzed the night away, Cary Grant and Audrey Hepburn in a movie called *Road Trip*.

We went home to find Lily and Ted crumpled on the couch in their bulky bathrobes, their heads swathed in turban-like towels, looking disgruntled. They were all showered up and ready for bed but had decided to wait up for us, since this was to be our last night with them. We'd fucked up their schedule by staying out so late, but they weren't going to make any overt complaints.

We told them about our night on the town and they talked about their day at work. I looked at Lily sitting across from me with her knees tucked under, droning on about her drab job, and I could not help but marvel. How could I ever have thought that what I felt for her was love? This incredible thing I had with Shay was the real thing. How could I ever have confused what I felt for Lily with *this?*

I don't remember what took us to Boston but I remember the art exhibit we stumbled upon there, the nation's first major exhibit of photorealism. Each painting rendered, with absolute precision, a scene from everyday American life: a woman washing a car in some suburb, an escalator in a mall, a pimped out 1957 Chevy at a drive-in. I saw no reason to keep looking at these paintings, and yet I could not look away.

"Usually," Shay mused, "when you like a painting, you're thinking wow: I've never seen anything like *that* before. But here, you're thinking wow, I've seen *that* before. Somehow that's what makes it good."

She took the words right out of my mind. But then, gazing at Bechtle, Estes, Goings et al, I realized something more. Every other work of art I had seen either looked down at the world or up at the world. It either revealed unappreciated beauty or exposed unsuspected ugliness. Either it was praising or it was criticizing; either it was glorifying or it was crucifying. The art in this show stood right at eye level with its subject, looked at it head on, and added no comment. The attitude, if any, was yours. The judgment, if any? Yours.

I remembered the epiphany I had at Chris Montague's house in Utah, as I was falling asleep that night: life felt good, life felt bad, but what was life really? The answer: neither. Both. No way of knowing which way the scales tipped. The evidence would never tell you. The evidence would always go both ways. What was the world out there *really* like? No way to see "the world out there" except through the filter of your own eyes, your own life story.

I looked at Shay standing next to me. What was happening with us? Were we at this moment in the process of losing each other? The evidence went both ways. The evidence always would. The choice was mine: I could believe in us or give in to doubt. What I chose would alter what was real in ways I could not predict, control, or know.

The Others

My mother lived in a Washington DC suburb called Laurel. When we got there, a letter was waiting for Shay. Not from Helga, not from Ron and Helga, nor even from the two of them to the two of us. No, this letter was just from Ron and just to Shay. She opened it that evening and read it slowly, then wrote in her journal for a long while. And I wrote in mine. Perhaps she was writing to Ron, I didn't know. I didn't ask. Asking would have intruded on her privacy, which would have violated our ethos.

Both my siblings had come home for Christmas. My mother and my sister Rebecca were meeting Shay for the first time. When we opened presents Christmas morning, Shay got a dress my mother had made. My mother was a good seamstress, but she had some odd ideas from time to time and this dress she gave Shay was one of them. It was made of many colorful patches of fabric painstakingly sewn together, and Shay looked chunky in it. I have pictures of her posing for family snapshots in my mother's gift, looking resigned.

It never occurred to me that Shay's presence here could be interpreted as an audition. To my mother, however, here was the woman with whom I might spend my life, the woman who, in any other context, would be called a wife. How could I explain to her that "wife" was a disrespectful term, that this was not even my "girlfriend" (another disrespectful term) but my Primary Relationship?

Girlfriend was disrespectful because it contained the word "girl." A conscious man never called a grown woman a girl. I could not remember the last time I had called a female of *any* age a girl. I was shocked, therefore, when my mother took me aside one day to say, with a cheerful grin, "Shay is not what I expected. In your letters you kept calling her a woman. She's not a *woman*!"

"She's not? What is she?"

"She's a *girl!*"

I looked around furtively, hoping Shay had not overheard my mother's shocking gaffe.

The day after Christmas, Shay and I decided to smoke the second of our iconic joints and go hear Dizzy Gillespie at the Cavern, a D.C. jazz club. We included Riaz in our plan because he was one of our kind: he listened to rock and jazz, he smoked weed—he went to Evergreen State, after all. We never dreamed of inviting my sister Rebecca along (much less my mother!) because, I mean, for heaven's sake! really! Their music was Streisand and Sinatra, Mozart and Schubert. Why would we take them?

Dizzy Gillespie lived up to his legendary reputation. He blew us out of our front row seats. We went home transported—only to find my mother and sister waiting up in their pajamas, looking very much like Ted and Lily the night we came home from the John Hancock Building. Our glowing, grinning radiance seemed to ruffle my mother. I assumed she was taking exception to us being stoned. Many months later, in a letter, she told me no, she was upset that we had left Rebecca out of our expedition.

But even that wasn't the actual story. It took me years to realize that the real source of her foul mood that night might have been Shay.

Well, not Shay per se, but what Shay represented. My family had already been split by the divergence between Afghanistan and America, a divergence that had carried my father out of our lives. Now apparently it had split again. Shay and I, as well as Riaz, belonged to one culture. Rebecca and my mother belonged to another. We were part of that mystical band that not only knew something was happening but were making it happen. My mother and sister were out there in the cold with Mr. Jones: they didn't know what it was. They were not part of the community. They were going to be among the Left-Behinds. Shay represented the culture that turned my mother and sister into outsiders.

We left D.C. before New Years in a gloomy mood, but the clouds lifted as soon as we were once again tooling down the highway without a destination or a care, crammed together in that cozy little VW, alone with each other, each the other's lover and best friend, the one person so privy to the other's secrets that we were practically the same person.

How marvelous that in spite of such a bond—thanks to our daring experiment in multiple relationshipping—each of us was able to make the other person more free. How many couples could say that?

Descending through the greenery of Virginia, we basked in a companionship that rendered words unnecessary, content to merely gaze at the scenery and, on our periodic stops and side trips, marvel at the shifting cultural ambiance.

At a no-name diner near Richmond, for example, where we stopped for some fried chicken, Shay noticed that every "salad" on the menu featured meat: chicken strips, ham, bacon. I noticed that all the sandwiches were named after confederate generals, the most elaborate of them being the Robert E. Lee. Never anywhere had I seen a sandwich named after a Union general.

Everywhere else in America, the Civil War was part of history but here in the South it felt like part of daily life. I knew about Vicksburg and Shiloh and Antietam, but here, every few miles, we passed the site of some Civil War battle I'd never heard of, at places like Proctor's Creek, Boynton Plank Road, Drewery's Bluff, or Peeble's Farm. When we needed groceries, we got it from a place called Winn-Dixie. Yes, even the supermarkets seemed to still be cheering their side in a war that ended a hundred years ago.

One time, I asked a local about some curious plants I noticed bristling in a ditch and he gave me an earful. These weeds, he said, appeared after Sherman marched his army from Atlanta to the sea, ravaging the land so utterly that nothing else would grow in this soil. "In the north, y'all can forget the War Between the States," he scowled. "Down here, even the weeds'll remind you."

That sense of entering a foreign country deepened as we drove. The soil turned red as we crossed into Georgia and then kept growing redder. The air grew ever heavier and more moist.

At gas stations and grocery stores, restaurants and motels, people's speech slowed down until we could barely make out what anyone was saying.

We passed through cities that looked burned out. Smack dab in the middle of Montgomery, the poverty felt rural and this poverty had a color. In the north, African Americans were sequestered in ghettos. Here, black people were ubiquitously visible, but always in menial roles: mopping floors, cleaning toilets, shining shoes.

Then, at some gas station, when the attendant asked me how many gallons we wanted, his accent startled me. He had no southern drawl. His syllables were clipped. Each whole sentence had a musical lilt. We had crossed another border. We were in Cajun country now.

I had always thought of myself as the foreigner, not because I was from another culture but because "foreign" *was* my culture. In Afghanistan I was the American kid, in America the Afghan kid. Everywhere, I was The Other, which was probably why I embraced the newly-minted culture of those Americans who called themselves "freaks"— to me, being a freak felt normal. But here, both Shay and I found ourselves submerged in so many layers of otherness, it was eerie. The south was like a foreign country within the United States, this corner of Louisiana was like a foreign country to the south, and we were foreign to both layers, to all three if you counted American mainstream culture. All this foreignness shut Shay and me into a bubble of shared privacy, the intimacy of which I found ravishing.

New Orleans

We pulled into New Orleans on a Saturday afternoon and got ourselves a cheap motel room just outside the French Quarter, five minutes' walk from Bourbon Street. If a Motel 8 is somewhat classier than a Motel 6, this must have been a Motel 4.   All we had was a cheerless bed, a stick or two of graceless furniture and an uninviting bathroom. No TV but who needed TV? Bourbon Street was five minutes from the door. Even with the door closed, the jazz came wafting in. As soon as we had unloaded the minimum we rushed out to find excitement.

Being in New Orleans was like the realest possible experience of pretending to be in New Orleans. It was much like that time my father took me along to find the alabaster mountains beyond the Desert of Death and I played that I was in the world of *King Solomon's Mines*. Here, sitting at a sidewalk cafe, looking at the row of houses across the street, red bricks, black window frames, blue shutters, the wraparound second story porches fenced with ornate balustrades of wrought iron painted white, I was in a Faulkner novel or even was myself another Faulkner, dissipated and brilliant, tossing back booze and pouring out masterpieces, the only difference being that I was not pouring out masterpieces.

I was writing, but only in the journal I would be trading with Shay when this road trip ended. I tried to write with no regard for her reactions, the whole point being to pour thoughts so uncensored into these private receptacles that when we traded journals, we'd truly be giving each other the gift of our deepest, most authentic selves.

And while I wrote, Shay was writing too. Writing in our journals had become a way of spending silent, companionable time together. Scritchety scritch scritch. A way of sharing.

Though not a perfect way. Perfect would have been if we were two lovers so infatuated with each other that no one else existed for either of us, in which case we would always know who the other was writing about and the only question would have been: what are they saying? For two consciously non-monogamous people multiple-relationshipping, the activity had a hitch. We never knew who the other was writing about. Looking up from my notebook, I'd see Shay utterly absorbed, a faint smile clinging to her lips, and it would give me a shudder. What if she was writing about *him?* Then she'd frown and I would quail. What if now she was writing about *me?*

That night, we had a good time strolling on Bourbon Street, but the next morning Shay reminded me that Ron and Helga were coming to join us here for Mardi Gras, which was still a month away, so shouldn't we settle in a little, find a room and some temporary jobs?

We checked out the Times-Picayune: no jobs. We looked for sublets: none to be found. We tooled around town looking for New Orleans's version of the Scribe. Surely every good-sized city had a newspaper with classified ads placed by communal houses seeking roommates and columns on how to live for free on stew made from road kill, and updates on revolutionary workers' actions around the country. But no: New Orleans seemed to have no such rag.

What we needed, we decided, was to find "our people". We figured they'd be around the universities, so we took buses to Xavier, Loyola, and Tulane, but roaming those massive, immaculate campuses, we saw nothing but buttoned down students headed for law school and business careers. There were no coffeehouses, no leaflets tacked to telephone poles announcing demonstrations against The Machine, no organic grocery stores—the apocalyptic sense of an old civilization crumbling and a new one rising—the essential flavor of Portland—did not exist here. Perhaps—chilling thought—it didn't exist anywhere outside of Portland.

Most of New Orleans seemed to be a buttoned-down Catholic wasteland, so we decided to stick to the French Quarter and enjoy whatever it offered.   Surely we could wring a month's worth of enjoyment out of this place.   Mardi Gras was still weeks away, but the French Quarter was already crazy jammed. Was it always like this? No, someone told us. This weekend was special because an "important" football game was coming up. The concept of a football game being "important" made us smile. This particular game was called the "Super Cup" or the "Super Bowl" or some such. Whatever it was called, this impending game had turned the French Quarter into one big street party.

But there was less to the carnival than met the eye. The French Quarter boiled down to endless iterations of the same four attractions: music bars, eateries, souvenir stores, and strip joints. Every night we wormed our way into crowded venues to listen to the music New Orleans is famous for. All the bars had bands, all the bands were good, and all of them were playing Dixieland jazz. If all you ever wanted to hear was Dixieland Jazz, this was the place.

We were foodies long before the term was invented, and New Orleans was food heaven. From Brennan's with its turtle soup to Antoine's with its white tablecloths to funky dives specializing in frog's legs to red beans and rice from a street vendor's cart, it was all to die for. But a person can only eat so much food.

We avoided the souvenir shops because, like all tourists, we said (indignantly) "We're not tourists."

Which left strip joints. Portland had only a handful of such places, all clustered on streets where derelicts hung out in ragged clothes, sharing wine bottles and beating each other up, in front of porno movie theaters that looked too filthy to enter and adult bookstores that were all, for some reason, painted yellow. But in New Orleans's French Quarter, the sexual objectification of women (and men) was considered a charming tourist attraction. The strip clubs were right there among the hoity-toity restaurants and clubs featuring exquisite jazz.   They projected a sanitized naughty.   They all had barkers who kept opening the doors to afford glimpses of naked flesh undulating inside. The moment a door was opened, a line of gawkers formed right across to the opposite sidewalk.   The gawkers were perfectly respectable-looking people of all ages, men and women, young and old, Americans and foreigners, ogling and craning over one another's shoulders. When a barker deemed his line long enough, he shut the door and began singing his spiel: "Come on in, folks, two dolluh cover, cheap at twice the price, bring both your wives, heh heh. Your girlfriend too."

Persistent glimpses of nudity blending with the sounds of jazz and the aroma of gumbos formed a rich broth of sensory arousal. Sex, however, was like saffron: even a little bit and the whole dish tastes like saffron. Here in the French Quarter of New Orleans, there was more than a little pinch. Sex bathed the crowds and mingled with the music, flavored the food, colored the blinking signage, permeated the street and spurted out in the croaks and bleats of the hawkers and barkers. It goaded us into a state of constant erotic agitation that wasn't actually pleasant. I began to crave release, but Shay, ever the optimist, thought we should give New Orleans more time. Once we got settled, we'd discover layers of truth and beauty not apparent to the naked eye. I didn't trust her optimism. I worried that she might be clinging to New Orleans only because Ron was coming and she wanted to be here for him. This suspicion was like those weeds that sprang up in the wake of Sherman's armies. Once it sprouted, nothing could kill it.

One day that important football game was played and that night the Quarter went particularly insane. Shay decided our problem with New Orleans was money--we weren't spending enough. We vowed to spend $50 apiece by midnight or die trying. In 1974, a seven-course meal at the most expensive restaurant meal in Portland cost seven dollars so... you do the math.

We smoked the third of our iconic joints and waded into the chaos of Bourbon Street. A black man was tap dancing on the sidewalk for coins. An anachronistically hairy hippie guy was thwacking at a guitar and screaming: "Wild thing! You make my heart sing." Women on balconies were snatching up their shirts to reveal their breasts. College boys were crashing through the crowds in sweating herds. The streets were full of hot dog vendors, pushing carts shaped like hot dogs in buns, drooling mustard, and I wondered how in God's name they could make money—who would buy a hot dog in a place so redolent with the fragrance of jambalaya? Then I got it, and it wasn't just me. Shay saw it too. The carts were giant simulacrums of penises. These vendors weren't selling hot dogs, they were selling arousal like everyone else. "Only in New Orleans," Shay beamed.

The two of us pushed into a jam-packed hole-in-the-wall for some seafood gumbo, and if food were sex, this would have been orgasm. At one point, we lifted our forks to our mouths at the same moment and Shay chuckled, because she had a crab leg poised on her fork and I had a crab leg poised on mine. "Looking at you is like looking in a mirror," she said.

I heard that as a bigger truth. For two months now, we had been right next to each other 24/7. Everything I had seen, she had seen, and from very nearly the same point in space. Our perspective had differed by two feet. Our moods had gotten synchronized. If I was tired, she was tired. If I had just woken up refreshed, she had just woken up refreshed. If she was sick, I certainly didn't feel good. To know how I felt, I could look at her.

I longed already for that future moment when we would trade journals. I wanted to be on the other side of that mirror, reading her account of this moment. I wanted to be inside her in a way that even sex could not enable: I wanted to be looking out through her eyes, at me.

Then Shay said it. "We've only been here, what: a week? And Mardi Gras is still..."

"I know. A month away."

"A whole month," she said. "I've been thinking..."

"You've been thinking?"

"Yes. We're having fun right now but I don't know. A month in this place? I don't know if I can take it. I was thinking we could write to Ron and Helga and tell them how awful it is. They'll understand if we move on..."

My heart turned somersaults. "Move on to where?"

"I don't know. Someplace quiet. You have any ideas?"

I did, actually. I had an idea. A year or two earlier, on a trip to Mexico, my brother Riaz had spent a few days at a place called Tulum. When he came back, he described it as paradise. He said the corruptions of civilization were unknown there. He said the beach was the cleanest he'd ever seen and the water so warm, you could swim in it at night. Tulum, he told us, was the last refuge of the Mayans, the place to which they fled after their great cities of Uxmal and Chichen Itza had been destroyed, the place where nobody could find them. A place where nobody could find us. It was situated halfway down the end of the thumb that is the Yucatan Peninsula. To get to it you had to go to Villa Hermosa and from there take a ring road that hugged the coast. If you went one way, you passed through Merida and approached Tulum from the north. If you chose the other direction, you went through Chetumal and approached Tulum from the south. Either way, Tulum was the furthest you get to anywhere in Mexico from anywhere in the United States. Once you passed Tulum, you were on your way back.

"How about Tulum?" I said.

Ends of the Earth

Once we boarded the bus for Villa Hermosa, my cares dropped away. Now at last Shay and I were headed for the ends of the earth where we could be with no one but each other. On the bus, we were surrounded by Spanish conversations we couldn't understand. All the foreignness compressed us again into a bubble of shared intimacy. When the bus stopped at dusty little towns, we disembarked to buy tamales and churritos from street vendors and felt pleasantly dusty.

Unfortunately, what we'd boarded was a local bus, which stopped in every town and village. People got off and on at every stop, but the bus always ended up packed. The others could take it, as they were only going twenty or thirty miles. We were going the full thousand, to Villa Hermosa. For us the ride turned brutal. The seats were narrow, the windows wouldn't open, and we were on that bus all day, all night, all the next day, and much of the next night. It was during that 1000 mile ordeal that Shay told me, guess what: when she'd called Ron and Helga to tell them we were leaving New Orleans, they'd decided they'd try to meet up with us in Tulum. Cool, huh?

I tried to calm my nerves. What were the chances Ron and Helga would connect with us? They'd have to leave right away, they'd have to fly to Mexico City and take a bus, and then in Tulum, they'd have to find us. Even we didn't know where we'd be staying there: our guide book didn't mention Tulum and the travel agency in Brownsville couldn't give us a list of the hotels. Our plan was just to get there and then see. No, no, where we were going--*the last refuge of the Mayans*--Ron and Helga would never find us. No chance. None.

At Villa Hermosa, we spent several midnight hours in a grungy station. When we finally climbed onto the bus heading into the Yucatan, it was so late, it was early. I could hardly doze on that rattling vehicle, slumped against Shay, who may have dozed a bit, slumped against me. In Chetumal, I surfaced just long enough to register an impression of tidy, pastel-colored adobe houses gliding past the windows and of dawn breaking over the Caribbean Sea, a sight that somehow made me sad.

The next time I woke up, the bus was still jam-packed but our fellow passengers no longer looked like the folks up north. We had entered Mayan territory. The men were small of stature with smooth brown skin and round, beardless faces. Virtually all the women wore white dresses with a flame of brilliantly colorful, floral embroidery at the neckline. Everyone was silent and solemn and seemed faintly melancholy.

An old man across the aisle from us had three live chickens bound together at the ankles. He was carrying them upside down as a single item. Once in a while the chickens flapped and squawked, but for the most part they accepted their fate quietly.

Around noon, a man with a rifle boarded the bus, dragging a dead animal behind him, a ring-tailed jungle cat of some kind, which left a thin, smelly trail of blood behind as the man made his way up the aisle.

Outside, there was nothing to see. The bus hurled along in a monotonous corridor cut through a jungle so dense that nothing was visible on either side but a seamless facade of green. We saw no towns or villages, and yet the bus stopped every so often for people waiting patiently by the side of the road.

The pitted two-lane blacktop narrowed to one lane eventually, and then the asphalt gave way to gravel. The bus slowed down, rocking and creaking as it moved over this rutted surface. Finally it stopped. I peered out. No one was waiting by the side of the road, and there was still nothing to see out there except jungle. The driver leaned out of his seat and called toward the back: "Tulum, gringos!"

We looked around for these gringos, but saw only Mayans. Who were these gringos? "Tulum!" our fellow passengers clamored.

Oh. We were the gringos? We stumbled out into broiler-level heat, dragging our suitcases along. The bus took off in a spurt of gravel, leaving us at a featureless crossroads. From where we were standing, one road ran north, one south, one east and another west, all four flanked by an impenetrable wall of jungle, all four shrinking to a vanishing point. Gertrude Stein wasted a good phrase on Oakland. It must have been Tulum she meant when she said "There is no there there."

"We'll have to get on the next bus." I muttered. "Get to Merida somehow or back to Chetumal, whichever bus comes first."

But Shay said, "Hold on." She ambled a few paces east, on the road that ran toward the sea. "What's that?"

I looked where she was pointing and saw a little cantina tucked into the jungle. It was little more than a patio, really, under a thatched roof held aloft by poles, but it had about twenty little tables, most of them occupied. The babble we heard when we got close was international: Swedish, German, French—every European country seemed to have coughed up at least one backpacking Bohemian to luxuriate in this spot. We stood clutching our suitcases and gawking until a tiny waiter in a dusty little suit came zipping up. In this heat, a suit.

He showed us to a table and slapped down menus but we couldn't tell what anything was, and our phrasebook didn't help. Its minimal dictionary told us *ropa viejo* meant "old clothes" which surely couldn't be right. It told us *filette de res* was meat but not what kind of meat. I couldn't stop picturing that ring-tailed jungle cat on the bus. Finally, from the beverage column, we ordered two "soldados" ("soldiers" according to our phrasebook) and from the food column a couple of "mantequillas," whatever they were. The waiter looked astonished and tried to talk us into buying something more, but we weren't falling for his sales pitch. "Mantequillas," we insisted firmly.

Soldados turned out to be cold chocolate milk in bottles shaped like tin soldiers. Delicious! Mantequillas, it turned out, was butter. We each got a big pat. That's when we broke down and ordered the extra item the waiter had been pushing: tortillas.

An English-speaking French couple at a nearby table told us there was no actual town hereabouts. The crossroads and this cantina—this was it. Tulum referred only to some small nearby set of Mayan ruins that no one ever visited. Bohemians came here because one could walk to the beach and camp anywhere. Shay and I enjoyed a good chuckle at our own naive stupidity, scarfed down our simple meal, and started trudging east, lugging our entirely inappropriate suitcases. The road ran between two wide trenches filled with slimy green water and amazing heaps of rotting household garbage that must all have come from that single cantina. The jungle had been cut way back from the moats, but one could almost feel it growing back. It was still too far away to provide the least bit of shade on the road, however. The sun beat down like a hammer and the extra bottles of soldado were soon gone. Getting to the sea turned out to be an ordeal.

Our road dead-ended not at the beach but at a wall of vegetation. We could smell the water, but it was on the other side of a tangle of greenery that might have made me think of Joseph Conrad, if only heat, dust and thirst had not stripped me of all capacity to think.

"We have to get to the water," Shay croaked.

"How? We can't go around this jungle!" I moaned. "It might go on for miles."

"We'll have to go through."

She was right, of course. There was no real entry point, but the brush did thin out a little in one place and it was there that we pushed in. The beach could not have been more than 50 feet from the road, but 50 feet of tropical jungle is a lot when your only instrument for chopping through it is your body. We struggled with vines and fought bugs, and the thing is, improbably enough, it started to feel like fun. The jungle was tropical the way it is in the movies, with the wildlife screeching and cawing from a thousand bursting overflows of vegetation, and I was Tarzan of the Apes, and here was my apple-cheeked Jane, determined as hell, pushing and struggling next to me or just ahead of me, her face aglow with anticipation.

When we broke through to the beach, the sight left us gasping. Our highest hopes fell short of this. What met our eyes was the cover of the first Tarzan book, come to life, the one I read when I was 12 and shared with my buddy Ralph. He and I had talked then about finding that beach someday, and living there, and at 12, we couldn't tell if that was an impossible fantasy or one of many possible life choices, like deciding to become a dentist. Now it turned it wasn't a fantasy at all, because here I was, and with my best friend, who wasn't Ralph, as it turned out, but Shay.

The real-life scene had, however, one tremendous advantage over any book cover. No piece of art could convey the color of the light given off by that sea: the luminescence that saturated the air and washed over the world. It looked green when you were thinking blue and blue when you switched to green. Later, when I tried to do a painting of that sea, I discovered traces of yellow in that blue, and orange, and even black.

Here by the beach, the sun shed the same bombastic light but not the same heat. The sand was always mysteriously cool to the touch and soft as powdered milk, and just as white.

We did not set up a campsite or unpack. We just dropped our gear, shed our clothes, and dove into the water. Naked? You bet. Why not? We were utterly alone. Oh, there had to be others in this wilderness, we'd seen so many of those young European Bohemian backpacker types at the cantina, but the jungle was so vast that hundreds of such groups might be scattered through it without any of us seeing any of the others.

We swam till the sea sank below the treetops and the heat lost its edge, and then got out—only to discover another way in which this scene differed from any book cover or post card. Our towels were sandy, so we couldn't dry off. Swimming in salt water left our skin itchy, but we couldn't alleviate it by scratching. The heat had dropped, but the humidity remained so high, the air felt like someone else's breath. What we saw was still beautiful, but what we felt was sticky, icky, sandy, sweaty and itchy.

"This is fun, huh," Shay grinned. "We're so good together. Aren't we, Tamim? I swear! This wouldn't be fun with anyone else."

"Fun" wasn't what I had been thinking, but as soon as she said it, I felt it. Sticky, sweaty, itchy, and icky was all just part of the adventure. Even Tarzan must have felt this way at times. Being anywhere with Shay was fun. As long as Ron wasn't there.

We didn't have a tent, we didn't have any sleeping bags, but we didn't need them. We'd bought a double-hammock along the way. Right where the sand met the jungle, I found two trees spaced conveniently apart and we slung our hammock between them. Nearby was a patch of sand that would always be in the shade. In the heat of the day, we could spread our towels there and nap, or loll, or read, or write in our journals. Perfect.

The heat had waned enough that we could trek back to the cantina for dinner and another round of soldados. Money was no object: the peso was so cheap, we could order anything on the menu. But just as I was getting ready to head back to the beach, Shay got busy writing something in a page that she had torn from her journal.

"What are you doing?"

"Writing a note for Ron and Helga."

I had almost forgotten about them

"Ron and Helga are never going to make it to Tulum," I chuckled. "Even if they do, how are they going to find your note?"

"We made a plan."

"We? A plan? What plan? Who's 'we?'"

"Helga and me. And Ron. We said whoever gets here first should leave a note somewhere and mark it with something blue." She rummaged in her luggage and pulled out a handful of blue ribbons. "See?"

I nodded, trying not to look sullen, and helped Shay find a good place to leave her note. Then I watched silently as she tied one of her blue ribbons to it.

"What's wrong?" said Shay. "Cheer up, it's going to be okay. They'll find us."

"I'm just not feeling cheerful."

Shay didn't ask why. She knew there were topics we could not afford to step on here. "Smile," she suggested. "If you act cheerful, you'll feel cheerful."

"I don't know how to smile."

"Use the Stanislavski method. Think of something funny. You can think of something funny, can't you?"

I pictured Ron and Helga boarding the wrong bus and riding along completely unaware that they were headed for Guatemala.

"See?" Shay exulted. "It works!"

The Paradox

When we climbed into our hammock that first night, we discovered yet another flaw in paradise. The hammock wasn't designed to hold two people at a time, even though it was called a "double hammock". The moment we got in, it sagged into a mesh-screen cocoon that wrapped around us so tightly, we became like a single immobilized organism with two heads facing in different directions: neither of us able to move independently—or, indeed, at all.

Then the mosquitoes started in. Dangling in mid-air in a bag of mesh made us like shish kebab on a spit for them, open to assault from every side. They feasted on our scalps and gorged on our feet. Because of the heat, we had made the mistake of wearing very little, so they could access our deepest crannies and most hidden places.

I could not turn my head, but the 'skeeters passing before my eyes looked as huge as helicopters. One fed on my hand, inches from my eyes, and I couldn't move. I simply had to watch its belly swell to the size of a pea. By the time it took off, it was too heavy to fly. Flapping its futile wings, it spiraled down until it crashed in a splish of blood.

Then, in the light of a full moon, I noticed that the ground below our hammock seemed to be in constant shimmering motion, like the waves of a black sea, which frightened me until I realized what I was looking at: insects, endless varieties of insects, scurrying every which way. We must have been very close to the world headquarters of insect research and development. One bug the size of a thumb had an ant-like back end, but a head that was big and round and pink, like a baby's. The locals, I learned later, called these creepy creatures *ninos de los terras*: "Earth babies." I wasn't scared but I was grossed out; and I stayed grossed out until

I saw an enormous black scorpion scuttle across an open space. Then I was scared.

By the second morning, we had mosquito bites everywhere. By the third, we had mosquito bites on our mosquito bites. We spent our days waist-deep in the salt water to soothe the itching, but we spent our nights in a nightmare Neverland of buzzing, scratching, and fitful dreaming.

We couldn't leave, however, because Ron and Helga were coming. It wouldn't be nice to desert them. Every day, therefore, around one o'clock we walked to the cantina to meet the bus. It was the hottest hour of the day, and the worst time to walk to the crossroads, and the bus wasn't actually due until around two-thirty, but we couldn't take a chance on missing them. While we waited, we ate lunch, guzzled soldados, and wrote in our journals. When the bus came, Ron and Helga were never on it. Sometimes, to avoid making the same trek twice in one day, we ate an early dinner—often ropa viejos, which turned out not to be old rags, but a tasty dish made of shredded meat—and then returned to our jungle nest. On the way back, Shay usually found another conspicuous spot to leave a note marked with another of her blue ribbons.

Paradise had another flaw: it was dull. Not as dull as the Sant Bani Ashram, but close. There wasn't much to do except stare at the lovely sea and swim in the placid water. The ruins provided about one afternoon's worth of amusement. Tulum was not a city like Chichen Itza but a single complex: a few pyramids and a smattering of buildings with oddly tiny doorways as if the place were built by giants, for children.

One day we procured a few groceries from a "nearby" village. "Nearby" meant two miles, a monstrous trek in that heat. The village was a collection of small huts inhabited by subsistence farmers, some of whom had a few surplus items for sale. We bought some finger-sized bananas and a yam-like root. One hut did have a table set up outside its front door, with a random assortment of Scandinavian canned goods on display, each of them one of a kind. From that family, we bought several tins of Norwegian meat.

That night, we built a small fire to roast our vegetable and heat our meat, which brought nocturnal insects surging in, the moonlight glinting off their millions of glistering legs and wings. After dinner, Shay crawled to the edge of our campsite to throw away our banana peels, whereupon, "Hey!" came her guttural whisper. "Tamim! Come here! Look." I crept up next to her on my hands and knees. In the beam of her flashlight crouched a jungle cat about three feet long, with black stripes on its nose and a tail that made rustling sounds slapping against the bushes. It blinked into our light. We stared back. It was close enough to touch, but we didn't try to touch it. There was no hostility between us, but the cat was reluctant to leave. I guess it smelled the canned meat and wanted some. We stood our ground, however, and the cat finally slunk away.

That close encounter stirred us both. Afterward we discussed why we had confronted it. "The hunger has made us feral," I speculated. "That scrap of meat it wanted? That was *our* little scrap of meat, goddamn it."

Shay smiled. "Maybe Ron and Helga will bring something better to eat. Honestly, I am so hungry."

The lyricism of the moment died. I wished Shay had not spoken those two names. Then again ... *I'm not in this world to live up to your expectations and you're not here to live up to mine.* Wasn't that the premise of our relationship? And the glory of it?

Shay noticed my silence. "Now what's wrong?"

I fed a damp twig into our tiny fire and watched it smoke. "I'm wondering what's going to happen if they ever come."

"If who comes?"

"Who do you think. Are you going to sleep with him here?"

"You don't have any reason to be jealous," she murmured. "You are my primary relationship."

"Will you, though? Just tell me."

"I don't know." I could feel her closing up. closing me out, resisting the intrusion of my demand. "How can I know?" She shook her head in frustration. "I can't predict how I'm going to feel in some future moment. Even if I do—I've told you—it doesn't mean he's more important to me. You're two different people! It's two different relationships!"

But I couldn't let it go. "I'm having some trouble with this."

"Oh, no," she said softly. "All things considered, I think you're being very good about all this. You're strong. Emotionally strong."

I used to bask in this kind of praise, but the pride wasn't kicking in this time. She was wrong about my strength. "It can't go on like this." I couldn't help how sullen I sounded.

"It's hard right now, but think how it will be," she said, "once we learn to *do* this kind of relationship. Once we master it." Then she added, "You are, you know: still my primary relationship."

The word *still* made me queasy. "You say that now, but how will you feel a month from now? A year from now? Tell me it won't be Ron a year from now. Promise me."

She was silent for a moment. It was like the silence that follows a sonic boom. What I was asking went against every belief we held dear. No one could know how they would feel in the future. Nothing could be worse than shackling the impulses of the future to the needs of the now. Civilization was crumbling, and no one could know how anything would be a year from now, or two years from now, or ten. Adaptability was the cardinal virtue: a boundless willingness to embrace change. Blocking another person's freedom to grow by asking them to pledge their future self to the needs of this passing moment was ... the cardinal vice.

Shay's eyes had gone bleak. It's curious that four decades later, I still remember a momentary expression in another person's eyes. "I don't know how I will feel a year from now," she ground out. "You can't ask me to make a promise like that. It's not what we do. You're so good about never crowding me. Now you're crowding me."

But I was tired of being good. "This is going to break us up," I predicted. I said it because I knew I actually was important to her. I said it was a threat.

She shook her head. She would not let go of her optimism. She would not stop believing in my generosity, my greatness of spirit. "We'll get through this," she vowed. "We'll come out of this stronger. Trust me."

"I trust you. I do trust you, I will trust you," I said. "But you have to promise me you won't violate my trust."

Another long silence ensued. Finally: "If that's what you want me to promise," she said, "It means you don't trust me."

She had a point. We had reached the paradox that could never be resolved.

Crossroads

Staying in Tulum was pointless after that. We hung on for another day or two, but soon enough we swam in the Caribbean for the last time and shortly after that dragged our silly suitcases to the crossroads to catch the bus to Merida. All along the way, I noticed blue ribbons we had tied to bushes, but we didn't collect them. For a conscious man, I was strangely unaware of how disconsolate I felt. I only knew how Shay felt: I knew she felt hot and spent and mosquito bitten, and I figured I must too. We sat in the shade of the cantina silently, waiting for the bus. I knew what Shay was thinking: how ironic it would be if Ron and Helga were to step out of *this* bus?

To me, however, they had been on every bus. I had dragged us to the last refuge of the Mayans but it wasn't far enough. We couldn't outrun them. Ron and Helga had always been right with us, the invisible presence throughout this road trip, the elephants in the Volkswagen.

At that moment, I noticed that parts of the bush next to my elbow were fuzzy and I thought maybe something had gone wrong with my eyes. But it wasn't my eyes. The bush was full of hummingbirds.

When the bus came, none of the people getting off were Ron and Helga. We climbed aboard and went to Merida, where we basked for a couple of days like survivors of a disaster, luxuriating in a bed, sleeping under a ceiling fan, taking frequent showers.

We also sat in outdoor cafes, drinking beer, and eating flavors of ice cream I didn't recognize. I was wishing to hell we'd skipped Tulum and come to Merida in the first place. On one of those lazy afternoons, at an outdoor cafe overlooking a charming square, Shay was writing in her journal. I went to get another dish of ice cream, and when I came back, I paused behind her chair. Had I looked over her shoulder, I would have seen what she was writing. She felt my presence and clapped her journal shut.

Which startled me, and I felt hurt. Because of course I wasn't going to look at her journal. What did she take me for? But also: weren't we trading these things when the road trip was over? So that we'd know each other's deepest feelings? And that's when I realized: there would be no trading of journals. Of course not. Never.

Nothing changed after that. We were still far from home and the road trip went on for a good long while. We were still good together, mostly. We had more fun and accumulated more anecdotes to tell our friends back home. Like that time in Texas when a couple of cops stopped us for no reason and played good cop/bad cop on us, one of them snarling at us to open our trunk and get out of the way, he was going to search our car, while the other one sat beside us, rolling his eyes and telling us that his partner was so overzealous, but what could he do? When bad-cop started rummaging through our glove box, I blurted, "What's he *looking* for?"

"Illegal immigrants," said good-cop.

"In our glove box?"

"You'd be surprised."

We kept accumulating memorable images too. I remember an eerie stretch of highway cutting through a Texas desert filled with tumbling tumbleweeds as far as the eye could see. And a lovely little motel room in Las Cruces tiled entirely in Mexican mosaics. And the town of Taos, where everything, even the Safeway, was built of adobe. We talked about moving there. We speculated that maybe this was Home. And I remember Disneyland, where we smoked our fourth and final joint in the chair-lift that crossed the park. And I remember Joshua Tree National Monument, which looked like a set for a Star Trek episode, so bleakly beautiful with its endless variety of cacti. Yes, we continued to have a great time on that road trip, except for the ocean of unmentioned melancholy through which we were sloshing.

When we landed back in Portland, Shay wanted space and I knew the feeling. We sprang apart like negatively charged particles. She rented a room somewhere, and I rented a room somewhere else. It wasn't over between us though, not by a long shot. We came together often over the next year and a half. Sometimes we went a week without seeing each other, then crossed paths somewhere, and saw each other every day for days. We even moved in together for a while in that period; six months maybe; and then we moved apart again.

I have no idea when Shay became an abstraction to me. It's sort of strange in retrospect. We broke up explicitly at one point, but that was not at the end, it was somewhere in the middle. After the breakup, we went on pretty much as before, tangled up in each other's lives, feverishly working on our "issues", sometimes spending nights together... The end was just as indistinct as the beginning. We gave each other space, and the "space" kept increasing, until space was all we had. Years later, when we met again, only the affection remained, and we were back to what we had been before we got involved, what all couples claim they'll be after a breakup: we were friends.

After the road trip, I went back to the Scribe and there, right away, I was a big dog again; but the kennel felt oh my God so small. And things were changing. I and my ideological soulmates tried to keep money out, but despite our best efforts money started coming into the paper. Despite our best efforts, a few people began to be paid. Despite our dogged opposition, a structure began to take shape: people acquired job titles, some began to specialize, and we even agreed to regard one of ourselves as our "managing editor": a charismatic guy who had worked as a mainstream newsman, traveling the world as a photographer for A.P. Under his tutelage—despite our best efforts—some of us started turning into actual journalists. I was hardly aware of the melancholy I was swimming through, like the leftover resonance of some dream one can't quite remember.

I found myself writing bonafide news stories, and not just about "the community." I did an investigative series about the shenanigans of real estate developers in Portland. Some of us struck up a relationship with a group of prisoners at the Oregon State Penitentiary and we began to publish "letters from prison." We covered the trial of Leonard Peltier, an Indian activist accused of murdering someone in southern Oregon, and thus rubbed elbows with radicals flocking from distant places to support him. I covered the trial of Frank Giese and Jim Cronin, who were accused of bombing a federal building in Portland. Then, with the 1976 elections coming up, I began to write about the presidential campaigns just as if it mattered who was president of a country verging on extinction.

Meanwhile, being poor was getting old, and I was tiring of endless policy meetings. Worst of all, civilization as we knew it was simply refusing to hurry up and goddamn it collapse already. One day, I decided to drive down to L.A. to see if I *could* get a mainstream job in publishing, should I want to *someday*. My car broke down in San Francisco, which was okay, I had people to crash with; but as long as I was waiting for the car to get fixed, I decided to poke around at the job possibilities here. My ears twitched when someone told me about an outfit called the Asia Foundation. I knew of them: they'd been active in Afghanistan. In fact, my friend Ralph's father had worked for them In Lashkargah when I was twelve!

I ambled over to their headquarters and told the woman at the desk I was looking for a job writing or editing. She got quite discombobulated. Well, she stammered, as a matter of fact, the Foundation did publish a journal about Asian politics and culture, and they did happen to be looking for an assistant editor but unfortunately the person they hired had to be from Asia.

I couldn't believe my ears. From Asia? Why, I was born in Afghanistan! Which *was* in Asia! This was too perfect! My naïve enthusiasm so steamrollered the poor receptionist that she called the vice-president of the foundation to ask if he'd be willing to see one more applicant right away. Then she told me to go on back.

As I slouched outside the vice president's office, waiting to be called in, a woman passing by said, "Oh—are you interviewing for the editing job? Did you know that Mr. James used to be a journalist himself. Why, he broke the Korea War story."

She walked on, leaving me baffled. How could someone "break" the story that a war had begun? Didn't most people notice the bombs and bullets without help from the media? When I was called in for my interview, I took a seat across the desk from an old fellow with a bulbous nose, but before he could ask me anything, I just had to satisfy my curiosity on one point. "How did you break the Korea War story?"

For the next hour, I didn't say a word except, "Huh!" "Really?" "Interesting!" Mr. James did all the talking. Then our time was up, and I wasn't sure he had

even gotten my name. But as I walked away, I overheard him telling someone, "Smart young feller, that 'un."

My car was fixed by then, but I had lost my appetite for L.A, I just wanted to get back to Portland. Frankly, I forgot about The Asia Foundation. I had done the interview as a lark, I had no intention of working there. Guys like me don't work at places like that. The following Thursday, the Foundation called to say I was hired and could I start Monday?

I had no plan to leave Portland just then. Quite the opposite. I had just found a new five-room apartment with a garden for $50 a month. You don't walk away from a deal like that. And I had just started seeing a new woman. You have to give a thing like that a chance. And I had just agreed to edit a special issue of the Scribe. People were depending on me.

"Okay," I told the voice on the line. "I'll be there."

The next day I gave away everything I owned except what would fit in my VW, broke up with the new woman I was seeing, quit the Scribe, found another tenant for my apartment, and headed to San Francisco.

Divided Life

It was all so sudden. Friday morning, I was still living in Portland. By midnight Saturday I was living in San Francisco. On Sunday, I found a room-in-a-house. On Monday morning I put on a ridiculous collection of motley suit parts acquired from thrift stores and made my way to the Asia Foundation in downtown San Francisco to join the mainstream.

The room was just a place to land. It wouldn't work long-term. We were three roommates in a three-room flat, and two of us had to go through the bathroom to get to the kitchen, our only common space. I could never bring a date back to this place, but then again, what date? What did I know about "dating"? Neither Afghanistan nor the Portland community had taught me anything about this mysterious ritual. I started my life in San Francisco with hardly any clothes, no utensils, and no furniture, not even a mattress. I slept on the foam pad that had replaced the back seat of my Volkswagen when Shay and I did our big road trip.

Was I depressed? Not one bit. In Portland it never stopped raining; in San Francisco, it never seemed to start. I didn't care that we were in a drought. How could a man be depressed in such a place? The only thing I had was endless possibility, but what else does one need? Anything I coveted I could eventually buy: I had a salary for the first time ever! Best of all, three minutes from my front door was Minichellos, a bar that claimed to carry beer from a hundred countries. In there you could road-trip your way around the world the easy way: by drinking a different beer every night. It all felt like a dream, however. Nothing had emotional resonance. Everywhere I looked was a place where nothing had happened. Portland felt real. Only Portland.

Several months into my new life, I went looking for a better place to live. I followed an ad to a flat that was looking for a roommate. The place was above a failing paint store on Valencia Street, a dive neighborhood said to be gang-infested. An elfin woman answered to my knock. She introduced herself as Debby, invited me upstairs, and led me past an enormous living room with Corinthian columns and a wall-sized plate-glass window overlooking the street. She led me through a cozy wallpapered sitting room that opened into a greenhouse brimming with luxuriously well-kept house plants. We strolled on into a sumptuous dining room paved with Mexican tiles, beyond which, through an open doorway, I could see a well-appointed kitchen. The bedrooms were on another whole story above. Was this a Fellini movie? Holy cow.

If accepted as a roommate here, I would be living with three women. One was a critical care nurse, another was a teachers' aide by day and a jazz singer by night, and the third was the lively imp who had opened the door to me. She worked as a clown in a children's circus, if you can call that working. When the women of 1049 Valencia Street called to offer me the room, I felt like I had gotten into Harvard.

The home didn't depart drastically from the life I had lived in Portland except for one thing. The Community factor was missing. No one to judge me, no one to track my movements, no one to care what I did. But also no one with whom I was building an apocalyptic future. For the next many months I inhabited two worlds, each one ghostly to the other, a split-screen quite familiar to me from a lifetime of straddling incompatible spheres.

In Lashkargah, where I spent my formative preteen years, I went to school all day with Afghan boys and pretended not to even notice the creatures clad in bat-like black in the corner, whom rumor reported to be females—they were the first few girls to study with boys in Afghanistan. After school, I went home and from 4 pm onward lived as an American boy whose thoughts were bent toward getting a kiss from one of those same formerly-bat-like creatures, a girl whose mother was American like mine and who after hours dressed in a skirt and blouse and left her face naked.

Now in San Francisco, it was another version of the same thing. By day, working downtown at the Asia Foundation, I felt like a spy behind enemy lines. The executives were mostly former state department officials and military people, many of them conservative Republicans: not a single transgender Maoist-Leninist or ex-convict organic marijuana farmer in the lot. All the men wore suits; all the women wore hose and lipstick.

I picked up eventually that men's suits had styles and that my thrift store suit-parts were recognizably from the forties, so as soon as I had money, I bought myself some new threads. When I slipped into one of those three-piece pinstriped disguises, I could move around among the right-wing Republicans without arousing any suspicion. Internally, however, I was still that Portland community guy, who had somehow wormed his way into the belly of the beast and was filing each day's events as anecdotes to tell his friends in the real world when he got back among his own.

After work I switched to jeans and mingled with counterculture radicals and self-proclaimed "revolutionaries". At one such gathering, the guests included several men who had gone to prison for building bombs in their garage and had just gotten out. They were connected to a bunch of lunatics called the Symbionese

Liberation Army. (Don't bother looking for the little-known nation of Symbion on any map.) It turned out that I knew people from my Scribe days who knew these people. Our mutual acquaintances included Jack and Miki Scott, an odd couple who had sought radical glamour by claiming they had helped hide Patty Heart during the months when that poor kidnap victim of the SLA claimed she was a "revolutionary" named Tania.

Now, at this San Francisco party, one of the revolutionaries suddenly, loudly demanded that I tell him what I thought of Jack Scott. The whole room fell silent. I hardly knew Scott, and I certainly didn't know what the issue was. I stammered, "Well, he seems sincere, but who really knows." Devoid though it was of content, this statement did the trick. The party resumed. I was thereafter ignored.

A few nights later, at an Asia Foundation party, I found myself sitting on a couch behind a couple of senior citizen colonels who'd been drinking hard. One of them was saying to the other, something like, "So I told Lon Nol, goddamn it, you put some men out there to protect that supply line or we'll come in with a couple of B-52s, and turn your jungle into a goddamn bonfire..." It dawned on me that this man might be chatting about his role in the bombing that destabilized Cambodia and led to the horrors of the Kampuchean killing fields.

The Berkeley bombers by night, the Pentagon bombers by day: such was my divided life. And all the while, Portland trailed along behind me like a wisp of fog filled with whispers.

A Wedding

A year after I moved to San Francisco, I went back to the real world for a wedding. Who was getting married? None other than Nick and Harriet, the pioneers most radically devoted to the ideals of non-monogamous multiple-relationshipping. These two were getting hitched to each other and only to each other.   What the hell?

On the drive north, I had Herman Hesse's novel *Journey to the East* with me. The protagonist is part of a great mythic movement of people heading toward some mystical destination. But the movement loses momentum; disputes arise; some drop out, some go off on tangents, and the whole thing dissipates. Years later, our hero runs into one of his compatriots from the old days and they get to reminiscing. *What happened to us?* our guy laments. *Why did that great movement fade away?* The question amazes his old friend. *What do you mean? You alone dropped   out. You alone forgot. Everyone else is still on the journey.*

The news of Nick and Harriet's wedding shocked our tribe the way the news of two people not getting married would have shocked our parents. The old tribe was scattered from Portugal to Pensacola, but lots of us announced that by God we were coming back for *this* event, if only to rub our eyes in disbelief. And lots of us did. Everyone who had something of themselves to give the happy couple made of their talent a wedding gift. Genoa chefs June and David catered the wedding. TK threw pots for them. Jan De Weese got a group together to play English country music.   I took notes, thinking I would write up a little wedding book.   But when I read my document later, I realized it would not make a an appropriate gift. It was too dark.

I wrote about seeing Shay at the wedding and giving her *Something Blue*, a novella I had written about a couple named Max and Molly who have a passionate but "open" relationship, much like the one Shay and I used to have. Max and Molly were fictional but the story was about "our issues." They go on a four-month road trip, just as we did in 1974. They end up in Tulum, just like us.   They are planning to meet another couple there, but since none of them have been in Tulum before, they don't know where to say they'll meet. Finally they agree that whoever gets there first will leave a note in some conspicuous spot and—to catch the eye—mark it with something blue.

In Tulum, my fictional Max does something very wrong. He reads Molly's journal. There she has written the words he has wanted to hear: that she loves him and wants to marry him. For Max this discovery comes one second too late: by reading her journal, he has blown the relationship out of the water. When Molly discovers what he's done, she decides to leave Tulum on the next bus.

> *Her face was pale, but behind her features was a darkness. "I need space," she said, as the bus doors closed. "I need some time." Twelve years have passed and I continue to give her space and time. I have no idea where she lives now or how she fills her days, but I know we'll meet again. It will happen in a strange city far from home, where neither of us speaks the language. I don't know exactly which bar or which hotel, but it won't matter, because when the time comes, both of us will know what to do. Whoever gets there first will leave a note and mark it with something blue.*

The story was fiction, but there was a real-world truth I was trying to get at, something about the dynamics of "multiple-relationshipping." I gave the story to Shay because I thought that she of all people would be able to tell me if I had nailed it.

The next day bunches of us packed into numerous cars and drove out to the wedding venue, somebody's fabulous house and garden in a Portland suburb. Harriet assured us that at this wedding, we would not be subjected to all the usual tired clichés: for richer or for poorer, etc. Nick and Harriet had designed their own rituals. We were asked to form a huge circle and hold hands. Some of us were shaggy survivors from the old tribal days, but at least half of us were crusty parent-age folks decked out in suits and ties and fancy dresses and old-folk hats. I wound up between Steve Brummel and Shay. Looking around, I could tell that the "grown-ups" were feeling awkward. They didn't know what was coming and worried that they might screw up their parts. The people at the four quadrants of the circle were entrusted with objects of ritual significance, which they were instructed to pass on when the moment felt right. The items traveled slowly from hand to hand, right to left, around the circle. I received a couple of owl feathers tied together with locks of the couple's hair. Next came a rough gray stone with a hole in the middle. Then something wrapped in cloth. Someone said rather too loudly, "What is this? What am I supposed to do with this?"

While the sacred objects were making the circuit, a garrulous old woman to my right was blaring away about a restaurant she'd just been to where she didn't even get bread. An older guy a few places to my left was examining the pumice stone. It struck me that we had managed to give new meaning to the phrase "meaningless ritual."

My sister Rebecca had gotten married six months earlier. Hers was the first mainstream Western-style weddings I had ever attended, though I had seen such weddings in movies. Our father came from Afghanistan for the ceremony, his brief presence exploding forever the myth that we were a family. In the middle of that unraveling of myth, Rebecca said to Bob: "I do." And in that moment, my breath caught and I felt like a little boy again, as I listened to my sister say: "Goodbye." Families were reconfiguring, spheres of intimacy were shifting, the universe was altering. The words those two spoke to each other—"for richer...for poorer...in sickness...in health...till death do us part..." were so familiar they should have been clichés, but instead they possessed awesome force—not in *spite* of having been spoken millions of times by millions of couples but *because* of it.

Now, at Nick and Harriet's wedding, the sun poured down blazingly bright. It was a beautiful day for something. The hum of dragonflies interwove with the voice of that old woman bellowing about tipping: how much was right if you didn't even get bread? David stepped out from the circle and recited a fine Lou Welch poem about drawing a circle in the grass and finding a hundred marvelous things inside it.

Then it was time for the vows. I was too far away to catch Nick's words, but when Harriet's turn came, she made a strong statement, not just to Nick but to the circle. She told us she and Nick were declaring their love for each other publicly; but this did not alter the relationship either of them had with any of us. It sounded like she was saying the wedding wasn't going to change a thing.

The heavens did not split asunder as she spoke. But the garrulous old woman fell silent, and the honeybees suddenly seemed exceptionally loud. And then—it felt as if the universe did shift. Turns out, it didn't matter what was said. What mattered was the saying. Just by uttering vows—any vows—Nick and Harriet had stepped across a line.

After the ceremony the group fragmented and we each clumped together with whom we knew. I found myself face-to-face with Shay.

"I read your story," she said.

I nodded, giving her space to say more, but she didn't say more. I recollected that once, before our relationship began, she had said to me, "All feelings are mutual and obvious— eventually." At the time those words had sounded profound. Now, I wasn't sure they even held water. "Obvious" is the one thing feelings aren't, so who's to say they're ever mutual?

When the food came, we went gladly to long tables crowded with countless splendid dishes. We stuffed ourselves until we collapsed on the grass, groaning with pleasure. We wallowed in a sense of tribal fellowship—which was no longer real. From this wedding, we would disperse into myriad separate lives and some of us would never cross paths again.

The next morning I got up shortly after dawn to get an early start. I thought I might stop in Ukiah to see my dear friend Maggie, the only important one from the old days who didn't make it to Nick and Harriet's wedding.   I called her from a gas station, but someone else answered the phone. "Maggie's at the hospital."

"Oh my God! The hospital! What happened?"

"She went into labor."

Oh. I knew Maggie was pregnant but somehow it hadn't sunk in that being pregnant meant she would someday have an actual baby. Hers was the first baby born to anyone from the old tribe— just as Nick and Harriet had been the first of us to get married.

There was nothing to do now but keep driving. And I felt content to just keep driving.   I didn't even want to stop for gas. I wanted to get back to our flat at 1049 Valencia. I wanted to get back to my adorable roommates, my stimulating job, the women I was dating, the streets I knew. I wanted a burrito from El Faro. I wanted to quaff a beer at Vesuvio's. In short, I wanted to go home. And the miracle was, I could do that. I had a home to go to.

Epilogue

The Real Thing

Moving to San Francisco was a good choice. I fell in love with my roommate Debby, and this time it was the real thing. From San Francisco, I also blasted off on one more grandiose road trip, across the Islamic world at the height of the Iranian revolution, hoping to get a story that would turbocharge my journalism career. The journalism part came to nothing. I ended up at a seaside town in Turkey, drinking Czech beer and scribbling notes for *Sinking the Ark,* a novel about the Portland years. But when I got home, Debby and I did what normal people do. We got married, launched careers, bought a house, and had two children. And the years passed. And the years were good.

In 2000, Debby and I had been married for 19 years. Our older daughter Jessamyn was graduating from high school. Our younger daughter Elina was hitting her stride in elementary school. Our friends were mostly the parents of our kids' friends. We lived in a cozy Edwardian house, tucked away in a quaint San Francisco neighborhood called Bernal Heights. I was working in educational publishing as a writer. Debby had left clowning behind: she was producing conferences now for an economic research organization.

That year, however—the year I turned fifty—I found my thoughts drifting back insistently to people I had known in Portland long ago, to the acid trip, to Lily, to the community and Tulum... All the craziness of those crazy years were gone without a trace. None of it mattered now and none of it had mattered for years. And this gnawed at me a little because, if none of it mattered now, did it matter that these things had happened at all? If not, did anything matter once it was over and done? If not, did *anything* matter? Since, after all, everything will eventually be over and done?

Just as such thoughts started percolating in my head, I got a postcard from Reed College reminding me that my 30th-year class reunion was coming up. To the soundtrack of my friends' hooting and derision, I decided to do the corniest thing known to humankind: go to a college reunion.

But the reunion was just an excuse, frankly. I wasn't going back to Portland to catch up with old "college buddies." My real mission concerned the novel I had started writing in that hotel room in Turkey. *Sinking the Ark* was about six characters much like me and my friends, who work for an "alternative" newspaper in Portland called the Ark. I got a first draft done in 1982 but I wasn't sure I had corralled what I was after. *Sinking the Ark* was a work of fiction, none of the six characters was any actual person, but as I wrote the book, Sval, Zoe, George, Raoul, Marica, and Martha became more vivid to me than anyone I had actually known in the era of tribal communes and collectives. *Sinking the Ark* was fiction but in it I was trying to capture something real. How close had I come? I couldn't tell. I figured the only way to know for sure would be to go back and compare my imagined

Portland to the real thing—walk those same streets, revisit the old haunts—the Unitarian church that housed the Ark—excuse me, the Scribe ... Rose's Deli where we used to gobble pastries on Thursday nights, just for the sugar rush we would need to put the paper to bed... Ken's Afterglow, where we danced the night away on Fridays after the paper hit the stands... I would have to huddle with friends who had stayed in Portland so that we could correct our memories of the times we'd shared. And I was always planning to do that, but life got hectic, more pressing projects kept coming up and then one day my fiftieth birthday had come and gone and I had not touched *Sinking the Ark* in a decade. Goddamn it, the time had come.

The Reunion

I made it to Reed early Friday afternoon, checked into the dorm room they were giving me as an alum, and then went down to the coffee shop, where Robinson Hobbes used to fulminate about the Theory of Difference Arranging. The first reunion event was already under way on the lawn just below the steps where Lily was sitting the first time I saw her, reading *The Adventures of a Rock*.

At the lawn party, I saw one or two dozen clumps of alumni. This reunion was for every class that graduated in a year ending with the number zero—so the classes of 1990, of 1980, of 1970, and so on back. I simply gravitated to the closest clump of folks who looked like me, but I didn't recognize a single one. Had we changed so much? Or had I simply been friendless at Reed? The group was staring at me, so I asked. "Who are you guys? Did I know any of you?"

"Duuude," cackled one of the women. "We're the class of 1990!"

Oops. Ha! Duuuude! Twenty years younger than me? I looked around and saw another group of folks who looked distinctly, and I do mean distinctly, older. Were those my peers? Oh my gosh, we had not aged well. I sidled over and stared around, but I didn't recognize any of them either. "What class are you guys?"

"Class of eighty," said one.

Holy Moly! Even these dignified elders were ten years younger than I? Just how the hell old was I? Again I looked around, and this time I saw—oh, no way. No fuckin' way! That clump of geezers? Some of them with canes? All of them white haired or balding? Or bald? Most of them chunky, even fat? Those were my peers?

Yes. They were.

Wandering over to this circle, I recognized a few folks, though it wasn't easy. "Neil ...?"

"Yes. Are you...? Tamim?"

"The very same. So, um—what are you doing these days, Neil?"

"I'm an attorney."

I love how those guys never call themselves lawyers. Neil was one of the wild disreputables who lived in a broken-down old hippie mansion known as Troll Hall. "Let me guess," I twinkled. "Drug lawyer?"

He stiffened up to his full, imposing height. "Tax attorney."

Another fellow in the group turned out to be Jim Potosi. I worked with him at the Scribe and didn't even know he'd been my fellow Reedie. He was the seed from which grew Ray Perkins, a character in *Sinking the Ark*. Jim, like Ray, was a graphic artist and dreamed of making the paper a moneymaking tabloid that would serve Portland hipsters and pay salaries to its staff. You can be sure we got rid of him and his mercenary cronies in one of the earliest battles for the paper's soul.

Jim gave me his business card. He and his wife had a small shop that sold "erotic accessories"—handcuffs, leather jock straps, latex garter belts, stuff like that. Jim complained about the problems of running a small business— the complexities of the tax code, the government licenses required... And then—trying to get a mail-order revenue stream going? Fugeddaboutit. Jim's life was that of any hard-working small businessman. The fact that he sold handcuffs and crotchless panties was irrelevant. His life would have been the same no matter what he sold.

All Fiction

Then it was time to make my way into the Portland I knew after college, the city I lived in as a counterculture stalwart, as a member of the snowflake, as a roommate in the infamous old Everett Street House, as part of the Macondo Experiment, as a writer for the Scribe, as a citizen of the world I had created in *Sinking the Ark*.

I didn't have to take the book along. The fiction was inside me, all of it: the hillside rope course where Marica and George went hiking on that fateful morning. The basement workshop where Raoul was building his aquarium the night Zoe decided to sleep with him. And Sval, standing on Taylor Street, looking up at Zoe's window, knowing she was up there with another man. I didn't need to know anything more about the fiction. What I needed was the real thing to set beside the fiction. How close had I come?

Rose's, the venerable Jewish deli across from Ye Olde E-Street mansion was the obvious place to start. I could still remember groups of us E-Streeters piling into Rose's late at night, stoned, hungry, and giggling. I still had a fond spot in my heart for those shiny red, faux-leather vinyl booths, the dim lighting, and the 1940s big-band music that was always wheedling faintly in the background. There was an actual Rose too in those days, an older woman with dyed blond hair all poofed up, pancake makeup heavily slathered onto her face, and well-lipsticked lips, and long fingernails, and a cigarette burning between her fingers, a Zap Comics figure. She would certainly be gone by now, but I fully expected to see her daughter standing in her place, looking like Rose, because her daughter would be about the same age today as Rose had been back then.

But there was no Rose's at 23rd and Everett, only a large, grey, windowless box of a store selling hardware, squatting right where the deli and its parking lot had been. It was certainly the right address because the three-story mansion across the street had to be the old E-Street house—no mistaking the overall structure, that deep porch, the many gables. It had been renovated, though. It was no longer a residence but a mini-business complex. Our old music-room on the ground floor, where Karl Friedrich used to unload gunny sacks of peyote buttons upon returning from buying runs to the southwest, housed an insurance brokerage now. Upstairs, a law firm seemed to be operating out of my old bedroom.

I stopped a guy passing by. "What happened to Rose's Deli?"

"It's on Glisan Street, closer to 22nd."

"When did it move?"

"It's always been there."

I didn't correct him. "What about that building across the street? Do you remember when it was a hippie house?"

"Like ... a commune, you mean?"

Commune! The word sounds so formal—as if a group of people drew up a manifesto and organized a household to make a political statement. "Yeah," I sighed, "a commune."

"It's never been a commune."

Always. Never. I drove back to the east side of the river and parked a block from Harper Richardson's old Methodist Church. In my day, the Scribe had occupied the whole third floor of the church. The United Farmworkers were on the second floor, as was the Draft Resistors League. Down in the basement was the Ninth Street Exit coffeehouse, which gave underage teenagers a cool place to hang out so they wouldn't try to sneak into bars. Folksingers played at the Exit every Friday night.

There must have been at least ten other right-on projects of various sizes headquartered in that church, because Pastor Richardson believed religion wasn't about singing psalms on Sunday but on working with "the community" to better people's lives. That's why he gave the Scribe a free office—we were after all "the community newspaper". It said so right on our masthead. I knew the Scribe had folded long ago, but I was curious to know what Pastor Richardson was sheltering now, under his great wings.

The answer turned out to be—nada. The church had been razed. The whole block was an empty lot with the muddled beginnings of new construction at one end—stray lumber, a few bags of cement, some rebar, and some construction machinery.

Intellectually, I was not surprised. Emotionally, however, the sight of that empty lot made me crave a beer. Fortunately, I was just a five minute drive from good old Ken's Afterglow. You could still park within a block of anywhere in Portland, so I pulled into a spot on Hawthorne Street. Strolling east from there, I saw the familiar sign and felt a flush of affection. Well, at least one thing had survived.

But the moment I walked into the Afterglow, I smelled the stale beer and as my eyes adjusted, discerned sticky tables and old sawdust ground into the dance floor. A few ratty plants still hung from grimy beams here and there. The handful of customers scattered about the room were huge and intimidating and sported tattoos and wore leather. The Afterglow was a biker bar.

Well, I'd go visit Nick, I decided. We'd sit on his porch, toss back a couple of cold ones, and reminisce, because it was pretty evident at this point that "the real thing" didn't exist in any *place*. It existed only in psychic space, the collective memory of we who had shared that world.

Nick and Harriet lived in a small house in north Portland, which they were constantly expanding and remodeling. Nick had trained as an architect after our hippie years, and he worked for the city planning department now, but remodeling remained his passion, and he practiced it relentlessly on his own house. I told him of the shock I felt, seeing how Portland had changed, particularly Ken's Afterglow, which had once embodied the feelings we all had about "the community" in Portland—did Nick remember how green it was in there, with all the plants? Like a cross between a tavern and a rain forest?

"You're thinking of Produce Row," he said. "That's on Belmont."

"Uh uh, Ken's Afterglow. Don't you remember the night it opened, you and me walking home afterwards, past the recycling center?"

"Must have been someone else. I was in New Mexico around then. But remember the night Sid came up with the idea for Macondo—?"

"No way! Macondo was born at the Genoa one night, when Sally—"

"Well, whoever thought of it first—if only we'd gotten it open and run it for a few years, we could have sold like we said and bought some land on Hornby Island...I wonder where we'd be now if—"

"Sell it! That was never the plan! Don't you remember? When Shay and I wrote the Macondo Manifesto—"

"You mean the business plan? I thought Rosie wrote that."

We stopped talking then and just sipped beer for a while. We both had sharp memories of the same events but they weren't the same memories. And there was no way to determine who was "right". Old journals? Most of us just gushed about our feelings, failing to record a single concrete event. And those who, like me, kept factual logs recorded only the main points. But real life doesn't consist of main points. When it's happening, real life is a torrent of trivia, all of which matter in the moment, none of which can be ignored, and most of which are forgotten by dusk. Most of life is forgotten.

And of the remembered life, each person carries an idiosyncratically unique collection of moments. When memories conflict—as they always do—there is no way to know what "actually" happened. When Einstein realized there was no way to detect the existence of space and time apart from measurements of the distance between events, he concluded that absolute space and time do not exist. I had a similar epiphany at this moment about the past. The past does not actually exist. It never did.

I had spent so many years, re-imagining the Portland of the '70s. I had peopled it with so many characters who evolved as I moved them through those streets and homes and co-ops until I lost control and couldn't tell them what to do anymore, it was they who started telling me. They were forever, those guys. So were their experiences and the meanings I ascribed to them. The day Sval missed the big collective meeting because the wheel popped off his van when he was on the freeway? The time George dragged him to the food stamp office where a crazed gunman was allegedly holding hostages? The fact that comically enough they went to the wrong food stamp office? And then, most hilariously of all, it turned out Zoe was sleeping with some random hitchhiker that night? None of that will ever happen any differently than it did in the novel. Than it does. Than it always will.

What exactly did it mean, then, to check my novel against the Real Thing? If the Real Thing was not in any place, nor in any artifact, nor in the collective memory of people who were there— where was it? Didn't *Sinking the Ark* have a status equal to any other version of the Real Thing? In fact, wasn't *Sinking the Ark* as real as it gets?

Stages of Life

I woke up the next morning in a world I now knew would not be real until I had turned it into fiction. In this dream world, Debby called to tell me that our daughter Elina had left the ground. Elina had wanted to come to the reunion with me, and I had said yes, because I remembered my own self as a kid, heading out on adventures with my father, and I wanted my daughter to have adventures too. Debby and I agreed that once I was in Portland, she'd put Elina on a non-stop flight, and I would meet her. At the age of eight, she'd be flying solo for the first time—a big adventure indeed!

In the year 2000, you could still go right to the gate to meet your loved ones; terrorism had not yet been noticed by America. It was the last year of the time before. Elina came sailing out of the jetway all confident eight-year-old strut. She was in that toothy stage kids pass through: a few of her bicuspids had fallen out, two new front teeth had come in, and they looked huge—adult teeth in a child's face. With the side teeth gone, the new ones had relaxed to hog all the available space, opening a gap in the middle. She looked adorably eight-years-old.

"How was the flight?" I asked.

She shrugged the shrug of the jaded traveler. "It was good."

"Was it exciting?"

But my little girl was too cool for exuberance. "It was *good*," she repeated firmly. "I sat with two girls. They were flying alone too. One was 6, one was 7. I was the oldest. Oh no! I lost my tag! It shows who's going to meet you."

"Well, he's met you now, so you don't need the tag anymore."

"Oh." She saw my point. "I guess." She stopped for a moment to see if she could balance on one foot. She could.

Back at Reed, she changed into her bathing suit because she had seen the pond in the middle of campus. When I was studying here; the pond had just been scenery to me; but college kids and eight-year-olds look at the world with different eyes. We made our way down a squiggly dirt path, and Elina eased herself into the water. I was taping her with my new video camera, the first one I had ever owned. "Ah…! Mud," she exclaimed happily, scooping up a handful to show me. "Nice, squishy mud." She started stepping in place, and each time she did, her foot sank into the soft pond bottom. "Oh … *this* is fun!" Then she paused to look around. Trees bent gracefully over the still waters. A couple of ducks trailed V-ripples, moving smoothly toward the opposite shore, their means of locomotion invisible below the surface of the water. "It's beautiful here," Elina remarked.

This was true, although I had not noticed it before. After a while, I made Elina get out and dry off. I got her a bottle of

Snapple and we sat under a tree, next to Foster dormitory, not twenty feet from the window that I used to climb through every night, thirty years ago, when Lily was my girlfriend. Elina sipped her drink and gazed into the distance. I was still taping her when she mused: "Life has many stages."

"Does it?" I wondered what an eight-year-old's take could be on this profound topic. "What are some of the stages?"

"Well," she said, "Okay." And she began to enumerate them. "First? You're born and you don't know anything. Then? You get to be a little kid, like three and four and five and you know *some* things. Then you get a little older, six or seven, and you know *more* things. After that you go through another stage, which is eight through ten. Then comes eleven and twelve."

At least she could count. "Eleven and twelve is another stage?"

"Daddy! Eleven and twelve is a *whole* other stage, because after *that* you get to be a teenager and you go to high school." She paused to take a sip of Snapple, and I figured she must now have cited all the stages an eight-year-old could imagine; but no, she was just getting started. "Then you go to college..." she ruminated. "College is a whole other kind of work... you leave your family then. You start living on your own. You're almost an adult. And after college, you're pretty much *considered* an adult, and you have the hard job of finding a job." She frowned over this unpleasant necessity, until a sunny new thought struck her. "If you're lucky, though, you have kids! And if you're really lucky, you got married a little before that."

"What happens after people have kids? Any more stages?"

"Then, you just go through the stage of *raising* your kids. And once your kid is an adult you go through the stage of *missing* your kid."

"What are you saying? The moment your kid is an adult, she leaves?"

"Yes," Elina explained patiently. "Kids grow up and go away and after they're gone...you wonder if you should be relieved that you don't have to go through so much work and stuff, or should you feel really sad 'cuz your kid is gone. If you're smart, you choose to miss your kid but just go on with your life."

"But what is your life, if you don't have kids?"

"Hmmm. That's weird. Yeah... I don't know *what* your life is like with no kids. There wouldn't be much to do."

"You could go to movies in the afternoon."

"But your *kids*—" she protested. "You have *fun* with your kids. You *like* your kids!"

"Of course you do. You love your kids."

"Anyway..." she went on, "after you've chosen what to feel like, you go into being a senior citizen. You probably retire. You have time to do what you want. And if you're lucky, you're still with someone, if not married, so you do what you want with your husband or wife or whatever you've got, and you get old and then … " She gave one last diffident little shrug. "You die."

"I see. And is that pretty much it?"

"Pretty much. But all these stages go on for a very long time, Daddy."

"But if that's the case, does it feel like: what a waste, why even bother?"

"No, because you have *fun* in all those stages, Daddy."

The Letters

That night, Nick and Harriet invited us over for dinner. Shay was there too, with her husband Sam. Shay was an ecologist now, with an MBA and a law degree. They were there with their son Calvin, a gleeful, handsome little fellow. He and Elina sat at a table together, making art, and they got along famously.

At the end of the evening, as I was collecting my stuff and getting set to leave, Shay drifted up. "Hey, incidentally," she said, touching my arm. "We're moving to Hawaii, and I was going through some old boxes, throwing out stuff I don't want to keep— which is pretty much everything, because I'm trying to thin out the clutter and live lighter. Anyway, I found a bunch of old letters

from you, and I thought: 'Tamim's into all this memoir stuff...
maybe he'd want them. Are you interested?"

I shrugged. What letters? Back then, Shay and I had either
lived together or lived a few blocks from each other. Our
relationship had consisted of live interaction, not correspondence.
Nonetheless I said, "Sure, I'll take them."

Shay fetched the folder and it was surprisingly thick, but I
didn't dwell on the surprise. We were all too busy trading goodbye
chatter just then. Shay walked me to my car and Elina climbed
into the front seat. I tossed the files onto the back seat and gave
Shay a friendly farewell hug. We drove away.

Elina and I were staying with one of the dozens of Afghan
cousins of mine who were now living in America. Late that night,
after everyone toddled off to bed, we unrolled our sleeping bags in
the living room, and Elina promptly fell asleep.

I had a problem, however. I can't fall asleep unless I first run
some print before my eyes, but I had finished all the books I had
brought along, and there was nothing to read at my cousin's house,
not even a scrap of newspaper.

Then I remembered the letters. Those might work. I got them
from the car and settled into my sleeping bag. Except for the beam
of light from a lamp perched on the low coffee table at the head of
my mattress pad, the room, the house, and the city were dark.

I didn't think the letters would hold me long—after all, what
could I have written to Shay? Quick notes? Reminders? To-do
lists? Still, they might be good for a laugh—glimpses of our days
of youthful folly! I riffled through the pages, ready to smile. But
even in skimming those pages, I registered the salutations, and
they jolted me a little: "Dearest Shay", "Darling Shay", "Sweet
Shay, My Closest Friend" Had we been on "dearest darling"
terms? Yes we were lovers, and sure we were friends, but had our
language with each other been quite that gushy? It wasn't how
Sval and Zoe talked to each other in *Sinking the Ark*.

I decided to slow down and delve into the letters more closely.
I was still ready to be amused, because none of this was new to

me. I had written all of this up in *Sinking the Ark.* I knew these
events and experiences to be amusing, because *Sinking the Ark*
was an amusing novel. Two lines into the first letter, however, my
amusement dried up. Five lines in, I was right back in 1974 and
emotions were coming up way too fast. What emotions? I'm not
sure. The same cocktail I had felt the night I wrote the letter I was
looking at, twenty-five years ago, as fresh as on that day, as if not
one minute had passed: love and hate and hope, longing and
misery and euphoria, all undiluted and industrial strength. Where
was it coming from? Had I not workshopped these emotions to
death back in that era?   Surely,   not one drop of intensity
remained to be wrung from them. What was going on?

I knew I should stop reading, but I knew I wouldn't. I felt like
I did that time I took too much LSD: the effects coming on, the
sudden intimation that I didn't know how uncontrollably strong
this would get, along with the knowledge that it was too late, I
was in for the full ride, wherever it took me.

> *Shay: Love letter: impossible. The pain,too*
> *muddling. Hey Shay, are you there? I like talking to*
> *you. How come you don't bore me, after all this*
> *time? Listen, I'm doing all right actually...*

The moment I started reading that letter, I remembered writing
it--we had just launched our non-monogamy experiment. I put it
down and looked at the next letter. It was the one I wrote after she
slept with Ron for the first time.

> *...As the shock fades I realize I have never been*
> *this in touch with my emotions, and I'm thinking,*
> *"Good. This is shit I have to confront." I figure if I*
> *play my cards right, I can turn all this shit into*
> *compost. I will grow visibly as a lover and as a*
> *person. Several inches a day.   Soon I will be the*
> *biggest lover in the business.   Other lovers will*
> *stand around, staring at my ankles. They will have*

*to construct special quarters for me, I will no longer
fit inside ordinary rooms. Are you having fun yet?
What about the interesting problem of the night
brain? I love you, Shay. Whenever I feel good, it's
like feeling good with Shay. Is this what has to end
with letting go? If it is, even so, I will learn to do it.
I'll let go. I'll be a sun, and you be a sun, and our
intermingling will be the intermingling of light from
two separate suns in the middle of deep space. We
won't be everything to each other, we'll be two
things in a much bigger everything. "We" will
happen under a canopy twinkling with stars, each of
them another sun. But I warn you, I will still love
you like we were everything to each other. I won't
be able to help it.*

I didn't actually remember writing that letter, but I remembered
the event that triggered it, because that event happened to Sval, in
Sinking the Ark, a wrenching moment and yet comical too,
because the whole novel was rather droll. Rather droll because
Sval, for all his earnest adherence to "principles," poor shlub, cut a
slightly ridiculous figure. As did they all—in *Sinking the Ark*.
But the letter wasn't from *Sinking the Ark*. It was part of real life.
And real life differed from *Sinking the Ark* in one key way. Real
life contained no irony.

The Real Thing

The letters did not remind me of a single forgotten fact. How
could they? I'm the guy who remembers what type of sandwich
he ate walking across Vancouver forty years ago.   Every
particular fact was in the files. The only thing I had forgotten was
the whole thing: the single reality that all of it was: how it was all
happening at once. Bend in the River, the *Scribe*, the interlocking
networks of Portland's vast "alternative" universe, Shay and I
multiple-relationshipping, Upepo playing the music of the
apocalypse, all our friends multiple-relationshipping, the corrupt

old civilization in its final days, the rise of the new world we were building—everything was intertwined, and there was no border where love ended and pain began or where pain ended and joy began. We knew we were the future, if only we could become better people. But becoming better people—ah! That turned out to be so hard!

What I saw as I read those letters of mine to Shay was not the two of us in isolation but two tiny figures in a much bigger landscape. I saw us embedded in a world huge with hope. I had forgotten that I moved to San Francisco in headlong flight from contradictions that could not be resolved and emotions too intense to bear. I couldn't bear that the old civilization was refusing to crumble. I couldn't bear that Shay loved anyone but me. I wasn't big enough to be a new kind of human being. I had not actually exhausted every drop of drama, not with Shay, not with Portland. I just stopped my ears to all further sounds from that direction. I threw it in a box, slammed the lid, shot the lock, threw the box in the ocean, buried the key, walked on and did what Dylan advised: never looked back. Good move! The moment the Ark sank, I got traction. The moment I moved on, I found true love, built a career, made a life. For me, San Francisco had been the city on the hill.

But when I walked away from Shay, I relinquished the whole world we were part of. When I walked away from Portland, I relinquished the whole idea of community that gave fire and light to our lives, and I relinquished the boy who believed in that idea. In fact, I forgot he ever existed, that boy. We all forget the boys and girls who once existed. Turning ourselves into fiction is the only way to hold onto the memory of having been alive at all, yet fictionalizing is the very thing that cuts us off from knowing it was all real, it was all real.

The great surprise was the voluminous correspondence I kept up with Shay after the move. I don't know what I thought our relationship was, but she was clearly still my closest confidante. She came to see me over the Christmas break, and we celebrated New Years Eve together at a place in Berkeley called La Pena, where we saw a reggae band. After Shay went home, however, our correspondence tailed off. We crossed paths briefly that summer at Nick and Harriet's wedding and I gave her my story *Something Blue*, about two people who go to Tulum—she never did tell me what she thought of it. On another trip to Portland, later that summer, I went to see her at the rustic shack she was sharing with several other nature-loving hippies in the Columbia Gorge, but we scarcely talked. That fall, I sent her one last major letter, after which we exchanged only pro forma social notes, and then... nothing at all. That letter then was the last thing the boy who no longer exists said to his Shay:

November 13, 1977
Dear Shay,

I noted a certain weariness breathing from your last letter. You seemed to think I had criticisms of your way of life, your choice to live in the gorge and be a country hippie, to pursue a countercultural life, to keep juggling many relationships at once. But I was not in fact voicing any criticism. What I see is a world too fragmented for anyone to say of anyone else's incomprehensible life program, "You're fucking up." Who's to judge? In this bucket of broken glass that seems to be our present world-historical moment, I can no longer picture a bigger quest. I assume everyone is busy trying in their own way to avoid the collapse into the self—or seeking it, as the case may be. And in the end, as I say, who's to judge?

You speak of the many "R's" that make your life so baffling. Your shortening of "relationship" to "R" bemuses me. I'm amazed that you are still hip-deep in multiple-relationshipping. I think back to last New Year's Eve, when we went to that reggae place. We both knew the rules. We were to wade into this party together but separate. I should never once by word or deed behave like you were mine; and you would do the same for me. And we both succeeded, but why was this our goal? With such a goal, how could being together ever have been any different than being alone?

I remember that Fritz Perls quote that used to be on posters everywhere: " I am not in the world for you, you are not in the world for me, etc." You know the one I mean. You leave me alone, I'll leave you alone was the gist of it. How beautiful. But there's more to life than just being left alone. People want something to be asked of them, I read somewhere. They want something in the universe to depend on them.

My own views are undergoing a metamorphosis. I still think about relationships a lot, but these are usually the international relationships that I write about, as for instance between Vietnam and Thailand. At any given time these days, I have too much to do and not enough time to get it done, and that's the way I like it. I don't dismiss the possibility of progress. Things could be different, and surely should be. But let's not overestimate our power as individuals to bring about these changes. The old civilization is not collapsing. It is like some dragon born at the beginning of time, as big as the landscape and as durable. Its corruption is not its weakness but its strength. We will never change the world.

It's not that the world won't change. It will. It always does. But it will change in spite of us, not because of us. Those visions we pursued in Portland came to nothing and were always destined to come to nothing. We were living in a dream, we just didn't know it. In the end the world goes on; it was only we who lost our way, only our community that dissipated. A hundred years from now, no one will know the world we lived in existed or that any of that stuff ever happened.

Part of my disillusionment comes from the discovery that my own most cherished goals are embarrassingly trivial and obvious. All I want, it turns out, is to not be lonely. All I want is to be respected by the society in which I live and to contribute something useful. All I want is to love someone truly and be loved in return. All I want is to feel at home somewhere.

Dawn was spilling over Portland. All hope of sleep was gone for the night, and one simple fact kept glowing like red kryptonite. The boy who wrote those letters wasn't fictional. It's true that he was gone. I was not that boy and Shay was not the girl he loved, but that boy did exist, and so did the vanished girl. And I, looking over his shoulder as he wrote those earnest letters, had no right to discount, dismiss, or minimize what he felt. He was as real as I, and his love for Shay as heartfelt as mine for Debby. He's gone now, but what of that? I'll be gone too someday. On that score, neither of us has the existential edge.

It's true that by 2000, I knew something unknown to that guy. I knew that chasing grandiose visionary goals only leads to disappointment. But the guy who wrote those letters knew something too. I wasn't wrong, but he wasn't either. Even as I write this, I'm remembering something that happened a few days ago: someone asked me what my wife does for a living, and I informed him that she organizes an annual conference for a research organization that promotes employee ownership. As the words left my lips, I thought: Good God. The Macondo project didn't die. There are people still working on it. One of them is my own wife! How could I not have noticed?

The letters were still on my mind when Elina and I headed home. Elina was having a great adventure, and I knew the feeling: she was living in a story, just I was doing that time my father took me along on the quest for that fabled alabaster mountain and I found the black stone. And it struck me that the little fellow who went on that journey with his father—he was as real as the little girl sitting next to me, having an adventure with *her* father. At one point, Elina interrupted her own excited chatter to pipe, "Is this a road trip, Daddy?"

"Yup," I assured her. "This is a road trip, honey." Not for me, to be sure: I had done my last road trip, but for her? Yes: her first of many, perhaps.

A few weeks later, Debby and I took the kids out for pizza. Walking back to our car in the gathering dusk, I watched the girls chasing each other down the hill, teasing, laughing, chattering, horsing around—and I was struck with wonder. Here I was, walking hand in hand with the love of my life, and here were my children, and behind me stretched half a century of life. How did I ever deserve this?

Long ago, in that last letter to Shay, that intense, despairing moment of transition, I had written that I was giving up on grandiose ambitions. I had listed my pitifully scaled-down goals: to love and be loved, to contribute something useful, to feel at home ... twenty-two years later I had all those things. It blew me away. I told several people about this in the days that followed, and they all waited for a last line, which didn't come. And when it didn't, they supplied it.

"Yet somehow you are not content."

It seems to be an obligatory expectation in our culture—one must never be content. But my experience was just the opposite. When I listed those goals, I thought they were trivial. Now they seemed huge. Far from discontented, I felt humbled, grateful. When I thought about other ways my life could have gone ...

I had an argument with my childhood friend Ralph once about what is real. He held that the world is *not* real; I held that it is. From his platform as an intractably religious guy, he argued that the world can't be real because it is impermanent. The Real, he said, cannot be transitory. Evanescence proves that another realm exists, a realm from which death and change are missing.

And I kept stubbornly saying, "Why can't it be real and yet keep changing?"

Today I concede that Ralph was onto something, and that I have always known it, but I still insist on the opposite as well. My earliest memory is of coming to the breakfast tablecloth (which was laid on the floor and surrounded by the 15 or 20 people who then comprised my closest family) and discovering that my hot chocolate was not already there, as I had come to expect. I was plunged into despair by the revelation that Life could contain such agonizing disappointments—No Hot Chocolate at a time and place where Hot Chocolate had "always" been. At that moment, I learned something stupendous, and I began to cry.

But *then*! Then a *hand* came swooping down from somewhere, and in that hand was a cup, and in that cup was hot chocolate topped with foam. And as this was set before me, a shaft of morning light came through the window, hit the foam, and turned each bubble into a tiny rainbow-colored dome! Oh my God! From the depths of hell to the vaults of heaven in a single stroke and with no transition! Here was a second revelation, coming fast upon the heels of the first, and a greater one—the world contains miracles!

But *then!* Then came part three of the experience: the bubbles were breaking. One by one by one, the rainbows were winking out. The glorious moment was not a glimpse of the Permanent Real. It was just one moment in an endless string of moments. This turned out to be what registered enduringly for me: the simultaneous impermanence of it all and realness of each moment.

For each moment becomes part of a past that will never have happened any differently than it did. The past we carry is a story that keeps changing with the ever-changing present we are in. But the actual past, that inaccessible, unknowable darkness that we trail behind us, the fountainhead of all story: that is the real thing.

Artist's Statement

I'm interested in the role that memory plays in giving meaning to existence. Since childhood I've treated nostalgia like an opiate, making a conscious effort to induce it in myself. The past exists in two visual records: in our minds' eyes and in snapshots. Photography sometimes causes us to experience our own pasts in 3rd person: the hard-edged images preserved in film mingle with the fuzzily emotional colors of neurological memory. Where story, photographic image, and recollection trisect--that's the terrain I'm exploring.

I first read Road Trips when I was nineteen. Seeing the world through my father's eyes when he was my own age was transformative. I now had a written record of the memories that shaped my father's mind—the mind that shaped my own mind. In a way, I felt like I could remember these things too, etched somewhere deeply in my genetic code. And the feeling I had been grappling with all my life—the reason I'd always been so fascinated with memory, and the driving force that urged me to make art—then crystallized. Memory is intangible. The very thing that tells us who we are and gives meaning to our lives is nonexistent in the physical realm and impossible to pinpoint or define in any realm. If memory exists only in our minds and is forever changing there, is it real at all? Or is memory perhaps the only real thing, while the present is transient and the future abstract?

Elina Ansary

39461349R00173

Made in the USA
San Bernardino, CA
27 September 2016